T0273971

TRAILS TO THE TOP

HELP US KEEP THIS GUIDE UP TO DATE

Every effort has been made by the authors and editors to make this guide as accurate and useful as possible. However, many things can change after a guide is published—trails are rerouted, regulations change, techniques evolve, facilities come under new management, etc.

We appreciate hearing from you concerning your experiences with this guide and how you feel it could be improved and kept up to date. While we may not be able to respond to all comments and suggestions, we'll take them to heart and we'll also make certain to share them with the author. Please send your comments and suggestions to the following email address: falconeditorial@rowman.com.

Thanks for your input, and happy trails!

TRAILS TO THE TOP

50 COLORADO FRONT RANGE MOUNTAIN HIKES

Susan Joy Paul

Stewart M. Green

FALCONGUIDES

ESSEX, CONNECTICUT

For the trail builders and trail blazers

FALCONGUIDES®

An imprint of Globe Pequot, the trade division of
The Rowman & Littlefield Publishing Group, Inc.
4501 Forbes Blvd., Ste. 200
Lanham, MD 20706
www.rowman.com

Falcon and FalconGuides are registered trademarks and Make Adventure Your Story is a
trademark of The Rowman & Littlefield Publishing Group, Inc.

Distributed by NATIONAL BOOK NETWORK

Copyright © 2023 by The Rowman & Littlefield Publishing Group, Inc.
Photos by Susan Joy Paul and Stewart M. Green unless otherwise noted
Maps by Melissa Baker and The Rowman & Littlefield Publishing Group, Inc.
Front cover photo of Longs Peak from Flattop Mountain Trail and back cover photo of Pikes Peak
from Mount Rosa summit

All rights reserved. No part of this book may be reproduced in any form or by any electronic
or mechanical means, including information storage and retrieval systems, without written
permission from the publisher, except by a reviewer who may quote passages in a review.

British Library Cataloguing in Publication Information available

Library of Congress Cataloging-in-Publication Data

Names: Paul, Susan Joy, author. | Green, Stewart M., author.
Title: Trails to the top: 50 Colorado Front Range mountain hikes / Susan Joy Paul, Stewart M.
  Green.
Description: Essex, Connecticut: Falcon Guides, [2023] | Includes bibliographical references. |
  Summary: "While Colorado's 14ers and 13ers are well-known and well-traveled, Trails to the Top
  guides readers off the beaten path to the very top of some of Colorado's lesser-known, yet
  no less impressive, mountains between 9,000 and 12,000 feet. The 50 unique routes covered
  in this guide feature amazing views with accessible trailheads for hikers of all skill levels, all
  located within a couple hours' drive of Denver, Fort Collins, and Colorado Springs. The best
  part about these hikes is that they don't stop short of the summit; they take you all the way to
  the top"—Provided by publisher.
Identifiers: LCCN 2022045694 (print) | LCCN 2022045695 (ebook) | ISBN 9781493048649
  (paperback) | ISBN 9781493048656 (epub)
Subjects: LCSH: Hiking—Colorado—Guidebooks. | Mountaineering—Colorado—Guidebooks. |
  Trails—Colorado—Guidebooks. | Colorado—Guidebooks.
Classification: LCC GV199.42.C6 P384 2023 (print) | LCC GV199.42.C6 (ebook) | DDC
  796.5109788—dc23/eng/20221013
LC record available at https://lccn.loc.gov/2022045694
LC ebook record available at https://lccn.loc.gov/2022045695

♾ ™ The paper used in this publication meets the minimum requirements of American National
Standard for Information Sciences—Permanence of Paper for Printed Library Materials, ANSI/
NISO Z39.48-1992.

The authors and The Rowman & Littlefield Publishing Group, Inc., assume no liability for
accidents happening to, or injuries sustained by, readers who engage in the activities described
in this book.

CONTENTS

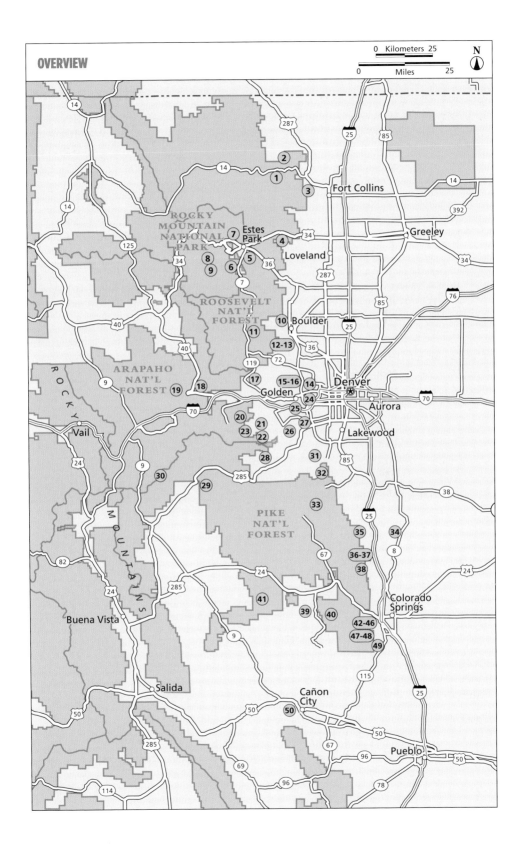

ACKNOWLEDGMENTS

Many thanks to all the people at Rowman & Littlefield, Globe Pequot, FalconGuides, and National Book Network, and all the bookstores and outdoor recreation retailers that carry our books.

Special thanks to our editorial director David Legere, acquisitions editor Mason Gadd, production editor Nicole Carty, map maker Melissa Baker, copyeditor Lauren Szalkiewicz, and proofreader Annette Van Deusen. We couldn't have done it without you.

—Susan Joy Paul and Stewart M. Green

MEET YOUR GUIDES

Susan Joy Paul has summited more than 700 peaks including all of the Colorado 14ers. She was the first woman to summit every ranked peak in El Paso County and Teller County and the thirty-sixth person to summit every Colorado county highpoint. Susan's memorable routes and peaks include the Keyhole Route on Longs Peak, the Knife Edge on Capitol Peak, the Maroon Bells Traverse, the Mountaineer's Route on Mount Whitney, the East Arête on Mount Russell, Otto's Route on Independence Monument, the Emmons Glacier on Mount Rainier, the Gooseneck Glacier on Gannett Peak, the Jamapa Glacier on Pico de Orizaba, the Ayoloco Glacier on Iztaccihuatl, and the Whymper Route on Chimborazo. Her books include *Touring Colorado Hot Springs* (2nd and 3rd), *Hiking Waterfalls Colorado* (1st and 2nd), *Climbing Colorado's Mountains*, *Best Lake Hikes Colorado*, and *Woman in the Wild: The Everywoman's Guide to Hiking, Camping, and Backcountry Travel*. Susan lives independently in Colorado Springs, Colorado.

Stewart M. Green has hiked, climbed, photographed, and traveled across the American West as well as the world in search of memorable images and experiences to document. Based in Colorado Springs, Stewart, a freelance writer and photographer for Globe Pequot Press and FalconGuides, has written and photographed over fifty travel and outdoor adventure books, including *Best Easy Day Hikes Colorado Springs*, *Scenic Driving Colorado*, *Best Hikes Colorado Springs*, *Best Climbs Moab*, *Best Hikes Albuquerque*, *Rock Climbing Colorado*, *Scenic Driving New England*, and *Rock Art: The Meanings and Myths Behind Ancient Ruins in the Southwest and Beyond*. His photographs and writing are also published in many magazines, books, catalogs, websites, and ads. Stewart is also a professional rock climbing and hiking guide for Front Range Climbing Company. Visit stewartgreen books.wixsite.com/stewartmgreenphoto for images and information.

INTRODUCTION

WELCOME! A MESSAGE FROM YOUR MOUNTAIN GUIDES

Few experiences come close to standing on a mountaintop. Blue skies, puffy white clouds, fresh mountain air, and never-ending views conspire to put a smile on the face of anyone willing to put one foot in front of the other, pace by pace, to rise above the rest. High above the parks, the prairies, and most of the people, lofty summits offer a respite from everyday low-elevation life.

Thanks to Colorado's unique geography and location along the Rocky Mountains and the Continental Divide, the lucky Coloradan has access to many, many high-elevation destinations. Our state has the highest mean elevation, at 6,800 feet, and the highest low point, at 3,315 feet of any state in the country. It has more land mass above 10,000 feet and more mountains with summits above 14,000 feet—including fifty-three ranked 14ers, or 14ers with 300 feet or more of prominence—than any other state. It's the only state that lies entirely above 1,000 meters (3,281 feet). The high point of the Rocky Mountains, Mount Elbert, is in the state's Sawatch Range, and the high point of the Continental Divide, Grays Peak, rises in Colorado's Front Range.

About one-third of Colorado is public land, including much of the higher elevations, allowing for mostly free and unfettered access to the state's multitude of peaks. This dynamic and legally accessible topography provides a wonderland of mountainous hiking adventures.

While the state provides thousands of peak destinations, getting to those mountaintops isn't always easy. Most do not have trails, and they require a degree of route-finding skill. While the intrepid hiker, climber, and mountaineer should take it upon themselves to learn map and compass, GPS, and other orienteering and land navigation skills, the process can take a lot of time. Meanwhile, many summit-seekers just want to get to the top of a peak. And they don't want to get lost.

It's these hikers that inspired this book. We offer people of all hiking abilities a fine collection of peaks to climb that have parking lots, trailheads, and trails. This doesn't mean the hikes can be done without preparation or a bit of research, and we'll get to all of that shortly. But compared to Colorado's thousands of pathless, remote peaks, these are accessible and navigable for even the beginning hiker. Plus, the peaks and their airy summits are pleasant enough that seasoned mountaineers will enjoy them too.

THE FRONT RANGE

The fifty hikes in this book are all within Colorado's Front Range, the longest contiguous uplift in the state. This mountain range defines the eastern edge of the Rocky

Mountains in Colorado, trending north-south from the Wyoming border to Cañon City and separating North Park, Middle Park, and South Park, west of the range, from the Great Plains to the east.

The Front Range crosses many counties and comprises many subranges, including, from north to south, the Rawah Range, Laramie Mountains, Never Summer Range, Mummy Range, Indian Peaks, Vasquez Mountains, Williams Fork Mountains, Platte River Mountains, Kenosha Mountains, Tarryall Mountains, Puma Hills, Rampart Range, and even the lowly South Park Hills, Gorge Hills, Grand Canyon Hills, and the McIntyre Hills.

Each peak in this book is below 13,000 feet. Many great books and websites exist that discuss routes on the 14ers and the 13ers of the state. We chose to focus on peaks that you can hike in a day or less, and whose trailheads lie within a couple of hours' drive of the Front Range's major cities. The summit of the lowest peak, North Table Mountain, is 6,575 feet above sea level, while the highest is 12,713-foot Hallett Peak. The shortest hikes, "Baboon Rock" and Grouse Mountain, are just 1 mile roundtrip, while the longest one, a loop hike over Dragons Backbone and past Robbers Roost on Cheyenne Mountain, is 15.4 miles. The Grouse Mountain hike also has the least amount of elevation gain at less than 200 feet roundtrip, while Mount Rosa boasts 3,988 feet of net elevation gain and more than 4,000 feet roundtrip. If you do every hike in this book you will cover, on foot, more than 260 miles of distance and gain over 60,000 feet of elevation.

HOW TO USE THIS GUIDE

The features in this book will help you choose the best hike for your location, fitness, and how much time you have available for your adventure.

The **Overview Map** shows all the peaks in this book on a map, so you can see their locations in Colorado. This section, the **Introduction,** offers information about the book's layout along with general guidelines for staying safe, being respectful to the areas you visit, and planning and packing for your hikes. The **Appendix** at the end of this book lists contact information for the hikes' various land management agencies beyond what's included within each chapter, along with other useful sites such as where to get park passes.

Each of the fifty hike chapters in this book is organized as follows:

Number and title: The hike or chapter number and the name of the peak. Most of the hikes go to the highest point of a peak, with a few exceptions. For example hike 49, Dragons Backbone and Robbers Roost directs you to two sub-summits of Cheyenne Mountain, as the true high point of the peak is not accessible by an established trail.

The name of each peak is what you will find on most maps, designated by the United States Board on Geographic Names, or USBGN. When the name is unofficial it is enclosed by quotation marks. Two hikes, Green Mountain (Boulder) and Green Mountain (Lakewood) are so named to differentiate the like-named peaks.

The official name of Mount Evans, a 14,265-foot mountain west of Denver, is undergoing a possible name change in 2023. The mountain, although not included as a hike in this book, is mentioned in several hikes and photo captions. At press time, the mountain was named for John Evans, a controversial territorial governor from 1862 to 1865. Evans authorized the Sand Creek Massacre in 1864, which resulted in the deaths of over 200 Cheyenne and Arapaho tribal members. The Colorado Geographic Naming Advisory

Board, tasked with replacing offensive names of geographic features, is considering six proposals in 2023 to rename Mount Evans. Mount Blue Sky, suggested by the Cheyenne and Arapaho tribes, is the leading candidate for the new name.

The hike name is followed by a short descriptive paragraph introducing the hike by their locations.

Start: The name of the trailhead where the route begins. Unofficial trailheads appear in quotation marks.

Difficulty: Ratings include Very Easy, Easy, Moderate, Strenuous, and Very Strenuous, depending on the distance, elevation gain, altitude, and terrain. Difficulty ratings are highly subjective, based on the hiker and current conditions on the peak. Use these ratings as a general guide to assess your hiking abilities and physical condition.

Trails: The names and numbers, where applicable, of the trails from trailhead to summit. Unofficial trail names appear in quotation marks.

Hiking time: The time it takes an average hiker to summit the peak and complete the route, trailhead to trailhead. This does not include rest stops or time spent on the summit, which may increase your own time considerably. Hiking time is estimated at roughly one hour per thousand feet of elevation on the way up, adjusted for steepness, distance, and terrain; plus about two-thirds that time on the way down. Hikers may experience much longer or shorter hiking times. Use the hiking time in each chapter as a rule of thumb and adjust your own expected times accordingly.

Distance: The distance in tenths of a mile roundtrip, from trailhead to trailhead. The type of hike, either out and back, loop, or lollipop loop, is also noted.

Elevations trailhead to summit: The elevation in feet above sea level at the trailhead and at the summit, and the net elevation gained from trailhead to summit. Note that some hikes lose elevation on the way up, which must be regained on the ascent as well as on the descent, adding more overall elevation gain to the hike, which is not accounted for in the net gain. To avoid confusion, these elevations are what you will find on current USGS maps. They do not reflect recent, unofficial adjustments established by LiDAR (Light Detection and Ranging) technology. Subsequent editions of this book will reference those newer elevations after the release of the USGS's updated maps.

Rank status: Peaks with 300 or more feet of prominence are noted as ranked and those with less than 300 feet of prominence are noted as unranked. Prominence standards vary between countries, and in the United States, 300 feet is the generally adopted standard.

Restrictions: Special considerations and precautions beyond the general guidelines for backcountry travel including fees, seasonal access, and whether or not dogs are allowed on the trails, and if they are required to be leashed. If the trailhead does not include a toilet, that is also noted. Routes that enter wilderness areas, where additional restrictions apply, are also called out in this section.

Amenities: Toilets, camping, and other services are listed here, including the nearest town for full services such as gas, groceries, and lodging.

County: The county or counties in which the trail(s) are located.

Maps: Details from three maps are included:

DeLorme Colorado Atlas & Gazetteer, 13th edition, including the page(s) and grid number(s) where the route exists. This is useful information for getting a "big picture" view of where you are going relative to where you are starting your drive.

National Geographic's Trails Illustrated Map, by map name and number. These maps are chockful of valuable information and are small enough to carry in your pack for a medium-size view of your destination and the surrounding area.

United States Geological Survey (USGS) Quad Map. This is a small, zoomed in view of the area. Print them from the USGS Map Locator and Downloader site, order hard copies from the site, or ask about USGS Quad Map print on demand services at your favorite outdoor retailer.

Land status/contact: The name and phone number of the associated land management agency. Additional information, such as websites, are included in the Appendix.

Finding the trailhead: Driving directions from the closest town or major highway, along with the GPS waypoint of the trailhead. If you have a GPS in your car or on a mobile phone, you can input the waypoints before leaving for the trailhead.

The Hike: A short description of the hike.

Miles and Directions: The mileage from trailhead to summit and back, in tenths or one-hundredths of a mile, with descriptions of each section and GPS waypoints for most entries. If you have a GPS, you can plug in the waypoints for easier route finding.

Note: The route defined within the Miles and Directions is, by default, a summer route and does not take into account snow or other conditions that may render the route susceptible to avalanche danger or otherwise unsafe. In winter and during the shoulder seasons of late fall and early spring, further research may be required to ensure the route is suitable for foot travel.

Extra Credit, Options, etc.: Some hikes include alternative route options and extra credit hikes to additional, nearby destinations and peaks.

In addition, a map of each hike is included along with photographs of the peak, the trail, and views from the trail and summit area.

WHAT TO WEAR

You may be hiking for many hours and in changing conditions, so comfortable layers are the rule of thumb when dressing for a summit hike. Layering allows you to adjust your clothing to match the varying outside temperatures and weather, as well as your own body temperature.

Ideally, wear your hiking clothes to the trailhead. If you have a long drive, dress comfortably and have other clothes you might need packed away in your daypack or in a duffle to put on at the trailhead. Here's a list of clothing items to consider:

A pair of shoes or boots made for the terrain. If you're sticking to dry trails in good weather, trail runners will do, but if the route crosses rocky terrain you may want something sturdier such as hiking shoes or boots with support for your feet and protection for your ankles. If you will be traveling on wet terrain, wear waterproof hiking shoes or boots.

Socks that retain their insulating ability when wet. Hiking socks and mountaineering socks are good choices—just make sure they fit your shoes or boots.

Layers for your torso and legs, including a thin base layer to wick moisture away from your skin, an insulating layer for warmth, and a protective wind and rainproof layer with a hood. Depending on the season and the weather forecast, you may need fewer layers, or you may need to double up on some of them.

A hat with a brim to protect your face from the sun and a snug-fitting cap to keep your head warm on cold days. You may also want to bring along a headband or earflaps for your ears and a buff to protect your face from the wind and cold.

Gloves or glove layers, depending on the temperature and conditions.

Additional items such as short gaiters to keep rocks out of your shoes in the summer, and knee-high winter gaiters for snowy hikes. Traction for icy or slippery trails are also extremely helpful on trails year-round, especially at higher elevations where snow may exist any month of the year. Choose spikes such as EXOspikes or MICROspikes, or similar traction, and make sure you get the right size for your hiking footwear.

Sunglasses or wrap-around glacier glasses for sun and wind, and goggles for extreme winter cold and wind.

WHAT TO PACK

Hiking gear and clothing can be expensive, so start with the active wear you have in your closet and add pieces as you need them for longer hikes in colder or more inclement weather. Here are some tips to get you started:

Get a pack that fits everything comfortably. The hikes in this book are day hikes or shorter, so you don't need a big backpack. A smaller daypack will do.

Build the ten essentials as you can afford them and make them staples in your pack: (1) a first aid kit, (2) fire starter, (3) extra clothing layers, (4) headlamp with extra batteries, (5) map and compass and/or a GPS (with extra batteries), (6) plenty of food, (7) sun protection such as a hat, sunglasses, and SPF 30 or higher sunscreen and lip balm, (8) an emergency shelter, such as a tarp, (9) water and electrolyte drink, and (10) any tools you might need for gear repairs, such as a small knife, duct tape, cord, and zip ties. You don't need to break the bank to acquire these items. For example, your first aid kit may be as simple as bandages and pain reliever, plus any medications you are on, and your fire starter may be a book of waterproof matches in a plastic bag, and a bit of cotton and petroleum jelly in a plastic bottle. Add items as you can afford them. You don't need to make a large upfront financial investment to enjoy the outdoors.

Add the eleventh and twelfth essentials: extra gear for the conditions and terrain and a bathroom kit. Extra gear may include trekking poles, spikes, a camera, and so forth. A bathroom kit may include toilet paper, wet wipes, a small trowel for digging a poop hole, menstrual products and feminine urinary/urination director/device (for women), and anti-chafing stick or cream. Pack them all in a waterproof bag and include extra waterproof baggies to stash used items in for later disposal in a proper trash receptacle.

Carry plenty of water. A general rule of thumb for a full day of hiking is to carry 3 liters of water and 1 liter of electrolyte drink, but this varies depending on the distance, elevation gain, difficulty of the hike, and the outside temperature. Use a water reservoir for sipping on the go in warmer temps, and insulated bottles or plastic bottles nestled in an insulated bottle "parka" or carrier for cold days. You will not find potable water on the trail, and most of these hikes do not pass by water for filtering, so be sure to carry enough for the whole hike.

For food, bring items that travel well and will not get crushed in your pack. In winter, pack foods that won't freeze or become too hard to chew. You should have a good combination of foods that supply energy and nutrition. Sweet and salty foods taste especially good in the mountains, where your appetite may be diminished by the altitude. You need to eat to climb, so carry foods that you will want to eat.

Tuck a card into your first aid kit with your personal information on it, and the contact information of a trusted friend. If you become sick or injured and require rescue, your hiking partners can communicate the information on your card to first responders, who will want to know how tall you are, how much you weigh, what medications you are on, and so forth. You can also keep your Colorado Outdoor Recreation Search and Rescue (CORSAR) card in the kit. The purchase of a CORSAR card supports local search and rescue teams that assist climbers in distress, and the cards may be purchased online or at your local outdoor recreation shop. Also pack a pencil and paper so that if there is an accident, you can note important information such as the location and condition of the victim and relay that information to rescuers. Use proper precautions to ensure a safe, unassisted ascent and descent of your peak, but know that if you become sick or injured and are unable to return to the trailhead on your own, SAR is your best bet for emergency assistance in the mountains. Contact the local ranger station or connect to SAR by calling 911 if you have cell service.

Carry a whistle to signal for help in the event of an emergency.

Devise a system for storing your items in your pack and stick to it. Over time, you'll figure out which items come out of your pack most often. Make them readily accessible. In general, store heavy items like extra water bottles and thermoses in the bottom of your pack, and food and clothing on top. Store batteries together, and if it's cold out, keep them in a pocket on your body, as the cold will deplete them. Having a storage "system" is helpful so you can retrieve items quickly, and without standing around in the wind and cold.

If you are hiking from late fall to early spring, you may need special gear and training in snow travel and avalanche safety. Additional gear may include snowshoes, skis, an ice axe, aggressive traction for your boots such as crampons, and extra clothing layers. Bear in mind that most of the hikes in this book are well-traveled year-round, making them more easily navigable in changing conditions than peaks without trails.

MOUNTAIN HIKING SAFETY AND PROTOCOL

The mountains are not designed with our safety or comfort in mind. For all their beauty, they are inherently dangerous and inhospitable places for humans, and people die on them every year. That's why we prepare for our hikes and keep our visits to the summits short: to increase our chances of a successful ascent and descent without injury or death.

This book is not a comprehensive guide to hiking Colorado's peaks, and there is no single book that encompasses everything you need to know to be safe and self-sufficient in the mountains. Following is some general information you need to know now, and an overview of the outdoor skills you should master over time, to become a responsible mountain hiker. Seek out other resources to build on your knowledge and experience as you advance from a beginner to an advanced mountain hiker. Plan to read books and take coursework specific to land navigation and route finding, weather, mountain travel, wilderness first aid, camping, backpacking, snow travel, self-arrest on snowfields, back-country group dynamics and leadership, and avalanche safety. Numerous licensed and insured organizations in Colorado offer these resources.

Advance Planning

Mountain hiking, even on peaks with trails to the top, requires planning. Depending on the season and the peak you are doing, you may need to plan your hikes days, weeks, or even months in advance.

Be prepared with the appropriate clothing, gear, food, and water you'll need for a safe hike.

Carry a written plan of your expected route, with directions to the trailhead and the summit, and the name of the trailhead and the peak.

Share a copy of your plan with someone you trust, along with the make, model, and license plate number of the vehicle you will be leaving at the trailhead, and a "latest time to call." This is the latest that your contact person should wait for you to check in before they contact emergency personnel. In the event of an accident, that person will know where you are, that you are overdue, and can contact first responders with that information. Your "latest time" should be realistic. For example, it may take you two hours to drive to the trailhead, three hours to get up the mountain, two hours to get down, plus two hours of breaks and time on the summit, and another hour to drive from the trailhead to a place where you have cell phone service. The more hikes you do, the better you will get at estimating your own "hiking times."

Check the Colorado Department of Transportation (CDOT) website (cotrip.org/) for road conditions and closures.

Call the ranger district of the forest service or wilderness area where you will be traveling for information on access and road closures on roads not covered by CDOT.

Check the National Oceanic and Atmospheric Administration (NOAA) website (noaa.gov/) for weather conditions and be sure that you won't be hiking through open areas or above tree line in extreme wind or if there's a danger of lightning. Lightning storms above tree line occur almost daily in the mountains, especially in the summer, and can move in very quickly. Note the temperature, wind speed and direction, precipitation, and lightning danger expectations for the day, and expect them all to be worse.

In snow, check the Colorado Avalanche Information Center (CAIC) website (avalanche.state.co.us/) for avalanche conditions. Even if you have all the gear and the training to survive an avalanche, do not underestimate the danger. Gear such as a beacon *may* save you, but more likely, it will only be useful to retrieve your body. A good rule of thumb is, if you will not feel safe doing a hike *without* a beacon, probe, and shovel, then don't do the hike with it.

Check the National Operational Hydrologic Remote Sensing Center (NOHRSC) website (nohrsc.noaa.gov/) for information on precipitation and snow depths. Even if avalanche danger is low or non-existent, you will want to know how much snow exists, so you are prepared with appropriate gear. Expect a much longer day snowshoeing or postholing in deep snow. The Open Snow website also offers lots of winter weather and snow accumulation information.

If you plan on camping at a national park or national forest campground, check recreation.gov for availability and reservations. For camping at Colorado State Parks, visit the state park website (cpw.state.co.us/) or call 800-244-5613 for a reservation. For backcountry camping, identify water sources along the route so you'll have water to filter for drinking and cooking. Some areas also require permits, WAG bags for packing out solid waste, and bear canisters for storing your food, and that you camp in designated sites only, so check before you go.

For more information about Colorado's expansive trail network, including statewide maps, trails, and trailheads, visit Colorado Trail Explorer (trails.colorado.gov/).

Check with your hiking friends, or on your favorite climbing website, for the latest trailhead conditions, or call the local National Forest Ranger District.

Be aware of the hunting calendar in Colorado, and wear blaze orange if you will be hiking in an area where hunters are active. Check the Colorado Parks & Wildlife website for calendar dates (cpw.state.co.us).

Gas up before you go and especially before getting on a long dirt road so you don't get stranded.

Clip your fingernails and toenails a day or two before the hike, and hydrate with plenty of water and electrolyte drinks.

On the Road

Sometimes the most dangerous part of a hike is just getting from your home to the trailhead and back. Colorado's busy highways are often filled with drivers on their way to work, the ski slopes, or out to the mountains, just like you.

Mountain hiking sometimes requires an early start, and the general rule of thumb is to be off the summit by noon to avoid lightning and precipitation. Plan your hikes with this in mind and be on the road in time to drive to the trailhead, gear up, and get to the summit before noon. Traffic on the major roadways is busier than you might expect in the early morning hours, and ski traffic can bring you to a halt. Leave early, or head to the trailhead the night prior and camp or get a hotel room.

Pack an emergency kit for your trunk, with food and water to sustain you for a couple of days in case you are stranded. Also pack a shovel for digging out of snow, and a small handsaw to cut tree branches that can fall across backroads and block your path. It is not a bad idea to have a tent, sleeping bag, and pillow in the trunk, even if you don't plan to camp overnight. In winter and spring, bring your snowshoes even if you don't plan to use them on your hike, in case you get stranded on a dirt road and need to wear them to get from your car to a service station.

Pack snacks and drinks for the drive, and for recovery after your hike. After drinking a lot of water on your hike, you may crave a salty snack like pretzels or chips. Bring trash bags for your recyclables and compost, and small bills so you can pick up extra items and use the restrooms at gas stations and convenience stores along the way.

If there is a fee and a self-serve kiosk at the trailhead or campground, bring your checkbook and a pen, or the exact amount in cash. Some kiosks accept credit cards, but don't count on it.

When driving to the trailhead, be aware of changing conditions, especially during inclement weather or disasters. Rainfall, snowfall, rock fall, mudslides, and wildfires can impact your route, so be prepared to turn around if conditions become unsafe.

Watch for runners, bicyclists, motorcyclists, and wildlife on the roadways. Deer, elk, bighorn sheep, antelope, and moose are especially active at dusk and dawn, when the lighting is bad and you are on your way to the trailhead, or on your way home.

On steep, narrow back roads, yield to uphill-driving traffic (traffic that is *below* you and heading *up*). If you are approaching a flat, single lane stretch of road and you have a convenient place to pull over, pull off and let other drivers pass. Drivers in the backcountry are usually much more considerate than those on the state's highways.

Don't overestimate your ability, or the ability of your vehicle, to make it to a trailhead. When in doubt, pull over and park completely off the road or turn around, and walk to the trailhead. Tows in the backcountry are very expensive.

After a hike, assess your ability to drive safely and without "nodding off." Mountain hiking can wear you out, so if you need a nap, take a nap in your tent or car. Don't drive home drowsy.

At the Trailhead

You may feel pressured to push off from the trailhead quickly, but take a moment to ensure you are properly geared up and prepared for the day ahead.

Put on sunscreen, and dress for the first couple of miles, so you can minimize clothing adjustment stops. Being slightly cold at the trailhead will probably have you feeling just right when you're hiking uphill. Unzip armpit zippers, and push sleeves and pull zippers and buffs up and down to adjust your body temperature, instead of constantly stopping.

Don't leave valuables or your garage door opener in sight in your car at the trailhead. Lock them in the trunk or glove box or take them with you. If you have an extra car key, give it to one of your climbing buddies in case you lose yours.

Information signs at the trailhead provide details on access and restrictions. Read them. Don't assume you can camp at a trailhead, or have a campfire at a trailhead, as the rules vary between trailheads and they can change.

On the Trail

Vigilance is as important on the trail as it is on the roadways. If you follow the trail or others in your group "blindly," you may get lost. Use every hike as an opportunity to hone your land navigation skills.

Reapply sunscreen during your hike. Don't neglect your ears and the inside of your nose. Reflected sun off snow will burn your nasal passages and the roof of your mouth, and you will likely not even realize it's happening until much later, when you get home and the inside of your nose starts peeling, and your mouth is sore. Use sunscreen and a buff to protect these sensitive areas.

Learn how to follow a simple trail map, how to use a map and compass, and how to use a GPS unit, if you have one. Keep your map handy and track your location along the route. Do this every time on good trails, in good conditions, until you can do it off-trail and in bad weather.

Travel in small groups to lessen impact in the backcountry. In wilderness areas, there is a limit on the number of people allowed to hike together.

Follow pet restrictions on trails, and where dogs are allowed, keep them on leash or on voice command. Do not allow them to chase wildlife, which can stress the wild animals, causing death. Wild animals may be responsible for feeding young ones, so killing a single adult animal can wipe out an entire family.

Do not approach wildlife. Although bear, mountain lion, and moose attacks are rare, they can happen, and are more likely when animals feel threatened. Even small animals carry diseases, so don't try to pet or feed them.

Leave berries and other native foods for the animals. They rely on these foods for their nutrition and survival. Bring and eat your own food.

You may share the trail with others, and a right-of-way protocol should be followed. Bikers should yield to hikers and horses, and hikers should yield to horses. Descending hikers should yield to those traveling uphill. However, use your common sense. If you are a single hiker climbing a trail and you see a large group heading down toward you, step off the trail and let them pass. Likewise, if you see a biker barreling toward you, even though you have the right-of-way, it's probably a good idea to move to the side of the trail and allow them to pass safely. Bikers who are coming behind you will usually let you know they are coming, so you don't accidentally step out in front of them.

Take extreme care when crossing streams. Use dry rocks and tree limbs to step across or take off your shoes and wade across. If you have to cross something deep, unfasten your pack straps so that if you are pulled in the weight of the pack does not carry you downstream, but if you are concerned about being carried away at all, find a shallower place to cross, string a safety line of rope and tie into it, or turn around. If you anticipate a deep crossing, pack some water shoes. Snowmelt and rain during the day can turn an early morning babbling creek into a roaring torrent later in the day, so be prepared for more difficult crossings on the way out.

Pack out all trash and personal items, including toilet paper. In some areas, you are also required to pack out solid waste, so be prepared with a suitable container.

Keep to established trails and avoid traveling off-trail or on social trails. Adhere to the Leave No Trace principles to lessen your impact and prevent resource damage. The Leave No Trace (lnt.org) principles are easy to follow and ensure a clean and pristine environment for inhabitants and future visitors to the peaks.

Do not cut "switchbacks," which destroys vegetation and causes erosion.

Leave everything on the trail as you found it. Do not remove rocks, plants, wildflowers, live trees, or historical artifacts from the wilderness, but leave them for others to enjoy. Per the Antiquities Act of 1906, removing artifacts is illegal and punishable with fines and jail time. Likewise, do not leave anything behind such as painted rocks or trash.

Tread lightly above timberline. Unlike alpine tundra in northern lands, Colorado tundra drains continuously, preventing the development of protective permafrost. High altitude plant life has a short growing season and so regrowth of damaged areas takes a very long time.

Purify creek water before you drink it, and if you're traveling around a mining area, don't use the water at all.

Rocks, tree roots, and even dirt are very slippery when wet. Keep your boots dry, but if that's not possible, use trekking poles for balance and traction for your boots to help keep you upright.

Stay dry. Clothing adjustments are time-consuming, but if it starts to rain or snow, cover up immediately, before your clothing gets wet and you get chilled.

Lightning, exposure, sunstroke, hypothermia, dehydration, and altitude sickness are killers. If a storm threatens, if you get cold or overheated, or if you are feeling sick, take immediate action. Remedy your situation by descending, drinking fluids, eating, adjusting clothing layers, or taking medication, and then reassess your condition and the situation, and make the decision to continue or to descend. Check with your partners regularly to make sure they're OK, too.

Eat and drink *regularly*, even if you're not hungry or thirsty, to stay hydrated, energized, and warm. If you wait until you feel thirsty you may already be dehydrated.

Don't separate from your climbing buddies. It's inconsiderate and can put all of you in an unsafe situation.

On the Peak

People die every year on Colorado's mountains. Injury and death are sometimes caused by a climber's inexperience and bad decisions, and sometimes it happens even when an experienced hiker has done everything within their power to be safe. Minimize the odds of an accident by following a few simple rules.

Keep an eye on the weather so you're not caught up in a storm. Lightning, rain, and snowstorms can come at any time of day, and in any month of the year, especially at higher altitudes. Make a habit of checking the sky for incoming weather.

Winds on Colorado mountains and passes can be ferocious, knocking you off your feet. Plan to descend immediately if the winds suddenly pick up.

Don't throw rocks, or anything else, from a peak. You could start a rockslide and kill someone, or the velocity of the thrown rock, in a long descent, could kill another hiker.

Some peaks have registers at the trailheads and on the summits—scrolls of paper, logs, or notebooks to sign, in waterproof containers—and this information is useful for those who track trail usage, and maintain the trails, and the information may come in handy for rescue personnel, too. It's OK to sign a register, but do not sign your name on rocks or anything else on a peak, and do not leave signs, water bottles, or anything else behind on the summit. There are no paid garbage collectors in the mountains, so clean up after yourself and carry out any trash you find.

Don't take shortcuts off peaks. Stay out of loose gullies, and don't climb down anything that you can't climb back up, or up anything that you can't climb back down. That's how hikers get "cliffed out" and have to be rescued.

Don't let "summit fever" or the herd mentality that often accompanies group hikes cloud your judgment. If the terrain or weather conditions are unsafe, or if you are not mentally or physically prepared to summit a peak, turn around. Your peak, your climb, your life: Don't hand that responsibility off to anyone else in the mountains.

Safe mountain travel always demands vigilance. The greatest dangers are unstable terrain, bad weather, poor judgment, and making poor decisions. Loose rocks can fall on you or give way under your feet. Snow can bury you in an avalanche, cornices can break away beneath you, and slick, icy terrain can cause you to slip and fall. Lightning is common in the mountains, especially on summer afternoons, and can maim or kill you. Exposure to heat, sun, cold, wind, and altitude can bring on many illnesses, including sunstroke, heat exhaustion, hypothermia, and even death. If you are new to hiking peaks, find a mentor or a small group of experienced climbers willing to join you on your forays to the summits, while you embark on a personal mission to get a thorough education on safe mountain travel and outdoor skills.

BEYOND THIS BOOK

This book is a good start for planning your adventures, but you will want to expand your knowledge with more resources. Lucky for you, the Colorado mountaineering community offers guidebooks, websites, and organizations to help you with your education.

Take some classes with formal outdoor education service providers and hire them to take you out and teach you advanced hiking skills. Non-profit organizations like the Colorado Mountain Club also offer classes to members, for a fee.

If you are going to be hiking in the spring or winter, take an avalanche safety course, and invest in a probe, shovel, and beacon, and learn how to use them. Make avalanche safety coursework and self-arrest practice part of your annual training. Don't take chances with snow, period. Non-profit organizations like Friends of Berthoud Pass also offer avalanche awareness and safety instruction.

Outdoor recreational shops offer workshops and presentations on hiking skills and safety. These are a good introduction and a refresher for formal coursework.

Front Range bookstores and gear shops carry FalconGuides like this one, covering a variety of hikes across Colorado. If you find that you are interested in a particular area or group of peaks, pick up a guidebook that focuses on your area of interest. Recommended FalconGuide books for more Colorado hikes include *Hiking Waterfalls Colorado*, *Best Lake Hikes Colorado*, *Hiking Colorado's Hidden Gems*, *Climbing Colorado's Mountains*, and *Best Hikes Colorado Springs*.

The website 14ers.com has amassed and organized volumes of information about the highest peaks in the state. Colorado mountaineer and site administrator Bill Middlebrook's website is free, but you can make an annual offering for his generosity in providing access to everything you need to plan a 14er climb. This is a great place to get up-to-the-minute route and conditions information from other climbers, and much more. It's also a good place to make climbing friends.

Lists of John (listsofjohn.com/), a website developed and maintained by prolific Colorado mountaineer John Kirk, is a database of all the mountains in Colorado and across the United States. You can discover which peaks are located in a particular county, or are of a particular elevation or steepness, or are on a number of other "lists." Basic information on this site is free, while additional services require an annual fee. Lists of John users are also a great resource for learning more about the peaks, and for finding climbing partners.

Other mountaineering websites like SummitPost (summitpost.org/) and Peakbagger (peakbagger.com/) are useful for discovering historical information and route details about the Colorado mountains and places beyond.

Finally, develop a network of friends who share your passion for mountain hiking, so that you will have other like-minded people as hiking partners to assist with planning, driving, and leading summit hikes. Hiking friends also motivate you to take more outdoor skill courses, read more guidebooks, and hike more mountains.

Now it's time to pick a peak to climb. Check out the overview map and choose a Front Range hike. See you on the summit!

MAP LEGEND

══25══	Interstate Highway	⊟	Bench
══285══	US Highway	■	Building/Point of Interest
══67══	State Highway	▲	Campground
════	County/Forest/Local Road	○	City/Town
= = = = =	Unpaved Road	×	Elevation
⊢+⊢+⊢+⊢	Railroad	ⵏ	Gate
▪▪▪▪▪▪	Featured Trail	▲	Mountain/Peak
- - - - - -	Trail	🅟	Parking
- - ▪ - - ▪ - -	State Border	🀤	Picnic Area
∼∼∼	Small River/Creek	👪	Ranger Station
∼∼∼	Intermittent Stream	🅺	Scenic View/Viewpoint
⬭	Body of Water	🯅	Tower
▭	National Park/Forest	①	Trailhead
▭	Wilderness Area	❓	Visitor Center
▭	State/County Park	⸙	Waterfall
⬚	Open Space		

1 MOUNT MCCONNEL

The hike up Mount McConnel, a peak above Poudre Canyon in the northern Front Range, follows a designated National Recreation Trail up steep slopes partially burned in a 2012 wildfire. McConnel's rocky summit offers 360-degree views of the Rawah and Mummy Ranges to the west and rough country in the Cache la Poudre Wilderness Area.

Start: Mount McConnel Trailhead, Mountain Park Campground
Difficulty: Moderate
Trails: Kreutzer Nature Trail #936, Mount McConnel National Recreation Trail #992
Hiking time: 2-3 hours
Distance: 4.0 miles, out and back
Elevations trailhead to summit: 6,652 to 8,020 feet (+1,368 feet)
Rank status: Ranked
Restrictions: Trailhead is a fee area at the day-use area at Mountain Park Campground; wilderness regulations apply; camping and fires prohibited within 1.4 miles of trailhead; group size maximum 12 people; leashed dogs only; pick up dog waste; no mountain bikes or motorized vehicles; winter trailhead on CO 14 at river bridge; no water available on hike
Amenities: Vault toilet at trailhead; Mountain Park Campground near trailhead; services in Fort Collins
County: Larimer
Maps: *DeLorme*: p. 19, D7; Trails Illustrated #101: Cache la Poudre, Big Thompson; USGS Big Narrows
Land status/contact: Cache la Poudre Wilderness Area; Roosevelt National Forest, (970) 295-6600; Canyon Lakes Ranger District, (970) 295-6600

FINDING THE TRAILHEAD

From Fort Collins, drive north on US 285 to the junction with CO 14 at Ted's Place. Turn left on CO 14 and drive 23.2 miles and turn left into Mountain Park Campground just past mile marker 99. Cross a bridge over the river and take the first right turn to Mountain Park Day Use Area, McConnel Trailhead, and a parking lot (GPS: 40.683326,-105.465057). Spaces 1 to 5 are designated for Mount McConnel hikers. An information sign at the trailhead on the south side of the parking lot has a map, trail details, regulations, and trail history. The winter trailhead is at the locked gate on the north side of the river bridge. Parking is alongside CO 14.

THE HIKE

The Mount McConnel National Recreation Trail, built by the Civilian Conservation Corps (CCC) in 1936, follows two trails—Kreutzer Nature Trail and Mount McConnel Trail—to the boulder-strewn summit of 8,020-foot Mount McConnel. Both trails form loops, with the 2-mile Kreutzer Nature Trail on the bottom and the 2.7-mile Mount McConnel Trail on the top. This description follows the western arms of both trails to the mountain summit. An alternative descent route follows the eastern arm of the Mount McConnel Trail, but it is for experienced hikers only with steep sections and drop-offs. See the Option below for miles and directions on this descent. The hike is popular in summer but is accessible year-round from the winter trailhead on CO 14 at the river bridge.

The first leg up Kreutzer Nature Trail begins at a trailhead in Mountain Park Picnic Site off CO 14 northwest of Fort Collins. After almost a mile, the next hike section

The trail swings around the west slope of "Little McConnel" high above the Cache la Poudre River's gorge.

climbs the Mount McConnel Trail up the peak's northern slopes in the Cache la Poudre Wilderness Area to the fire-ravaged summit and wide views across the Front Range. Much of the terrain burned in the High Park Fire in June 2012, leaving sections of pine, fir, and spruce forest lightly charred and completely burning other areas. The wildfire, sparked by a lightning strike, burned 259 homes and 87,284 acres in 21 days.

MILES AND DIRECTIONS

0.0 Start at the Mount McConnel Trailhead on the south side of the parking lot at Mountain Park Picnic Site. Go left and follow the trail up a hill.

0.1 Reach the road to Mountain Park Campground and cross it to the signed trail and an information kiosk at the upper trailhead (GPS: 40.682753,-105.463978). The first hike section follows the Kreutzer Nature Trail. Hike south and then southwest, slowly gaining elevation on north-facing slope burned by wildfire. After the third switchback, the trail climbs east to a blunt ridge, then turns south and ascends a sloping bench.

0.8 Reach a signed junction and the start of the Mount McConnel Trail loop. Go right on Mount McConnel Trail. The left trail is the second section of the Kreutzer Nature Trail, crossing high slopes and then descending to the Cache la Poudre River. The singletrack Mount McConnel Trail gains elevation on partially burned, northeast-facing slopes.

1.2 Reach an overlook on a high grassy ridge with fine views west of the V-shaped river canyon and distant snowcapped peaks in the Rawah Range (GPS: 40.677659, -105.466766). The trail continues climbing and swings across grassy slopes studded with dead snags.

The Mount McConnel Trail offers spectacular views in the Cache la Poudre River's deep canyon.

Standing stone ribs mark the highest point of Mount McConnel.

The summit area of Mount McConnel was burned in a 2012 wildfire.

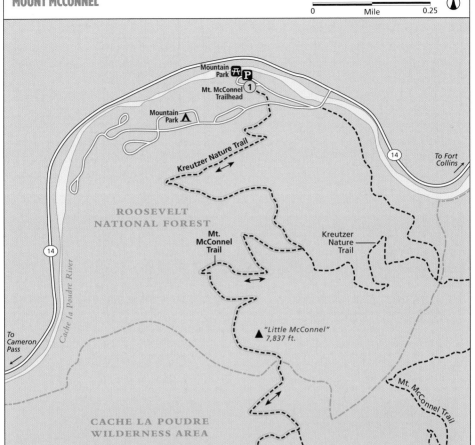

1.6 Reach a saddle between a knob on the left and Mount McConnel on the right (GPS: 40.675147,-105.463569). Follow the narrow trail south up McConnel's burned, north-facing slopes onto the east shoulder.

1.9 Reach a junction with a trail on the right signed "Mt. McConnel Summit" (GPS: 40.672967,-105.462805). Follow this spur trail west across burned terrain to a jumble of boulders that forms the summit.

2.0 Scramble onto the highest blocks of 8,020-foot Mount McConnel for stunning 360-degree views across the northern Front Range (GPS: 40.671982,-105.464591). Look for Clark Peak on the Continental Divide to the west, Greyrock Mountain to the east, and the deep Poudre Canyon twisting below. Afterwards, head east to the junction and go left to retrace your footsteps back down the mountain.

4.0 Arrive back at the trailhead (GPS: 40.683326,-105.465057).

Option: After summiting, go right on the Mount McConnel Trail and descend the primitive path for 1.6 miles to the Kreutzer Nature Trail, which is followed back to the river and trailhead for a 4.5-mile round-trip loop hike.

2 GREYROCK MOUNTAIN

Rising northwest of Fort Collins, the granite dome of Greyrock Mountain offers hikers a convoluted national recreation trail, expansive summit area, and scrambly finish to a rocky top.

Start: Greyrock Mountain Trailhead. CO 14 / Poudre Canyon Road
Difficulty: Strenuous
Trails: Greyrock Trail #946
Hiking time: 5–6 hours
Distance: 6.4 miles, out and back
Elevations trailhead to summit: 5,889 to 7,613 feet (+1,724 feet)
Rank status: Ranked
Restrictions: Dogs must be on hand-held leash; no bicycles on trail; no open fires or camping within 0.25 mile of the river or 200 feet of Greyrock Trail; no available water on trail; watch for poison ivy
Amenities: Toilet at trailhead; services in Fort Collins
County: Larimer
Maps: *DeLorme*: p. 19, D8; Trails Illustrated: #101: Cache La Poudre, Big Thompson; USGS Poudre Park
Land status/contact: Roosevelt National Forest, (970) 295-6600; Canyon Lakes Ranger District, (970) 295-6700

FINDING THE TRAILHEAD

From Fort Collins, take US 287 N for about 10 miles and turn left onto CO 14. Drive 8.4 miles on CO 14 / Poudre Canyon Road to a large, paved parking area on the left (GPS: 0.695002,-105.283328). The trailhead is accessed from the far northwest end of the lot (GPS: 40.694804,-105.284370). Cross the highway to the trail.

Greyrock's looming south face towers above the scenic Greyrock National Recreation Trail.

Boulders and bedrock on Greyrock's summit offer views west to the Rawah Range.

THE HIKE

The trail to Greyrock Mountain's summit starts out straightforward enough, but due to rock slabs and boulders that block your view of the trail on the steeper sections and an overgrown path over and between rock slabs on the summit area, good route-finding skills are recommended. Start early and leave plenty of time in case you accidentally get off-trail so you can find your way out before dark. Bring a headlamp and extra water in case the hike takes longer than expected. On the steep descent from the summit area, remember that the trail hugs the southeast face for a long time, and that dropping down too soon will take you off-trail. If you lose the trail, hike up to locate it. Poison ivy exists along the trail. Due to the ups and downs on the trail, you will gain more than the net 1,724 feet of elevation on the way up and add a bit more on the descent—close to 2,000 feet overall.

The summit is rocky and very exposed, surrounded by a sea of lower elevation peaks with higher peaks on the distant horizon. On a clear day, you may be able to pick out 12,951-foot Clark Peak, the high point of the Rawah Range, 13,560-foot Hagues Peak, the high point of the Mummy Range, and 13,916-foot Mount Meeker to the southwest.

The pointed "Auguille du Greyrock" rises above the Greyrock Meadows Trail.

MILES AND DIRECTIONS

0.0   From the kiosk at the west end of the parking lot, take the steps north down to the road and carefully cross to the other side. Traffic does not stop. Descend more steps and cross the footbridge over the Cache le Poudre River.

0.5   At the official Greyrock Mountain Trailhead, turn left onto Greyrock Trail (GPS: 40.695424,-105.284933). Hike west with the river to your left and the hillside to your right. The trail rises gently and crosses a minor stream.

0.6   Reach trail junction with Greyrock Meadows Trail #947 to the left. Go right to stay on the Greyrock Mountain Trail and hike north (GPS: 40.695833,-105.295631).

1.9   The trail rises north, crosses another minor creek, and bends east, switchbacking through a burned area and climbing north again out of the canyon, finally offering views of Greyrock Mountain (GPS: 40.708569,-105.294615).

2.2   The trail levels out and meets the junction with the end of Greyrock Meadows Trail. Turn right to stay on Greyrock Mountain Trail (GPS: 40.711888,-105.294490). The trail enters a wooded area, curving east, west, and north before taking a northeast route, contouring across the southeast face of the peak.

2.65 Pay close attention to your route as the trail gets progressively rockier, steeper, and more difficult to follow. Expect to use your hands to scramble over rocky sections. The trail meets the rockface and continues northeast. If you have a GPS, taking waypoints through this section may come in handy for the hike out. It is important to remember that the trail hugs the peak from this point on; on your hike out, remember to stay close to the rockface to this point or you may descend too early, lose the trail, and end up on very difficult terrain (GPS: 40.716044,-105.290203).

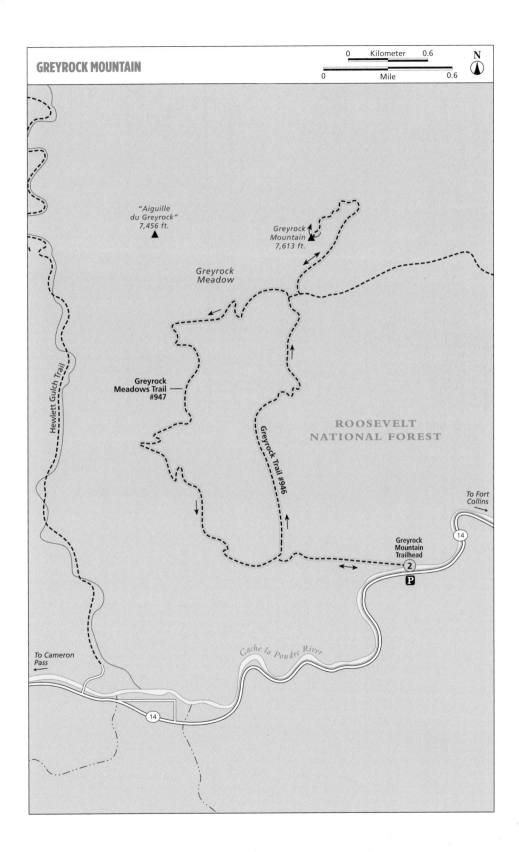

0   Kilometer   0.6

0   Mile   0.6

N

"Aiguille
du Greyrock"
7,456 ft.
▲

Greyrock
Mountain
7,613 ft. ▲

Greyrock
Meadow

Hewlett Gulch Trail

Greyrock
Meadows Trail
#947

Greyrock Trail #946

ROOSEVELT
NATIONAL FOREST

To Fort
Collins

14

Greyrock
Mountain
Trailhead
2

P

To Cameron
Pass

Cache la Poudre River

14

The Greyrock Trail passes through forests burned by wildfire below the peak's south face.

2.8 The trail steepens and ascends several rock "steps," taking a hard left (west). This is an important switchback, as continuing east here puts you on exposed terrain (GPS: 40.717369,-105.288704). Again, if you have a GPS, grab a waypoint here for your hike out. Look for a wooden post marked "TR 946."

2.85 The trail levels out and curves around a rocky slab on the right, then turns left heading west toward the summit area (GPS: 40.717354,-105.288912).

2.95 Follow the trail as it goes west, then east, then west again to a rockface on your right. Look for a short ramp running right to left up through rock to a wooden post (GPS: 40.717574,-105.289373).

3.15 From here, hike west over dirt trail and rock slabs. Look for occasional trail signs to guide the way. The trail curves south and southwest to a small lake or muddy lakebed, depending on rainfall and snowmelt. The summit lies straight ahead, but

Greyrock's distinctive granite pyramid is a northern Front Range landmark visible from the Great Plains.

there is scrambling to do first. Gain the rock slabs on the left (east) side of the lake/mud and scramble straight up (south), then bear right, continuing up and over the rocks and around the right side of a juniper tree near the summit. Take extreme care here, as there are large gaps between the boulders and major exposure on all sides of the rocky summit area.

3.2 Tag the highest point among the uplifted slabs, the 7,613-foot Greyrock Mountain summit (GPS: 40.715678,-105.292642). Return the way you came.

6.4 Arrive back at the trailhead (GPS: 40.694804,-105.284370).

EXTRA CREDIT: GREYROCK MOUNTAIN AND MEADOWS TRAIL LOOP

Turn this out-and-back hike into a longer, counterclockwise loop hike by ascending the Greyrock Mountain Trail and descending the Greyrock Meadows Trail. After summiting Greyrock Mountain as described in this chapter, descend to the upper junction at the base of the peak's pyramid. There, instead of turning left to stay on Greyrock Mountain Trail, continue straight (west) to get on the Greyrock Meadows Trail. This is a longer, gentler trail, but it is not all downhill. The trail rises several times, so you will lose elevation, regain it, and lose it again on your way to the lower junction with Greyrock Mountain Trail, where you will turn right toward the trailhead. The distance from the upper junction to the trailhead is 3.5 miles, versus the shorter, more direct route on Greyrock Mountain Trail of 2.2 miles, for a 7.7-mile total loop, including the summit. As another option, forgo the summit and do the loop only, ascending Greyrock Mountain Trail for 2.2 miles to the Greyrock Meadows Trails, then turning left to join that trail for the descent and a less strenuous 5.7-mile hike with no summit.

3 ARTHURS ROCK

Arthurs Rock, reached by a well-maintained trail in Lory State Park, offers 360-degree views of Fort Collins, Horsetooth Reservoir, Longs Peak, the Mummy Range, and the Rawah Range from its granite summit.

Start: Arthurs Rock Trailhead, Lory State Park
Difficulty: Moderate
Trails: Arthurs Rock Trail
Hiking time: About 2 hours
Distance: 3.4 miles, out and back
Elevations trailhead to summit: 5,635 to 6,780 feet (+1,145 feet)
Rank status: Unranked
Restrictions: Fee area; open daily from 5 a.m. to 8 p.m.; stay on designated trails; leashed dogs allowed; pick up dog waste; no mountain bikes or horses on trail; no open fires; no motorized vehicles; check Lory State Park Facebook page for updates on trail closures due to muddy conditions; no available water
Amenities: Restrooms, picnic tables, and info signs at trailhead; 6 backcountry campsites; services in Fort Collins
County: Larimer
Maps: *DeLorme*: p. 20, E1; Trails Illustrated (none); USGS Horsetooth Reservoir
Land status/contact: Lory State Park, (970) 493-1623

FINDING THE TRAILHEAD

From downtown Fort Collins, drive north on College Avenue / US 287 until it goes right at a roundabout toward Poudre Canyon and Laramie. Following signs for Lory State Park, continue straight on CR 54G (old US 287) through LaPorte to a left turn on CR 52D / Rist Canyon Road. Drive 1.8 miles to the east side of Bellvue and turn left on CR 23. Drive 1.3 miles south and turn right (west) on CR 25G / Lodgepole Drive. Drive 1.6 miles west and then south to a left turn at a Y junction and turn left into Lory State Park on Lory Park Road. Passing the entrance station and visitor center, drive 2.4 miles south on the dirt road to a parking lot and the Arthurs Rock Trailhead at the end of the road (GPS: 40.564355,-105.174851). The trailhead and vault toilets are on the west side of the parking lot.

THE HIKE

Arthurs Rock, along with Horsetooth Mountain to the south, is a landmark peak in the low mountains west of Fort Collins. The rocky peak, jutting proudly against the horizon above Horsetooth Reservoir, lies in 2,492-acre Lory State Park. The park, established in 1967, embraces three distinct plant communities—prairie grassland, mountain shrub, and a ponderosa pine woodland. The popular hike to Arthurs Rock's craggy summit passes through all three. Besides offering 26 miles of hiking trails, Lory State Park visitors also climb cliffs, ride mountain bikes, and picnic in the pines.

The trail, gaining over 1,100 feet of elevation, climbs steeply from the trailhead up Arthurs Rock Gulch. It crosses tall grass meadows and then switchbacks up sunny slopes to the base of a towering granite cliff. The last section ascends rocky steps up a short gully to an open alcove surrounded by rounded cliffs. Most hikers stop here, sitting on a rough boulder for a panoramic Front Range view. Wooded slopes plunge below to long hogbacks lining shimmering Horsetooth Reservoir and the glint of suburbs in Fort

Horsetooth Reservoir and Fort Collins lie east of the bedrock summit of Arthurs Rock.

Granite fins and ribs scatter across the corrugated top of Arthurs Rock.

Arthurs Rock, the rocky centerpiece of Lory State Park, lords over Arthurs Rock Gulch.

Collins. Look southeast on a sunny day for views of downtown Denver's skyline and southwest to towering Longs Peak and the Mummy Range.

To reach the mountain's high point, scramble west on a granite rib to Arthurs Rock's bedrock summit. This short jaunt is not difficult, but it is exposed and dangerous as it traverses above cliffs. Use extreme caution since a fall would result in severe injury or death.

MILES AND DIRECTIONS

0.0   Begin at the Arthurs Rock Trailhead on the west side of the parking lot. Hike west on the trail past a couple of information signs.

0.1   After crossing a footbridge, reach a T junction with West Valley Trail. Go left on signed Arthurs Rock Trail and hike west up Arthurs Rock Gulch in a narrow canyon.

0.3   Reach a Y junction with the Overlook Trail on the right at the east end of a meadow (GPS: 40.563437,-105.178195). Continue straight on the signed left fork and hike across the meadow with views west of craggy Arthurs Rock.

ARTHURS ROCK

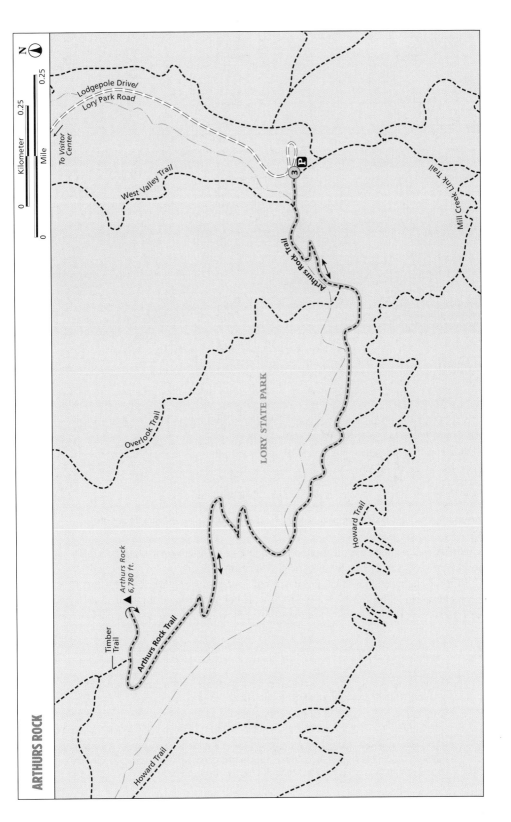

Lodgepole Drive/
Lory Park Road

To Visitor Center

West Valley Trail

Arthurs Rock Trail

Mill Creek Link Trail

Overlook Trail

LORY STATE PARK

Howard Trail

Howard Trail

Timber Trail

Arthurs Rock 6,780 ft.

Arthurs Rock Trail

N

Kilometer
0   0.25   0.25

Mile
0   0.25

The trail up Arthurs Rock crosses through open meadows and shady ponderosa pine forests.

0.6 On the meadow's western edge, reach a junction on the left with the Mill Creek Link to Howard Trail. Continue on Arthurs Rock Trail straight up Arthurs Rock Gulch through pine woods. Howard Trail is an alternate descent route to the trailhead.

0.8 From the bottom of the canyon, swing right and begin climbing the trail on steep, open slopes below Arthurs Rock.

1.1 Reach a signed junction on a ridge below Arthurs Rock (GPS: 40.566065, -105.184184). A short path goes right to a scenic overlook, while a climber access trail goes straight to cliffs on the peak's north flank. Go left on Arthurs Rock Trail to continue to the summit.

1.4 Reach the base of a high granite cliff that forms the south face of Arthurs Rock. Follow the trail west through tall ponderosa pines below the cliff.

1.6 Reach a junction with Timber Trail on the left (GPS: 40.568187,-105.188943). Continue straight on the trail signed "Arthurs Rock Summit" and climb rough stone steps up a narrow gully lined with broken cliffs.

1.7 Arrive at a flat area studded with pine trees and circled by low cliffs. Most hikers end their quest here. Find a bedrock seat and enjoy views east to Horsetooth Reservoir and Fort Collins. To tag the true 6,780-foot Arthurs Rock summit, scramble up a slab past a couple of large boulders and then tiptoe across an airy ridge to the high point of a granite fin (GPS: 40.568269,-105.188122). Note: This ridge scramble is airy, and a fall would result in severe injury or death. Use caution and control children. After admiring the views and eating a sandwich or energy bar, return down the trail.

3.4 Arrive back at the trailhead (GPS: 40.564355,-105.174851).

Options: Extend the foot adventure from the summit by descending twisting Howard Trail for 2 miles to Mill Creek Link, a side trail that jogs left to the Arthurs Rock Trail and the trailhead for a 4.3-mile round-trip hike. A longer option heads west from Arthurs Rock Trail on Timber Trail for 0.8 mile to Westridge Trail. Follow Westridge Trail for 1.9 miles to the top of Howard Trail, then down it for 1.3 miles to the Mill Creek Link, which leads to Arthurs Rock Trail and the trailhead for a 6.3-mile round-trip trek.

4 SHEEP MOUNTAIN

The Round Mountain National Recreation Trail twists up the east and south flanks of Sheep Mountain, a rugged peak looming above the Big Thompson Canyon between Loveland and Estes Park.

Start: Round Mountain Trailhead, Viestenz-Smith Mountain Park
Difficulty: Strenuous
Trails: Round Mountain National Recreation Trail #969, Summit Adventure Trail
Hiking time: 6–8 hours
Distance: 9.2 miles, out and back
Elevations trailhead to summit: 5,770 to 8,450 feet (+2,680 feet)
Rank status: Ranked
Restrictions: No motorized equipment; camping and fires prohibited along the first mile of both trails; leashed dogs only on the Foothills Nature Trail and the first mile of Summit Adventure Trail; no motorized vehicles or equipment; no available water; no nearby public camping
Amenities: Toilets and information board at trailhead; services in Loveland
County: Larimer
Maps: *DeLorme*: p. 29, B8 and p. 30, B1; Trails Illustrated #101: Cache La Poudre, Big Thompson; USGS Drake
Land status/contact: Viestenz-Smith Mountain Park, Loveland Parks and Recreation, (970) 962-2727; Roosevelt National Forest, (970) 295-6600; Canyon Lakes Ranger District, (970) 295-6700

FINDING THE TRAILHEAD

From the junction of US 34 / Eisenhower Boulevard and US 287 / Cleveland Avenue (southbound street) in Loveland, drive west on US 34 toward Estes Park for 12.9 miles. Just past the right turn for Viestenz-Smith Mountain Park, turn left into the signed parking lot and trailhead for Round Mountain Trail (GPS: 40.420313,-105.285208). After the highway enters the Big Thompson River's gorge, this left turn is 4 miles to the west. Trailhead address: 1211 US 34. If the parking lot is full, park at the mountain park across the highway and follow a signed connector trail to the Round Mountain Trailhead.

THE HIKE

The Round Mountain National Recreation Trail, divided into the Foothills Nature Trail and Summit Adventure Trail, climbs up 8,450-foot Sheep Mountain in the Front Range west of Loveland. The strenuous hike offers a long day on the trail with over 3,000 feet of cumulative (out and back) elevation gain, and gradual grades mixed with steep sections.

The hike begins in the city of Loveland's Viestenz-Smith Mountain Park by the Big Thompson River and rises into Roosevelt National Forest. Trailside plaques lie along the trail's first 3 miles, detailing geology, ecology, and natural history, with notes on the surrounding sagebrush, talus fields, and ponderosa pines. The trail climbs through a mixed conifer forest and open meadows to the hike's best section, a contouring traverse across the mountain's east face through jagged granite cliffs and views east to Loveland and the tawny prairie. Sheep Mountain's wooded summit yields no good views so soak in the scenery at overlooks along the trail. At the first trail junction, a right turn on

Palisade Mountain, walling the northern edge of Big Thompson Canyon, rises beyond the Summit Adventure Trail.

The trail levels out below the wooded east face of Sheep Mountain.

SHEEP MOUNTAIN

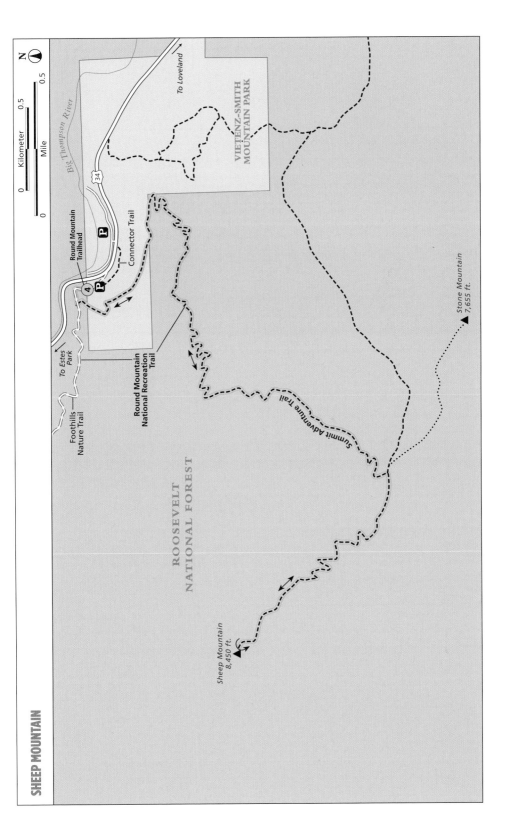

N

0   Kilometer   0.5   0.5

0   Mile

Big Thompson River

To Loveland

VIETENZ-SMITH
MOUNTAIN PARK

Round Mountain
Trailhead

P

Connector Trail

34

P

4

To Estes
Park

Foothills
Nature Trail

Round Mountain
National Recreation
Trail

Summit Adventure Trail

ROOSEVELT
NATIONAL FOREST

Stone Mountain
7,655 ft.

Sheep Mountain
8,450 ft.

A thunderstorm darkens the prairie east of Sheep Mountain.

Foothills Nature Trail (not part of this hike) provides a 1-mile, self-guided hike for kids and families that ends at a historic stone shelter overlooking the river.

The Civilian Conservation Corps (CCC) built the trail in 1934 and 1935 and the Loveland Ranger Force later improved it. The Loveland Mountain Club now maintains the trail with the US Forest Service. The name Round Mountain is confusing because the trail climbs to the summit of Sheep Mountain, the peak's official name as designated on USGS topo maps. The website Lists of John lists Sheep Mountain as one of more than forty ranked and unranked Colorado mountains with the same or similar name.

MILES AND DIRECTIONS

0.0 Start at the Round Mountain Trailhead on the northeast side of the parking lot. Hike past a locked gate and go uphill on the Round Mountain National Recreation Trail, a closed dirt road.

0.2 Reach a signed junction. Go left on the signed Summit Trail (GPS: 40.421165, -105.286552) and hike uphill on the wide track. The Foothills Nature Trail (not part of this hike) continues straight west from the junction to an overlook.

0.3 Reach a cleared area and the end of the doubletrack trail (GPS: 40.419608, -105.287206). Go left on the signed trail and hike east, contouring across a steep, north-facing slope. At 0.5 mile, the trail crosses a talus field and continues rising with occasional short descents.

0.9 The trail reaches a sign on the left detailing the partnership of the Loveland Mountain Club and the US Forest Service at a switchback to the right. This marks the end of the trail's north slope leg. The next section follows the peak's east ridge. Go right and begin climbing through an open pine forest.

1.0 Reach a sturdy wooden post marking Mile 1 (GPS: 40.416238, -105.279156). Continue west up the wide ridge.

The trail edges above granite cliffs and boulders on the east flank of Sheep Mountain.

The Summit Adventure Trail squeezes between cliffs and then climbs to the mountain's south slope.

1.3 The trail flattens and offers a view of the wooded eastern flank of Sheep Mountain. Continue west on the gently rising trail.

2.0 Partway up a steep section, reach the Mile 2 marker on a switchback (GPS: 40.413766,-105.290011). After climbing four more switchbacks, the trail turns sharply left. The next trail segment contours across the mountain's east face, offering scenic views to the east and threading through jumbled granite boulders and cliffs.

2.6 Reach a corridor flanked by high rock walls (GPS: 40.410893,-105.292992). Scramble through it and descend to the trail, which continues twisting southwest across the slope.

3.0 Pass a spring on the right and reach the Mile 3 post (GPS: 40.406791,-105.295380). Continue southwest and gently descend to a shallow valley. Climb slopes through a mature forest.

3.4 Reach a junction at a wide, grassy saddle. Go right on the main trail and head northwest up wooded slopes. The left trail heads up slopes for about a mile to the top of 7,655-foot Stone Mountain (not part of this hike).

4.0 Reach the Mile 4 post at a switchback (GPS: 40.406586,-105.304742). Continue up wide switchbacks and then head up gentler slopes through meadows and forest.

4.6 Arrive at a giant rock cairn on the flat summit of 8,450-foot Sheep Mountain (GPS: 40.412245,-105.310965). Thick forest on the mountain top blocks views of surrounding peaks. Return the way you came.

9.2 Arrive back at the trailhead (GPS: 40.420313,-105.285208).

5 KRUGER ROCK

An excellent trail, expansive views, and large summit area make Kruger Rock a popular destination for Estes Park locals and visitors to the area.

Start: Kruger Rock Trailhead, Hermit Park Open Space
Difficulty: Easy
Trails: Kruger Rock Trail
Hiking time: About 1.5 hours
Distance: 3.4 miles, out and back
Elevations trailhead to summit: 8,442 to 9,355 feet (+913 feet)
Rank status: Ranked
Restrictions: Fee area, pay per day or by annual permit; open seasonally from Mar 1 to Dec 20; no bicycles; no campfires; dogs must be on hand-held leash; no available water

Amenities: Toilet at trailhead; Bobcat Campground in Hermit Park (reservations at larimercamping.com); services in Estes Park
County: Larimer
Maps: *DeLorme*: p. 29, B7; Trails Illustrated #101: Cache la Poudre, Big Thompson, #200: Rocky Mountain National Park; USGS Panorama Peak
Land status/contact: Hermit Park Open Space, (970) 577-2090; for information after hours and during the off-season, (970) 619-4570

FINDING THE TRAILHEAD

From Estes Park, take US 36 / N St. Vrain Avenue east for 3.9 miles and turn right into Hermit Park Open Space. Purchase a day permit at the self-service station or see the office for an annual permit. Parking for Kruger Rock Trailhead is located 2.5 miles from the turnoff on the right side of the road. The trail begins on the west edge of the parking lot (GPS: 40.341774,-105.475596).

Kruger Rock lifts a craggy brow above meadows in Hermit Park.

The lower Kruger Rock Trail threads through open meadows and aspen groves.

A rocky overlook offers views from the Kruger Rock Trail to Estes Park and Lumpy Ridge.

To reach Kruger Rock's true summit, scramble up the easy gully to spacious views.

THE HIKE

The hike to Kruger Rock is straightforward on a good trail. You might be tempted to make short work of it but take your time to enjoy the scenic views at each opening in the trees along the trail. The horizon is lined with peaks, including Twin Sisters Peaks to the south, and Mount Meeker and 14,255-foot Longs Peak, the high point of Rocky Mountain National Park, to the southwest. Across the valley to the west rise Lily Mountain (Hike 6), and farther west are peaks along the Continental Divide including Flattop Mountain (Hike 8) and Hallett Peak (Hike 9).

MILES AND DIRECTIONS

- 0.0 From the Kruger Rock Trailhead, hike northwest on Kruger Rock Trail. Kruger Rock appears as a rocky fortress atop a forested hill in the western sky left of the trail.
- 0.4 At the junction with Limber Pine Trail, continue straight on Kruger Rock Trail (GPS: 40.344611,-105.480942).

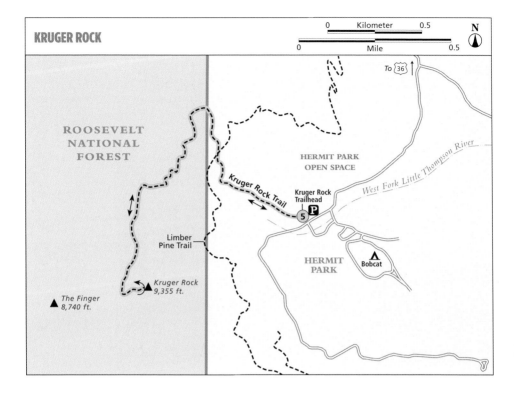

1.7   Reach the summit area of Kruger Rock. If you are comfortable with Class 2+ / Low Class 3 scrambling, reach the 9,355-foot rocky top by carefully making your way up a wide gap in the summit boulders. Take extreme care going up and down this section and on top, which is wildly exposed. Do not climb if the rock is wet or during inclement weather. A fall would result in injury or death. Return the way you came (GPS: 40.338374,-105.485689).

3.4   Arrive back at the trailhead (GPS: 40.341774,-105.475596).

6 LILY MOUNTAIN

The rugged trail and short, stiff hike up Lily Mountain seem hardly worth the trouble until you reach the lofty summit, where you're rewarded with exciting 360-degree views of Rocky Mountain National Park.

Start: Lily Mountain Trailhead, CO 7 / S St. Vrain Avenue
Difficulty: Moderate
Trails: Lily Mountain Trail #933
Hiking time: About 2 hours
Distance: 4.0 miles, out and back
Elevations trailhead to summit: 8,790 to 9,786 feet (+996 feet)
Rank status: Ranked
Restrictions: None posted, but the small parking lot fills quickly; no toilets at trailhead but are at nearby Lily Lake Trailhead

Amenities: Nearest camping at Longs Peak Campground; services in Estes Park
County: Larimer
Maps: *DeLorme*: p. 29, C6 and B6; Trails Illustrated: #301 Longs Peak: Rocky Mountain National Park (Bear Lake, Wild Basin); USGS Longs Peak
Land status/contact: Roosevelt National Forest, (970) 295-6600; Canyon Lakes Ranger District, (970) 295-6700

FINDING THE TRAILHEAD

From Estes Park, take CO 7 / S St. Vrain Avenue south for 5.8 miles to limited pullout parking on the right side of the road. The trail begins on the north edge of the parking lot (GPS: 40.313718,-105.535355).

Lily Mountain looms above Lily Lake on the eastern edge of Rocky Mountain National Park.

Evening light reddens the Twin Sisters above the Lily Mountain Trail.

The Lily Mountain Trail gives views south of the iconic Twin Sisters.

Boulders frame an overlook high on the Lily Mountain Trail.

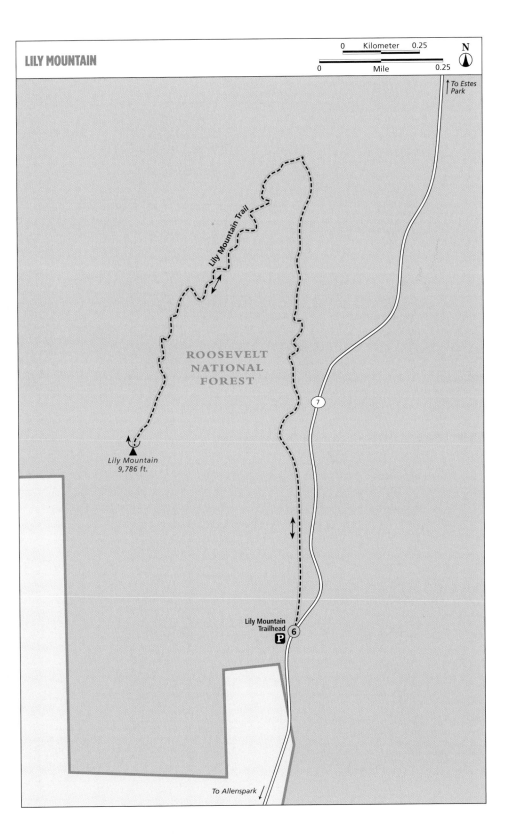

0 Kilometer 0.25

0 Mile 0.25

N

To Estes
Park

Lily Mountain Trail

ROOSEVELT
NATIONAL
FOREST

7

Lily Mountain
9,786 ft.

Lily Mountain
Trailhead 6

P

To Allenspark

Lily Mountain's rock-ribbed summit is a perfect lunch spot with spacious views of the Twin Sisters.

THE HIKE

Lily Mountain is a short, stiff hike that packs a punch. The small, rocky summit is flat but exposed, so stay clear of abrupt cliff edges. Views abound, with 11,428-foot Twin Sisters Peaks to the southeast and Estes Cone to the southwest. Beyond towers 13,911-foot Mountain Meeker and 14,255-foot Longs Peak, the highest peak in Rocky Mountain National Park, on the southwest skyline. Combine your trek with a circular hike around nearby Lily Lake, located 0.1 mile south on CO 7, where you can get good views of the peak you just climbed, for a full-value half-day adventure near Estes Park.

MILES AND DIRECTIONS

0.0 From the Lily Mountain Trailhead, hike north on Lily Mountain Trail. The trail rises above the highway, to your right, contouring the mountain north before turning south and climbing more steeply through the forest.

1.9 Shortly after passing a large cairn on the left side of the trail, as the trail reaches a high point, look for a side trail over and through rocks on the right. Switchback right and then left to reach the ridge. Carefully gain the ridge and scramble south (left) through rocks (GPS: 40.319596,-105.540774).

2.0 Reach the exposed summit of 9,786-foot Lily Mountain. Return the way you came (GPS: 40.319596,-105.540774).

4.0 Arrive back at the trailhead (GPS: 40.319179,-105.541295).

7 DEER MOUNTAIN

Deer Mountain divides Horseshoe Park and Beaver Meadows in Rocky Mountain National Park Wilderness and offers views of the Mummy Range, the Continental Divide, and Estes Park.

Start: Deer Mountain Trailhead, Deer Ridge Junction on US 36 in Rocky Mountain National Park
Difficulty: Strenuous
Trails: West Deer Mountain Trail
Hiking time: 3–4 hours
Distance: 6.0 miles, out and back
Elevations trailhead to summit: 8,926 to 10,013 feet (+1,087 feet)
Rank status: Ranked
Restrictions: Fee area; no toilets at trailhead; timed entry and reservation may be required (nps.gov/romo/planyourvisit/timed-entry-permit -system.htm); trail is day use only unless wilderness camping by permit (recreation.gov/permits/4675320); no overnight parking except for campground and wilderness camping in the park by permit only; no campfires; no dogs or bicycles allowed on trail; no available water on trail
Amenities: Toilets at Beaver Meadows Visitor Center (year-round), Moraine Park Discovery Center, and Fall River Visitor Center (seasonally); camping by reservation at Moraine Park, Glacier Basin, and Aspenglen Campgrounds (recreation.gov); services in Estes Park
County: Larimer
Maps: *DeLorme*: p. 29, B6; Trails Illustrated #200: Rocky Mountain National Park; USGS Estes Park
Land status/contact: Rocky Mountain National Park, (970) 586-1206

FINDING THE TRAILHEAD

From East Elkhorn Avenue in Estes Park, drive west on US 36 / Moraine Avenue for 3.6 miles to the Beaver Meadows Entrance / Toll Station at Rocky Mountain National Park and pay the fee or use your parks pass to enter the park. Continue for 3.1 miles to Deer Ridge Junction and roadside parking. The trailhead is on the right side of the road (GPS: 40.386967,-105.609900).

Deer Mountain, rising above Moraine Park meadows, is climbed by a popular trail in Rocky Mountain National Park.

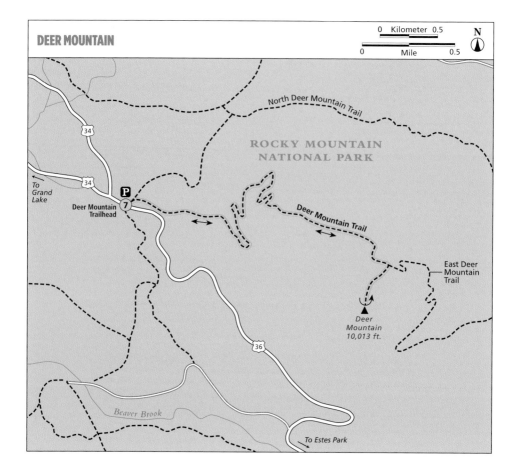

THE HIKE

This hike in Rocky Mountain National Park features enough elevation gain to provide a workout without wearing you out. The first mile crosses open terrain with a good trail and views south of the park's high peaks including Longs Peak, Pagoda Mountain, and McHenrys Peak. Looking north, left of the trail, the Mummy Range edges the sky. The trail gains most of its elevation in the forested, rocky switchbacks between the first and second mile. On the large summit, pull up a rock and enjoy more views of the Continental Divide to the west and Estes Park in the valley to the east.

MILES AND DIRECTIONS

0.0   From the Deer Mountain Trailhead, hike northeast on West Deer Mountain Trail.

0.1   The trail heads east with Deer Mountain in view straight ahead. At the trail junction with North Deer Mountain Trail, which leads to Aspenglen Campground, continue straight and east toward Deer Mountain (GPS: 40.387217,-105.608167).

0.8   Reach the first switchback. From here, the trail turns north and begins to rise steeply in alternating north and south switchbacks, east toward the summit ridge (GPS: 40.384017,-105.596717).

The Deer Mountain Trail offers mountain scenery like the crest of the Mummy Range.

2.1 Continue as the trail eases gently east-southeast (GPS: 40.386267,-105.593417).

2.8 At a trail junction, turn right toward the summit. The East Deer Mountain Trail to Estes Park (not your route) goes left at the junction, so don't miss this important right turn (GPS: 40.381483,-105.582700).

3.0 Arrive at the rocky summit of 10,013-foot Deer Mountain (GPS: 40.379200, -105.584450). Return the way you came.

6.0 Arrive back at the trailhead (GPS: 40.386967,-105.609900).

Peaks along the Continental Divide spread across the horizon beyond Deer Mountain's rock-strewn summit.

8 FLATTOP MOUNTAIN

A steady climb on good trails through Rocky Mountain National Park Wilderness rewards the hiker with two scenic overlooks and forever views on the final stretch to the flat-topped summit of Flattop Mountain astride the Continental Divide.

Start: Bear Lake Trailhead, Rocky Mountain National Park
Difficulty: Strenuous
Trails: Bear Lake Loop Trail, Bear Lake to Bierstadt Junction Trail, Flattop Mountain Trail
Hiking time: 5–6 hours
Distance: 8.8 miles, out and back
Elevations trailhead to summit: 9,452 to 12,324 feet (+2,872 feet)
Rank status: Unranked
Restrictions: Fee area; timed-entry reservations may be required to enter park (nps.gov/romo/planyourvisit/timed-entry-permit-system.htm); trail is day use only unless wilderness camping by permit (recreation.gov/permits/4675320); no overnight parking except for campground and wilderness camping in the park by permit only; no campfires; no dogs or bicycles allowed on trails; no motorized vehicles or equipment; parking lot fills early; take the free shuttle to Bear Lake Trailhead to avoid parking problems; no available water on trail
Amenities: Vault toilets and ranger station at trailhead; free shuttle from Park & Ride Transit Hub on Bear Lake Road; camping by reservation at Glacier Basin, Moraine Park, and Aspenglen Campgrounds (recreation .gov); services in Estes Park
Counties: Grand and Larimer
Maps: *DeLorme*: p. 29, C5; Trails Illustrated #200: Rocky Mountain National Park; USGS McHenrys Peak
Land status/contact: Rocky Mountain National Park, (970) 586-1206

FINDING THE TRAILHEAD

From Estes Park, take US 36 west for 3.8 miles to Beaver Meadows Entrance Station at Rocky Mountain National Park. Drive 0.2 mile past the entrance and turn left (south) on Bear Lake Road. Drive 9.4 miles up Bear Lake Road from the turnoff to a parking lot and trailhead at the road's end (GPS: 40.311960, -105.645968). The parking lot quickly fills in summer and on weekends. Avoid parking problems by boarding the Bear Lake shuttle at the Park & Ride Transit Hub on Bear Lake Road opposite Glacier Basin Campground and ride to the Bear Lake stop. The shuttle runs from late May to mid-October, with shuttles departing about every 15 minutes from 6:30 a.m. to 7:30 p.m.

THE HIKE

The hike to Flattop Mountain begins at Bear Lake, the busiest trailhead in Rocky Mountain National Park. After leaving the Bear Lake Loop Trail, climb the trail into a mixed conifer forest and head west toward the Continental Divide. The high-elevation trail holds snow through late spring, so unless you are hiking in mid-summer, be prepared with proper footwear, traction spikes, and trekking poles or even an ice axe for crossing mounds of snow in the forest and icy snowfields at higher elevations.

The hike offers breathtaking alpine scenery, but the summit plateau is anticlimactic with a wooden sign at a flat area pointing toward the North Inlet Trail and Tonahutu Trail on the other side of the mountain. These trails begin on Rocky Mountain National

Emerald Lake nestles in glaciated Tyndall Gorge below the Flattop Mountain Trail.

A trail sign marks the summit of Flattop Mountain on the Continental Divide.

Longs Peak, the highest mountain in Rocky Mountain National Park, rises beyond the Flattop Mountain Trail.

Park's west side near the town of Grand Lake and climb to the west slopes of Flattop Mountain. Access to the west slope was limited to only permitted backpackers after the 2020 East Troublesome Fire.

From the Flattop summit, located atop the Continental Divide, enjoy views of Hallett Peak to the southeast and Longs Peak, Storm Peak, and Mount Lady Washington visible to Hallett's left. Hallett Peak (Hike 9) is a short but difficult jaunt from Flattop Mountain, so if you have the time, the energy, and the skill to tag its summit refer to the next chapter for directions and details.

MILES AND DIRECTIONS

0.0   From the Bear Lake Trailhead located between the ranger station and the shuttle stop at the west end of the Bear Lake Parking Lot, hike northwest over a wide footbridge and bear right toward Bear Lake, past the junction with trails to Alberta Falls and Emerald Lake Trail, to get on the Bear Lake Loop Trail.

0.05 Bear right on the Bear Lake Loop Trail and hike counterclockwise around the east side of Bear Lake. The distinct angular east face of Hallett Peak appears on the skyline west-southwest of the lake, with the mellow mound of Flattop Mountain barely visible to the right of Hallett Peak (GPS: 40.312116,-105.646436).

FLATTOP MOUNTAIN/HALLETT PEAK

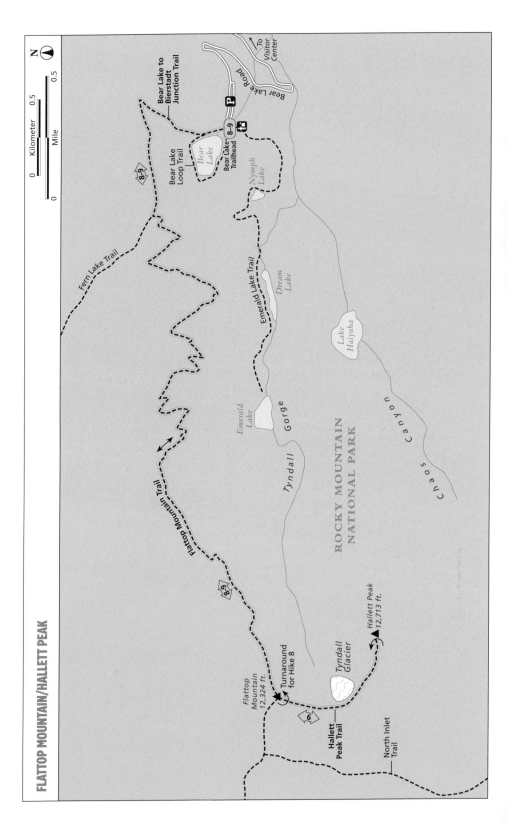

N

| 0 | Kilometer | 0.5 |

| 0 | Mile | 0.5 |

Bear Lake to Bierstadt Junction Trail

Bear Lake Loop Trail

8-9

Bear Lake

Bear Lake Trailhead 8-9

P

Bear Lake Road

To Visitor Center

Nymph Lake

Fern Lake Trail

Emerald Lake Trail

Dream Lake

Lake Haiyaha

Emerald Lake

Tyndall Gorge

Flattop Mountain Trail

ROCKY MOUNTAIN NATIONAL PARK

Chaos Canyon

8-9

Flattop Mountain 12,324 ft.

Turnaround for Hike 8

Tyndall Glacier

Hallett Peak 12,713 ft.

9

Hallett Peak Trail

North Inlet Trail

Hallett Peak's sheer northeast face lies beyond a jumble of boulders on the east flank of Flattop Mountain.

0.15   Turn right onto the Bear Lake to Bierstadt Junction Trail, signed for Flattop Mountain, Odessa Lake, Fern Lake, and Odessa Lake, and hike north-northeast past the Flattop Mountain information board (GPS: 40.313398,-105.646745).

0.5   Turn left at the trail junction, onto the Flattop Mountain Trail, and hike west (GPS: 40.317399,-105.643947).

1.0   Reach the junction with the Odessa Lake / Flattop Mountain Junction Trail and bear left to stay on the Flattop Mountain Trail (GPS: 40.316405,-105.653009).

1.7   Continue on the trail as it climbs west, switchbacking north and south to the Dream Lake Overlook (GPS: 40.312547,-105.659170).

3.0   The trail continues to climb west, slowly rising out of the forest to the final switchback and the Emerald Lake Viewpoint before curving northwest to southwest across boulder-strewn tundra (GPS: 40.314519,-105.670322).

4.0   Reach a horse rack above Tyndall Gorge with views of Tyndall Glacier and Hallett Peak ahead and left of the trail (GPS: 40.310315,-105.684213).

4.4   Arrive at the summit of 12,324-foot Flattop Mountain (GPS: 40.308909, -105.690247). Return the way you came.

8.8   Arrive back at the trailhead (GPS: 40.311960,-105.645968).

9 **HALLETT PEAK**

The hike to Hallett Peak is more difficult than other Rocky Mountain National Park hikes in this book. The final section, a faint path through talus and boulders, may challenge hikers used to well-worn paths but careful observation makes the journey possible and the skyscraping summit even more satisfying.

Start: Bear Lake Trailhead, Rocky Mountain National Park
Difficulty: Very strenuous
Trails: Bear Lake Loop Trail, Bear Lake to Bierstadt Junction Trail, Flattop Mountain Trail, Hallett Peak Trail
Hiking time: 7–8 hours
Distance: 10.2 miles, out and back
Elevations trailhead to summit: 9,452 to 12,713 feet (+3,261 feet)
Rank status: Ranked
Restrictions: Fee area; timed entry reservations may be required to enter park (nps.gov/romo/planyourvisit/timed-entry-permit-system.htm); trail is day use only unless wilderness camping by permit (recreation.gov/permits/4675320); no overnight parking except for campground and wilderness camping in the park by permit only; no campfires; no dogs or bicycles allowed on trails; parking lot fills early; take the free shuttle to Bear Lake Trailhead to avoid parking problems; no available water on trail; wilderness rules apply; no motorized vehicles or equipment
Amenities: Vault toilets and ranger station at trailhead; free shuttle from Park & Ride Transit Hub on Bear Lake Road; camping by reservation at Glacier Basin, Moraine Park, and Aspenglen Campgrounds (recreation. gov); services in Estes Park
Counties: Grand and Larimer
Maps: *DeLorme*: p. 29, C5; Trails Illustrated #200: Rocky Mountain National Park; USGS McHenrys Peak
Land status/contact: Rocky Mountain National Park, (970) 586-1206

FINDING THE TRAILHEAD

From Estes Park, take US 36 west for 3.8 miles to Beaver Meadows Entrance Station at Rocky Mountain National Park. Drive 0.2 mile past the entrance and turn left (south) on Bear Lake Road. Drive 9.4 miles up Bear Lake Road from the turnoff to a parking lot and trailhead at the road's end (GPS: 40.311960, -105.645968). The parking lot quickly fills in summer and on weekends. Avoid parking problems by boarding the Bear Lake shuttle at the Park & Ride Transit Hub opposite Glacier Basin Campground and ride to the Bear Lake stop. The shuttle runs from late May to mid-October, with shuttles departing about every 15 minutes from 6:30 a.m. to 7:30 p.m.

THE HIKE

The Hallett Peak hike follows the same route as the Flattop Mountain hike in the previous chapter for 4.4 miles, so if you do this hike, you can claim two peaks with one hike. However, the stretch of trail between Flattop and Hallett is less defined and the final 0.4 mile to Hallett's summit is technically more difficult. The trail crosses over loose talus and boulders, which adds time to the ascent. Take care on this somewhat unstable terrain. It's better to move slowly and choose your path carefully than to rush and risk twisting an ankle. If bad weather or darkness are approaching, turn back and do Hallett another day.

The sheer east face of Hallett Peak towers above Emerald Lake and Tyndall Gorge.

The hike up Hallett Peak follows the Flattop Mountain Trail with spectacular views of Longs Peak.

Hallett Peak's pointed summit lies above corniced ridges on Flattop Mountain and Tyndall Gorge.

But if you have the time and energy you'll be glad to add the extra 1.4 miles round trip to the Flattop hike, especially after reaching the rocky summit of Hallett Peak.

Hallett's summit yields expansive, 360-degree views. Flattop Mountain lies below to the northwest. Also, look for the shrinking Tyndall Glacier and Gorge; the Mummy Range stretching across the northern horizon; and a slew of Front Range peaks to the south, including Longs Peak, Pagoda Mountain, Chiefs Head Peak, McHenrys Peak, Powell Peak, Mount Alice, and Taylor Peak.

MILES AND DIRECTIONS

0.0 From the Bear Lake Trailhead located between the ranger station and the shuttle stop at the west end of the Bear Lake parking lot, hike northwest over a wide foot-bridge and bear right toward Bear Lake, past the junction with trails to Alberta Falls and Emerald Lake Trail, to get on the Bear Lake Loop Trail.

0.05 Bear right on the Bear Lake Loop Trail and hike counterclockwise around the east side of Bear Lake. The distinct angular east face of Hallett Peak appears on the skyline west-southwest of the lake, but don't worry—the trail approaches the peak from its gentler northwest side (GPS: 40.312116,-105.646436).

The Flattop Mountain Trail swings across open slopes to the Continental Divide and Hallett Peak.

0.15 Turn right onto the Bear Lake to Bierstadt Junction Trail, signed for Flattop Mountain, Odessa Lake, and Fern Lake, and hike northeast past the Flattop Mountain information board (GPS: 40.313398,-105.646745).

0.5 Turn left at the trail junction onto the Flattop Mountain Trail, and hike west (GPS: 40.317399,-105.643947).

1.0 Reach a junction with the Odessa Lake/Flattop Mountain Junction Trail and bear left to stay on the Flattop Mountain Trail (GPS: 40.316405,-105.653009).

1.7 Continue on the trail as it climbs west, switchbacking north and south to Dream Lake Overlook (GPS: 40.312547,-105.659170).

3.0 The trail continues climbing west, slowly rising out of the forest to the final switchback and the Emerald Lake Viewpoint before curving northwest to southwest across boulder-strewn tundra (GPS: 40.314519,-105.670322).

4.0 Reach a hitching rack above Tyndall Gorge with views of Tyndall Glacier and Hallett Peak ahead and left of the trail (GPS: 40.310315,-105.684213).

4.4 Arrive at the summit of Flattop Mountain. The Flattop Mountain trail continues west toward the North Inlet Trail and Tonahutu Trail on the other side of the mountain. The hike turns left here toward Hallett Peak. Continue south on the fainter Hallett Peak Trail (GPS: 40.308909,-105.690247).

4.6 At an unsigned junction, bear left to stay on the Hallett Peak Trail. The cutoff trail to the right joins the North Inlet-Flattop Junction Trail and goes in the wrong direction. To the left, the Tyndall Glacier drops into Tyndall Gorge. Do not approach the cliff's edge, as a fall would be fatal (40.306198,-105.691135).

The view north from Hallett Peak's summit includes broad meadows on the Continental Divide and a remnant of the Tyndall Glacier.

4.7   The trail rises and becomes hard to follow as it leaves the tundra and winds through broken rocks. Look for the dirt trail crossing the talus and boulders. Unofficial cairns have been placed from here to the summit, but they may be in the wrong places. Use caution following them to ensure you don't get off-route. Aim for the high point (GPS: 40.304588,-105.690831).

5.1   Arrive at the summit of 12,713-foot Hallett Peak (GPS: 40.303028,-105.685936). Pay attention to your exit point onto the flat summit area so you can locate it for the descent. Return back down the trail.

10.2   Arrive back at the trailhead (GPS: 40.311960,-105.645968).

10 MOUNT SANITAS AND "SANITAS MOUNTAINEER TOP"

Mount Sanitas, rising northwest of Boulder, is one of the city's most popular peaks with hikers and trail runners scrambling up its steep, rocky trails to a summit with forever views of Boulder and Denver's skyscrapers to the east, Green Mountain to the south, and the rugged Continental Divide to the west.

Start: Centennial Trailhead, Sunshine Canyon Drive
Difficulty: Strenuous
Trails: Mt. Sanitas Trail, East Ridge Trail, Sanitas Valley Trail
Hiking time: About 2 hours
Distance: 3.2 miles, loop for "Sanitas Mountaineer Top"; 3.5 miles for both summits
Elevations trailhead to summit: 5,555 at trailhead to 6,820 feet at "Sanitas Mountaineer Top" (+1,265 feet); to 6,863 feet at Mount Sanitas (+1,308 feet)
Rank status: Unranked (both summits)
Restrictions: Open daily from 1 hour before sunrise to 1 hour after sunset; hike on designated trails only; dogs must be leashed all the time and stay on trails; pick up dog waste immediately, do not leave baggies by trail; no open fires, camping, mountain bikes, marijuana use, or drones; no open carry or discharging of firearms; no motorized vehicles; stay on designated trails; no nearby public campgrounds
Amenities: Toilets and information sign at trailhead; services in Boulder
County: Boulder
Maps: *DeLorme*: p. 29, E8; Trails Illustrated #100: Boulder, Golden; USGS Boulder
Land status/contact: City of Boulder Open Space & Mountain Parks, (303) 441-3440

FINDING THE TRAILHEAD

From downtown Boulder and the Pearl Street Mall, drive north on Broadway and turn left on Mapleton Avenue. Drive 0.9 mile west on Mapleton, which turns into Sunshine Canyon Drive as the road enters a canyon. Turn left from Sunshine Canyon Drive into two parking lots for the Centennial Trailhead. The trailhead is on the east side of the parking lot and left of the restrooms at an information sign (GPS: 40.020256,-105.297632).

THE HIKE

Mount Sanitas, lifting wooded ridges above the city's northwest side, is Boulder's beloved backyard peak. Every day a host of hikers and runners tackle the famed Mount Sanitas Trail up the mountain's south ridge, gaining over 1,300 feet of elevation in a mere 1.3 miles. The trail offers steep, rocky sections with stone steps and tree roots interspersed with gentler sections and viewpoints that allow hikers to catch their breath. The descent drops down the steeper East Ridge Trail, scrambling over and between boulders. The final return route follows wide Sanitas Valley Trail down a grassy valley below the peak.

The peak's first hikers were tuberculosis patients at the Boulder-Colorado Sanitarium and Hospital near today's trailhead in the 1890s. The mountain's name is a shortened

Mount Sanitas, offering one of Boulder's most popular peak hikes, rears above the Dakota Ridge.

form of the word "sanitarium." The Mount Sanitas Trail reaches the mountain's lower summit, dubbed "Sanitas Mountaineer Top." To climb the higher 6,863-foot summit of Mount Sanitas, follow a short trail north through woods from the lower summit. The trails, open year-round, are busy on weekends and during the summer. Plan to arrive early in the morning or in the late afternoon for a parking spot at the trailhead. If it is full, more parking is east of the trailhead.

MILES AND DIRECTIONS

0.0   Start at the Centennial Trailhead on the south side of Sunshine Canyon Drive. Walk left past restrooms to an info sign and continue to a signed junction with Red Rocks Trail. Go left on the wide trail and cross Sunshine Canyon Drive on a diagonal cross-walk. Follow the Mount Sanitas Trail, which begins on the north side of the road, to a short staircase.

0.1   Reach the official Mount Sanitas Trailhead above the staircase. Descend steps and pass right of a picnic pavilion.

0.15 Reach a signed Y junction with the Mount Sanitas Trail on the left and Sanitas Valley Trail on the right. Start the clockwise loop by going left on Mount Sanitas Trail and climb timber steps to a junction with the right starting branch of Mount Sanitas Trail. Go left.

0.3   Climb the rough trail and timber steps to the base of a cliff at the south end of a hogback. Continue around and up the left side of the hogback's rocky crest, steeply gaining elevation in piney woods and alongside low cliffs. As the trail climbs, the ridge becomes more open with scenic views east across Boulder and south to Green Mountain.

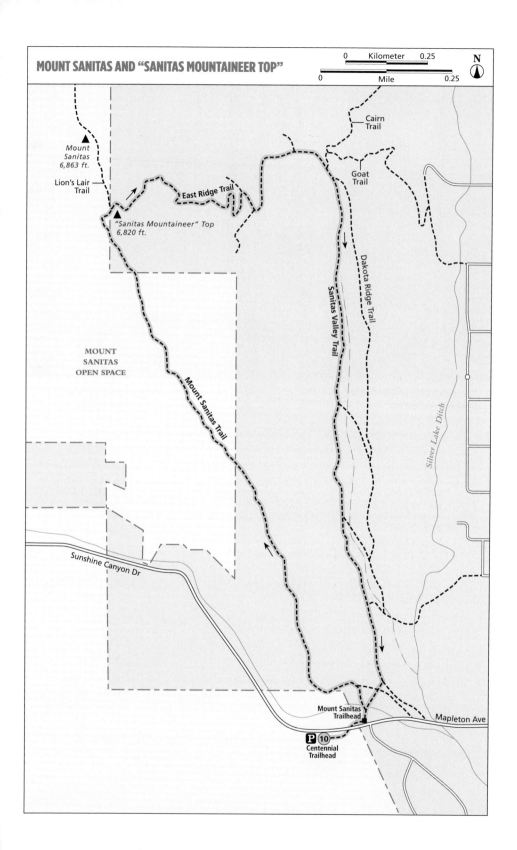

MOUNT SANITAS AND "SANITAS MOUNTAINEER TOP"

0　　　Kilometer　　0.25

0　　　Mile　　0.25

N

▲
*Mount
Sanitas
6,863 ft.*

Lion's Lair
Trail

Cairn
Trail

East Ridge Trail

Goat
Trail

▲
*"Sanitas Mountaineer" Top
6,820 ft.*

Santas Valley Trail

Dakota Ridge Trail

MOUNT
SANITAS
OPEN SPACE

Mount Sanitas Trail

Silver Lake Ditch

Sunshine Canyon Dr

Mount Sanitas
Trailhead

Mapleton Ave

P (10)
Centennial
Trailhead

The rocky summit of "Sanitas Mountaineer Top" offers sweeping views across north Boulder to tawny grasslands.

1.0 Past a sandstone outcrop, reach powerlines and a tower left of the trail (GPS: 40.030655,-105.303547). Continue up the trail to a final steep, rocky section.

1.35 Arrive at the bouldery summit of 6,820-foot "Sanitas Mountaineer Top" (GPS: 40.034407,-105.305258), the southern sub-summit of Mount Sanitas. See the **Option** below to climb the mountain's main summit to the north. A plaque on the top honors the volunteers that built the East Ridge Trail in 1990. Enjoy a rest and views from well-worn rocks on the top. Then head east on the signed East Ridge Trail, which scrambles down boulders, stone steps, and tree roots. At one section, the trail passes below the south side of an overhanging boulder, squeezes through a slot, and scrambles down a slab. Pay attention not to lose the trail here. As the trail descends, the angle eases and the footbed becomes less rocky.

1.75 Leave the trees and descend open slopes, following the trail which bends north and descends along the edge of a broad meadow.

1.95 Reach a signed junction with a spur trail (not your route) that goes north to houses (GPS: 40.035865,-105.298872). Keep straight (east) on the wide trail, which becomes Sanitas Valley Trail at the junction.

2.05 Reach a junction on the left with Goat Trail. Continue south on the main trail.

2.1 Reach a junction on the left with Dakota Ridge Trail. Continue south on the main trail, gently descending a grassy vale below Mount Sanitas. The Dakota Ridge Trail is a good 0.8-mile alternative return trail that rejoins Sanitas Valley Trail at its southern end.

2.5 Pass a junction with a spur trail to Dakota Ridge. Continue straight.

2.7 Pass a junction with a spur trail to Dakota Ridge. Continue straight.

2.9 Pass a junction with a spur trail to Dakota Ridge. Continue straight.

The East Ridge Trail passes under looming sandstone boulders.

Green Mountain, Flagstaff Mountain, and Boulder lie south of Mount Sanitas's grassy east slopes.

3.0 Reach a four-way junction with an information sign, trash receptacles, and directional signposts (GPS: 40.021492,-105.295758). Go straight (southwest) on the Sanitas Valley Trail, marked "To Centennial Trailhead." Descend a short hill.

3.05 Arrive back at the Mount Sanitas Trail and the start of the loop hike. Go straight.

3.1 Reach the Mount Sanitas Trailhead on the north side of the road. Cross the road and go right toward the parking lot.

3.2 Arrive back at the trailhead (GPS: 40.020256,-105.297632).

Option: To climb to the highest summit of Mount Sanitas from "Sanitas Mountaineer Top," descend about 100 feet down the ascent trail and go right on Lion's Lair Trail. Hike 0.15 mile north to the 6,863-foot summit of Mount Sanitas left of the trail (GPS: 40.037017,-105.306532). Return back to the Mount Sanitas Trail for a 0.3-mile round-trip side-hike.

11 SUGARLOAF MOUNTAIN

A short trail reaches the rocky summit of Sugarloaf Mountain, the high point of a ridge between Boulder Creek and Fourmile Creek, offering wide-ranging views of the northern Front Range and Continental Divide.

Start: Sugarloaf Mountain Trailhead, Sugarloaf Mountain Road
Difficulty: Easy
Trails: Sugarloaf Trail
Hiking time: About 1 hour
Distance: 1.4 miles, out and back
Elevations trailhead to summit: 8,445 to 8,917 feet (+472 feet)
Rank status: Ranked
Restrictions: Day use area open from sunrise to sunset; leashed dogs only; camping, fires, and smoking prohibited; no glass bottles or containers; illegal to carry or use firearms; no motorized vehicles, hunting, or drones; no nearby campgrounds
Amenities: None at trailhead; services in Boulder
County: Boulder
Maps: *DeLorme*: p. 29, E7; Trails Illustrated #102: Indian Peaks, Gold Hill; USGS Gold Hill
Land status/contact: Roosevelt National Forest, (970) 295-6600; Boulder Ranger District, (303) 541-2500; Boulder County Parks and Open Space, (303) 678-6200

FINDING THE TRAILHEAD

From the junction of Broadway and Boulder Canyon Drive / CO 119, drive west on Boulder Canyon Drive, which becomes CO 119, for 5.2 miles to a sharp right turn on Sugarloaf Road. Follow Sugarloaf Road / CR 122 northwest for 4.7 miles to a right turn on Sugarloaf Mountain Road, signed "The Switzerland Trail." Follow the narrow dirt road for 0.8 mile to a large parking lot at the Sugarloaf Mountain Trailhead (GPS: 40.025092,-105.424892).

Sugarloaf Mountain offers superb views of the Boulder area, including Green Mountain, Bear Peak, and South Boulder Peak.

The trail up Sugarloaf Mountain follows an old road that once accessed a fire lookout.

THE HIKE

The rocky summit of Sugarloaf Mountain, a prominent conical peak west of Boulder, offers spectacular 360-degree views of the northern Front Range including Longs Peak, the Continental Divide, the Indian Peaks Wilderness Area, and the lower mountains above Boulder. The short hike, following a closed road from a trailhead on Sugarloaf's west side, climbs through broken forest and open terrain to the summit. It's an ideal trail to the top for hikers of all abilities since it doesn't require lots of elevation gain, energy, and time like Mount Sanitas and other Boulder-area peaks.

The Sugarloaf Trail spirals up the west and south slopes to the peak's pointed summit.

Sugarloaf Mountain Trail, crossing Roosevelt National Forest and Boulder County land, is accessible year–round with wildflowers and blue sky in summer and wind-drifted snow in winter. The area to the west of the trailhead parking lot is popular for four-wheeling and mountain biking. The best track for those alternate activities is the Switzerland Trail, which follows an abandoned railroad grade that once linked Boulder to mining towns like Ward, Eldora, and Nederland between 1883 and 1919.

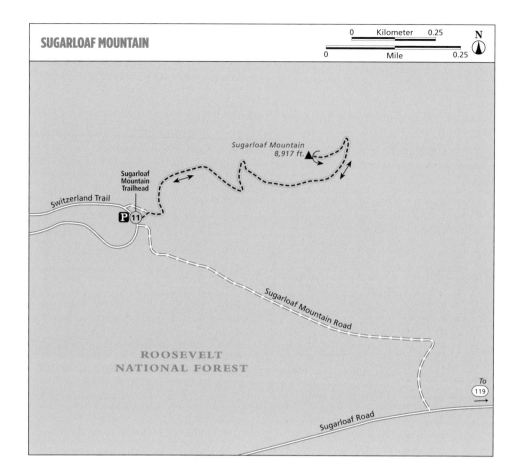

MILES AND DIRECTIONS

0.0 Start at the Sugarloaf Mountain Trailhead on the east side of the parking lot at the end of Sugarloaf Mountain Road. Hike up an eroded closed road, signed "No Shooting" and "No Motor Vehicles," and pass a gate. Continue up the trail on the west flank of Sugarloaf Mountain through a scrubby forest of pine, spruce, fir, and scattered quaking aspen.

0.3 Follow the trail through two switchbacks and head southeast across the mountain's open southern slopes.

0.4 Enter Boulder County Open Space land at a sign detailing park regulations. Continue gently climbing open slopes and pass a wooden bench (dedicated to "Michael 'Milo' Miller" No Stranger to Fun on the left). Continue up the rocky trail past talus slopes to a sharp left switchback and climb to the boulder-strewn summit.

0.7 Reach the high point of 8,917-foot Sugarloaf Mountain at four twisted, windswept limber pines (GPS: 40.026752,-105.418784). The summit offers wide views, including the Indian Peaks and Mount Audubon directly west, Longs Peak and Mount Meeker to the northwest, and Green Mountain, Bear Peak, and South Boulder peak to the east. Return down the trail.

1.4 Arrive back at the trailhead (GPS: 40.025092,-105.424892).

12 GREEN MOUNTAIN (BOULDER)

Green Mountain forms Boulder's iconic skyline, with the famed Flatirons pasted on the mountain's east face. The best hike to the peak's high summit follows a moderate trail through meadows and forests on its gentler west slope.

Start: Green Mountain West Trailhead, Flagstaff Road
Difficulty: Moderate
Trails: Green Mountain West Ridge Trail
Hiking time: About 2 hours
Distance: 3.7 miles, out and back
Elevations trailhead to summit: 7,693 to 8,144 feet (+451 feet)
Rank status: Ranked
Restrictions: Open daily from 1 hour before sunrise to 1 hour after sunset; hike on designated trails only; off-trail travel requires a permit; dogs must be leashed all the time and stay on trails; pick up dog waste; no open fires, camping, mountain bikes, glass containers, or drones; no open carry or discharging of firearms; no motorized vehicles; stay on designated trails; no nearby campgrounds
Amenities: None at trailhead; services in Boulder
County: Boulder
Maps: *DeLorme*: p. 39, A8; Trails Illustrated #100: Boulder, Golden; USGS Eldorado Springs
Land status/contact: City of Boulder Open Space & Mountain Parks, (303) 441-3440

FINDING THE TRAILHEAD

From the junction of Baseline Road and Broadway in Boulder, drive west on Baseline for 6.2 miles, passing Chautauqua Park and climbing Flagstaff Mountain on Flagstaff Road to the Green Mountain West Trailhead on a rise. Parking is on both sides of the road on the dirt shoulders. The signed trailhead is on the east side of the road (GPS: 39.983366,-105.323253).

THE HIKE

The popular Green Mountain West Ridge Trail, starting from a trailhead on Flagstaff Road west of Boulder, crosses meadows splotched with wildflowers in summer and a mixed conifer forest of ponderosa pine, Douglas fir, and Engelmann spruce. The mountain's summit, marked with a cairn on a blocky boulder, offers panoramic views of Boulder, the Great Plains, and the Continental Divide. A metal plate attached to the top of the cairn has stubby pegs that provide line-of-sight identification of major peaks to the west, including Longs Peak, Mount Audubon, North and South Arapaho Peaks, Mount Evans, and Mount Bierstadt.

The well-marked trail is easy to follow and open year-round. Watch for lightning in the summer and get off the high point if a storm threatens. Parking on the shoulder of Flagstaff Road can be a problem on weekends, holidays, and during the summer. Arrive very early or very late to grab a spot. This area in Boulder Mountain Park is a designated Habitat Conservation Area (HCA) to protect rare and easily damaged plants and animals.

A viewpoint looks west from the West Ridge Trail to wooded Green Mountain.

Deep canyons and steep ridges form Green Mountain's north slope.

Hikers must stay on the trail at all times unless they have a permit for off-trail hiking and dogs must be leashed. The state of Colorado named the western part of Boulder Mountain Park a State Natural Area for its rich biological diversity. Watch for turkey flocks, mule deer, and occasional black bears and coyotes.

MILES AND DIRECTIONS

0.0 Start at the signed Green Mountain West Trailhead on the east side of Flagstaff Road. Hike east on the rolling trail through meadows and scattered ponderosa pines and Douglas firs. Continue across north-facing slopes on the ridge's northern edge, with views toward Green Mountain.

0.9 Reach a junction with a trail on the right. Keep straight on the signed Green Mountain West Ridge Trail through meadows and trees on the wide ridge.

0.95 Reach a junction with the signed Green Bear Trail (GPS: 39.982573,-105.308766) which heads right to Bear Canyon (not your route). Continue straight on the main trail and begin climbing Green Mountain's west flank.

1.4 At a sharp switchback, go left and climb stone steps. Continue ascending the trail through a mixed conifer forest and open meadows that offer views south to South Boulder Peak and Bear Peak.

1.65 High on the mountain, reach a junction at a shoulder with Ranger Trail on the left (GPS: 39.982882,-105.303838). Stay right on the Green Mountain West Ridge Trail. Past here the trail steepens, climbing stone steps and scrambling up the boulder-strewn trail.

1.85 Arrive at the rocky summit of 8,144-foot Green Mountain. The actual high point is a huge walrus-shaped boulder with a cairn cemented in place near the top. Scramble

A metal plaque and pegs help hikers identify mountains seen from Green Mountain's summit.

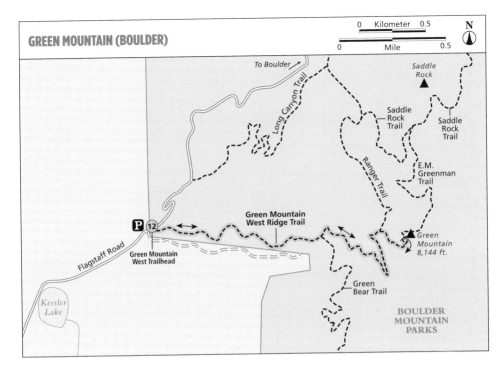

up a crack to the cairn. Otherwise, pick a comfortable seat on a boulder and admire the views east of the tops of the Flatirons and Boulder's gridwork below and the tawny prairie beyond. The Indian Peaks straddle the Continental Divide to the west and Longs Peak in Rocky Mountain National Park dominates the northwest skyline. The E.M. Greenman Trail, which heads northeast to Gregory Canyon, begins on the summit. After a snack and drink, retrace your steps down the trail.

3.7 Arrive back at the trailhead (GPS: 39.983366,-105.323253).

A giant boulder and cairn mark the highest point on Green Mountain.

13 SOUTH BOULDER PEAK

South Boulder Peak, towering above Boulder and Eldorado Canyon, offers a challenging hike up Shadow Canyon to its pointed rocky summit. The reward for your hard work is spectacular views across the northern Front Range from Mount Evans to Longs Peak and east to the Kansas horizon.

Start: South Mesa Trailhead, CO 170
Difficulty: Strenuous
Trails: Mesa Trail, Towhee Trail, Shadow Canyon South Trail, Shadow Canyon Trail, South Boulder Peak Trail
Hiking time: 5-6 hours
Distance: 8.0 miles, out and back
Elevations trailhead to summit: 5,620 to 8,549 feet (+2,929 feet)
Rank status: Ranked
Restrictions: Fee area for non-Boulder County residents; open daily from 1 hour before sunrise to 1 hour after sunset; hike on designated trails only; leashed dogs only; no dogs on Towhee Trail; no open fires, camping, mountain bikes, glass containers, or drones; no open carry or discharging of firearms; no motorized vehicles; off-trail hiking is prohibited on the Shadow Mountain Trail from Feb 1 to July 31 to protect nesting raptors; no nearby campgrounds; no available water
Amenities: Toilets at trailhead; services in Boulder
County: Boulder
Maps: *DeLorme:* p. 39, A8 and p. 40, A1; Trails Illustrated #100: Boulder, Golden; USGS Eldorado Springs
Land status/contact: City of Boulder Open Space & Mountain Parks, (303) 441-3440

FINDING THE TRAILHEAD

From Boulder, drive south on Broadway / CO 93 to the south edge of town. Continue south on CO 93 for about 1.5 miles and turn right on CO 170 toward Eldorado Springs. Drive west for 1.7 miles to the signed South Mesa Trailhead and forty-eight-space parking lot on the right side of the highway (GPS: 39.938804, -105.258170). If the parking lot is full, park across the road at the Dowdy Draw Trailhead. The parking lots are fee areas. If your vehicle is not registered in Boulder County, a daily fee is charged. Fill out an envelope and pay with cash at the Parking Fee Station. Parking is prohibited on CO 170.

THE HIKE

South Boulder Peak, the highest mountain on Boulder's western skyline, offers a superb but strenuous hike to its pointed summit. The 8,549-foot peak, anchoring the southern end of the escarpment, is climbed year-round but the trails to the top are never busy. Many locals use regular ascents of South Boulder Peak, with over 3,000 feet of round-trip elevation gain, as training for bigger mountains or for running high-altitude races. For most hikers, the trek is a toughie, with insecure footing, steep slopes, and a final short scramble over boulders to the peak's high point.

The hike's first half gently ascends wide trails, including the iconic Mesa Trail, to the base of Shadow Canyon. The second half clambers steeply up this steep-walled canyon, scrambling over rocks, twisting through a thick conifer forest, passing jumbles of house-sized boulders, and offering occasional views of Devils Thumb, a sheer pinnacle

The Matron on the south ridge of South Boulder Peak juts above the Towhee Trail.

South Boulder Peak, the triangular mountain in the middle, rises beyond lower ridges and sandstone slabs.

perched on a ridge above. The final pull up Shadow Canyon switchbacks across open slopes decimated by wildfire in 2012 to a saddle. Finish up the peak's northeast ridge, again climbing through burned tree snags to the boulder-strewn summit.

Expect the best views in the Boulder area from the summit, including Longs Peak in Rocky Mountain National Park to the north, the Indian Peaks and James Peak on the Continental Divide to the west, and Mount Evans to the southwest.

MILES AND DIRECTIONS

0.0 Start at the South Mesa Trailhead and hike north on Mesa Trail, crossing South Boulder Creek on a footbridge.

0.3 Reach a junction with the Homestead Trail on the left. Continue straight on the Mesa Trail, and then bend left, passing the Mesa Connector Trail on the right.

0.5 Reach a junction on the left with the signed Towhee Trail (GPS: 39.943031, -105.264302). Go left on Towhee and follow the singletrack trail west up a gorgeous valley, passing fields of flowers in summer. No dogs or horses are allowed on Towhee Trail. Near the head of the valley the trail switchbacks up open slopes and climbs onto a flat mesa top.

1.2 Arrive at a T junction with the Mesa Trail (GPS: 39.945722,-105.271101). Go left on wide Mesa Trail and hike west near the mesa edge.

SOUTH BOULDER PEAK

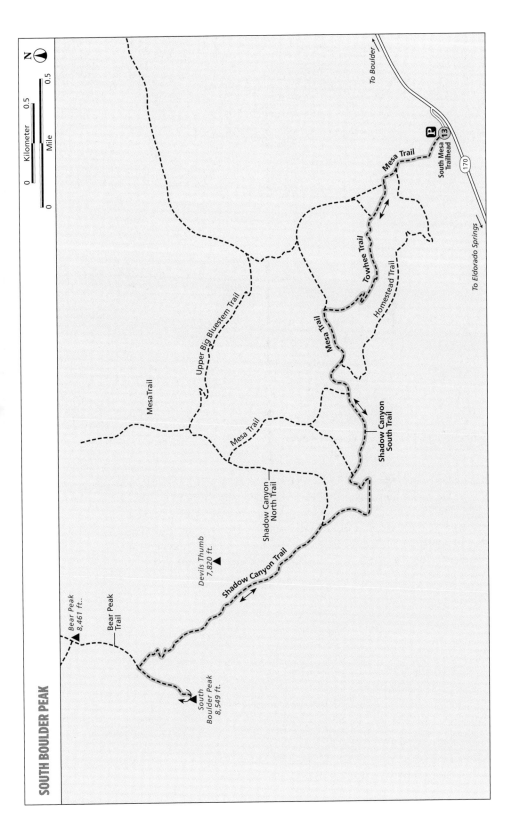

Kilometer

0   0.5

0   0.5

Mile

N

To Boulder

P

South Mesa Trailhead   13

170

To Eldorado Springs

Mesa Trail

Townee Trail

Homestead Trail

Mesa Trail

Upper Big Bluestem Trail

Mesa Trail

Mesa Trail

Mesa Trail

Shadow Canyon South Trail

Shadow Canyon North Trail

Shadow Canyon Trail

Devils Thumb 7,820 ft.

Bear Peak 8,461 ft..

Bear Peak Trail

South Boulder Peak 8,549 ft.

Summer wildflowers blanket meadows along the Mesa Trail.

Bear Peak towers behind a hiker crossing fire-ravaged slopes on upper South Boulder Peak.

1.4 Meet a Y junction with the Homestead Trail on the left. Continue straight on the Mesa Trail, slowly climbing through open pine woods and meadows.

1.6 Reach a signed Y junction with Shadow Canyon South Trail on the left (labeled "Shadow Canyon Trail") and Mesa Trail on the right (GPS: 39.944502,-105.276748). Go left on Shadow Canyon South Trail and hike into Shadow Canyon, a narrowing canyon floored by a trickling creek. Look west to see The Matron, a tall rock formation jutting above the canyon.

2.0 Meet a junction on the right with Shadow Canyon South Spur, which goes right for 0.3 mile to Mesa Trail (not your route). Continue straight on the wide main trail, which crosses the creek and climbs a hillside above.

2.1 Pass a junction on the left with a side trail at the top of a hill. Stay on the main trail and head northwest below The Matron, crossing open slopes with views east and dark woods. Pass an old homestead and dip down and cross the creek on rocks.

2.5 After crossing the creek, reach a T junction with Shadow Canyon North Trail (GPS: 39.946028,-105.286971). Go left on signed Shadow Canyon Trail. The next hike section is the toughest part of the ascent. Follow the steep trail up steep Shadow Canyon, clambering over boulders, threading through tall trees, and passing below Devils Thumb. The upper part of the trail crosses burned terrain. The area alongside the trail is closed in spring and summer for nesting raptors so stay on the trail.

3.7 Reach a signpost at a T junction at a saddle (GPS: 39.956687,-105.297214). For the last leg, go left on the South Boulder Peak Trail and hike southwest up the mountain's blunt northeast ridge. The trail steadily climbs through toppled deadfall from a 2012 wildfire. Finally, the trail ends at a small clearing below the final obstacle—a pile of boulders on the high point.

4.0 Scramble up the boulder pile (Class 2+) to the summit (GPS: 39.953595, -105.299386). Use caution on the boulders since a vertical cliff drops south of the summit. Enjoy spectacular views from the top, including Longs Peak to the

The Continental Divide scrapes the horizon beyond jumbled boulders on South Boulder Peak's summit.

northwest and the Indian Peaks and James Peak to the west. Afterwards, descend back to the saddle and the junction with Shadow Mountain Trail. Go right on it and descend steep Shadow Canyon and follow the ascent trails back to the trailhead.

8.0   Arrive back at the trailhead (GPS: 39.938804,-105.258170).

EXTRA CREDIT: BEAR PEAK

To climb unranked Bear Peak, after summiting South Boulder Peak, return to the saddle between South Boulder Peak and Bear Peak. Hike northeast on the Bear Peak Trail for 0.3 mile to its 8,461-foot pointed rock summit, then return to the saddle. This option adds 0.6 mile to the total hike length.

14 NORTH TABLE MOUNTAIN (LICHEN PEAK)

This hike climbs flat-topped North Table Mountain to rocky Lichen Peak, a volcanic outcrop that forms the mountain's high point, on the northern edge of Golden.

Start: North Table Mountain West Trailhead, CO 93
Difficulty: Moderate
Trails: North Table Loop Trail, Lichen Peak Trail
Hiking time: About 1 hour
Distance: 1.8 miles, out and back
Elevations trailhead to summit: 6,020 to 6,575 feet (+555 feet)
Rank status: Ranked
Restrictions: Park open daily from 1 hour before sunrise to 1 hour after sunset; stay on Lichen Peak Trail to avoid environmental damage; leashed dogs allowed; pick up dog waste and deposit in trash can; no camping, open fires, open carry or discharge of firearms, marijuana use, or motor vehicles; nearest campgrounds at Golden Gate Canyon State Park
Amenities: Toilets, water, maps, and info signs at trailhead; services in Golden
County: Jefferson
Maps: *DeLorme*: p. 40, C1; Trails Illustrated #100: Boulder, Golden; USGS Golden
Land status/contact: North Table Mountain Park; Jefferson County Open Space, (303) 271-5925; report violations to Jefferson County Sheriff's Office, (303) 277-0211

FINDING THE TRAILHEAD

From the junction of US 6, CO 93, and CO 58 on the west side of Golden, drive north on CO 93 for 2.1 miles and make a right (east) turn signed North Table Mountain Trailhead into two parking lots and the North Table Mountain West Trailhead (GPS: 39.782004,-105.229686). The trailhead is between two parking lots. Trailhead street address: 4788 CO 93, Golden.

THE HIKE

The highest point on North Table Mountain, protected in 1,998-acre North Table Mountain Park, is 6,575-foot Lichen Peak, a rocky knob perched on the northwest corner of the mountain's broad summit plateau. A rimrock cap of erosion-resistant basalt deposited over 62 million years ago in three separate lava flows forms the mountain's broad flat top above the historic town of Golden. The lava plateau once extended south onto today's South Table Mountain until Clear Creek excavated a deep valley between the two mountains.

North Table Mountain, a Jefferson County parkland, offers plenty of recreation including over 17 miles of trails and the Golden Cliffs, a popular rock climbing area overlooking Golden and Coors Brewery. The area is also a haven for wildlife, including mule deer, coyotes, mountain lions, and rattlesnakes. The mountain is a birding hotspot with over 130 species seen in the foothills shrublands ecosystem.

The hike to the mountain's highest point begins at the West Trailhead off busy CO 93 on the north side of Golden. When leaving the trailhead parking lot, all vehicles must

Hikers descend the North Table Mountain Loop Trail to the trailhead in north Golden.

turn right or north on CO 93 to avoid accidents. The short hike follows North Table Loop Trail up a steep, closed road that accesses North Table Mountain's plateau and finishes on Lichen Peak Trail. This hiker-only trail crosses a sensitive ecosystem, including an open grassland and volcanic bedrock covered with lichens, a slow-growing organism formed by a symbiotic relationship between fungi and algae. Stay on the trail to avoid damaging fragile vegetation and lichen.

MILES AND DIRECTIONS

0.0   Start at the North Table Mountain West Trailhead at a kiosk and sign on the east side of the two parking lots. Go right on signed North Table Loop Trail and hike south beside a rail fence.

0.1   Reach a junction with a closed asphalt road (GPS: 39.781020,-105.229255). Go left on it and follow the wide track, which turns to dirt, up a long, steep hill on the west side of the mountain.

0.5   Reach the top of the hill and a junction on the right with a climber access trail to the North Quarry Climbing Area (GPS: 39.776658,-105.223323). Continue east on the flat North Table Loop Trail on the mesa top.

0.55   Arrive at a major junction with Tilting Mesa Trail and continue straight east on it. North Table Loop Trail goes right at the junction (not your route).

0.6   After a short distance, reach a junction with signed Lichen Peak Trail (GPS: 39.776412,-105.221934) on the left. Go left between boulders on the hiker-only Lichen Peak Trail to an interpretive sign about Lichen Peak. Hike north on the single-track trail. Stay on the trail to protect the fragile grassland and lichens alongside it. The trail gently climbs toward the summit, a rocky knob.

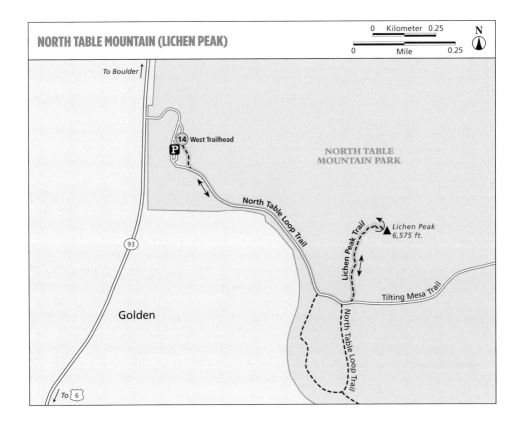

NORTH TABLE MOUNTAIN (LICHEN PEAK)

0   Kilometer   0.25

0   Mile   0.25

N

To Boulder

14 West Trailhead

P

NORTH TABLE
MOUNTAIN PARK

North Table Loop Trail

Lichen Peak Trail

Lichen Peak
6,575 ft.

93

Tilting Mesa Trail

Golden

North Table Loop Trail

To 6

Lichen Peak, the high point of North Table Mountain, offers views north of the Front Range escarpment.

The Lichen Peak Trail climbs to the highest point on North Table Mountain.

0.9   Arrive at a viewpoint just below the highest point of 6,575-foot Lichen Peak (GPS: 39.778904,-105.220480). To reach the summit, scramble up basalt boulders to the small top. After admiring spacious views, follow the trail back down the mountain.

1.8   Arrive back at the trailhead (GPS: 39.782004,-105.229686).

15 "WINDY PEAK"

"Windy Peak," the second highest ranked summit in Golden Gate Canyon State Park, offers a moderate trek up its southern and eastern slopes to a rock-strewn overlook and 360-degree mountain views.

Start: Bridge Creek Trailhead, Golden Gate Canyon State Park
Difficulty: Strenuous
Trails: Burro Trail
Hiking time: About 4 hours
Distance: 6.4 miles, out and back
Elevations trailhead to summit: 7,820 to 9,141 feet (+1,321 feet)
Rank status: Ranked
Restrictions: Fee area; daily or annual state park pass required; open day use from 5 a.m. to 10 p.m.; leashed dogs only; no water at trailhead; hikers only on Summit Trail; hunting allowed in fall—use caution when hiking
Amenities: Vault toilets and picnic tables at trailhead; Reverend's Ridge and Aspen Meadow Campgrounds in park; services in Black Hawk and Golden
County: Jefferson
Maps: *DeLorme*: p. 39, B8; Trails Illustrated #100: Boulder, Golden; USGS Black Hawk
Land status/contact: Golden Gate Canyon State Park, (303) 582-3707

FINDING THE TRAILHEAD

From the junction of US 6 and CO 93 in Golden, drive north for 1.9 miles on CO 93 toward Boulder. On the north side of Golden, turn left on Golden Gate Canyon Road, signed "Golden Gate Canyon State Park." Follow the twisty, paved road for 12.7 miles to a junction with Crawford Gulch Road on the right at the visitor center for Golden Gate Canyon State Park. Turn right on Crawford Gulch Road and drive northeast on the narrow paved road, passing through a section of private property, for 2.3 miles to the Bridge Creek Trailhead and two strip parking lots on the left (GPS: 39.846473,-105.378038). The signed trailhead is 120 feet north of the right-hand parking lot (GPS: 39.846473,-105.378038).

The Burro Trail climbs the south face of "Windy Peak" through ponderosa pine groves and open meadows.

A cliff composed of Precambrian metamorphic rock towers above Burro Trail on "Windy Peak."

A rock outcrop offers a view down Ralston Creek's canyon to Ralston Butte and the tawny prairie.

THE HIKE

The rocky summit of "Windy Peak," the highest mountain in the eastern part of Golden Gate Canyon State Park, is easily reached by the Burro Trail from Bridge Creek Trailhead. The popular, 12,119-acre state park, lying in the Front Range about 15 miles northwest of Golden, offers twelve trails, a visitor center, two campgrounds with 132 sites, backcountry shelters and tent sites, and 125 picnic sites. The trails are named for area animals and signs depicting that animal's footprint mark each trail.

The well-marked Burro Trail steadily climbs to "Windy Peak's" summit, crossing open meadows and threading through a mixed conifer forest of ponderosa pines, Douglas fir, spruce, and lodgepole pine. While a cairn designates the mountain's highest point on its broad summit, the trail ends just to the south atop a rocky outcrop that offers stunning views of the snowcapped Continental Divide to the southwest.

MILES AND DIRECTIONS

0.0   From the right-hand parking lot, walk 120 feet north to the signed Bridge Creek Trailhead. From the left parking lot by toilets, walk east for 250 feet to the trailhead. Cross a footbridge over a creek and follow Burro Trail up south-facing slopes covered with grass and ponderosa pines.

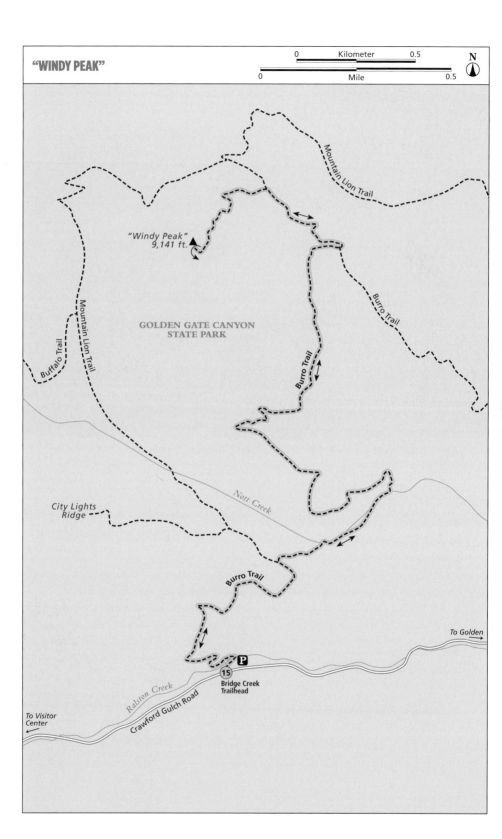

Kilometer

Mile

N

"Windy Peak"
9,141 ft.

Mountain Lion Trail

Buffalo Trail

Mountain Lion Trail

Burro Trail

Burro Trail

GOLDEN GATE CANYON
STATE PARK

Nott Creek

City Lights
Ridge

Burro Trail

To Golden

15
Bridge Creek
Trailhead

Ralston Creek

To Visitor
Center

Crawford Gulch Road

The Burro Trail traverses through piney woods on the lower slopes of "Windy Peak."

0.7 Reach a junction with Mountain Lion Trail on a ridge (GPS: 39.849633,-105.374973). The next segment of Burro Trail follows Mountain Lion Trail. Go left on the signed Mountain Lion Trail / Burro Trail and hike northwest.

0.75 Reach a junction with the Burro Trail, also marked "Windy Peak." Go right on Burro Trail and descend through a spruce and aspen forest, then cross Nott Creek on a wooden bridge. Continue northwest along the creek's north back.

1.1 Arrive at a Y junction and keep left on the signed Burro Trail to "Windy Peak" (GPS: 39.852640,-105.370489). Head up a dry ravine and then climb through meadows and a Douglas fir and ponderosa pine woodland on the southeast slopes of "Windy Peak."

1.8 Reach the base of a white cliff broken by vertical cracks. At the cliff's east end, dip around another rock buttress and climb past two switchbacks. The rising trail swings past a viewpoint that looks east down Ralston Creek's canyon toward the prairie and heads north through a mixed conifer forest on "Windy Peak's" east flank.

2.55 Reach a junction on a wide ridge (GPS: 39.861703,-105.372776). The Burro Trail splits here with a section going left to "Windy Peak" and Mountain Lion Trail and a section going right and descending south to Nott Creek. Go left and hike northwest on Burro Trail on the south side of a broken rock ridge.

2.85 Reach a signed junction with the Burro Trail segment to the "Windy Peak" summit (GPS: 39.863922,-105.376369). Go left on it and hike the rocky trail up the peak's north slope.

"Windy Peak's" summit offers a dramatic view west of wooded Tremont Mountain and the Continental Divide.

3.2 Arrive at 9,141-foot "Windy Peak's" spacious summit. A small cairn right of the trail marks the official high point. After tagging it, follow the trail for 50 feet to an excellent overlook on boulders (GPS: 39.861702,-105.380040). Look west to wooded 10,388-foot Tremont Peak, the park's high point, and 13,294-foot James Peak on the Continental Divide. After enjoying the views, retrace your footsteps back down the mountain.

6.4 Arrive back at the trailhead (GPS: 39.846268,-105.377766).

Option: Rather than doing an out-and-back hike as described above, hikers can also make a loop hike by following a short section of the Burro Trail north to Mountain Lion Trail, which is followed counterclockwise back to the Burro Trail. Besides climbing the mountain on the Burro Trail from the Bridge Creek Trailhead, "Windy Peak" is also climbed on the Burro Trail from the Nott Creek Trailhead and the Buffalo Trail from the Rifleman-Phillips Trailhead. Check the park's trail map for hiking details.

16 "NORTH RALSTON PEAK"

The hike up "North Ralston Peak" lies in Golden Gate Canyon State Park, a 12,119-acre parkland in the mountains northwest of Golden and Denver. Three trails up the mountain offer fun hiking and stunning views from the summit.

Start: Blue Grouse Trailhead, Golden Gate Canyon State Park
Difficulty: Moderate
Trails: Blue Grouse Trail, Mule Deer Trail, Black Bear Trail
Hiking time: 2–3 hours
Distance: 4.2 miles, out and back
Elevations trailhead to summit: 8,422 to 9,340 feet (+918 feet)
Rank status: Unranked
Restrictions: Fee area; daily or annual pass required; open day use from 5 a.m. to 10 p.m.; no water at trailhead

Amenities: Picnic tables at trailhead; toilets at Kriley Pond south of trailhead on CO 46; Reverend's Ridge and Aspen Meadow Campgrounds in park; services in Golden and Black Hawk
County: Gilpin
Maps: *DeLorme*: p. 39, B7; Trails Illustrated #100: Boulder, Golden; USGS Black Hawk
Land status/contact: Golden Gate Canyon State Park, (303) 582-3707

FINDING THE TRAILHEAD

From the junction of US 6 and CO 93 in Golden, drive north for 1.9 miles on CO 93 toward Boulder. On the north side of Golden, turn left on Golden Gate Canyon Road / CO 46, signed "Golden Gate Canyon State Park." Follow the twisty, paved road for 12.7 miles to a junction with Crawford Gulch Road at the visitor center for Golden Gate Canyon State Park. Continue west on Golden Gate Canyon Road / CO 46 for 1.3 miles and turn right (north) on Mountain Base Road. Drive 0.2 mile, keeping right after 180 feet at a Y junction, to the Blue Grouse Trailhead and parking area (GPS: 39.835561,-105.429738).

The Mule Deer Trail climbs below "North Ralston Peak" and rocky Ralston Roost.

Aspen shadows fall across snow on the Mule Deer Trail.

THE HIKE

"North Ralston Peak" is the high point of a wooded ridge that stretches south from Promontory Ridge to Ralston Creek on the southern side of Golden Gate Canyon State Park. Farther south on the high ridgeline are two more rocky bumps—9,334-foot Ralston Roost and 9,260-foot "Son of Ralston." Both points are reached from the Black Bear Trail but require rock scrambling to reach their summits. The hike to "North Ralston Peak" follows a good trail up south-facing slopes to an aspen forest, and then finishes on a boulder-strewn ridge to marvelous mountain views. The hike's three trails, named for local animals Blue Grouse, Mule Deer, and Black Bear, are marked with signs showing the animal's footprint and they are easy to follow.

Golden Gate Canyon State Park protects a swathe of wooded mountains and grassy valleys in the Front Range's lower-elevation mountains. The park, open year-round, offers two campgrounds for overnight stays, a visitor center with displays and programs, and over 42 miles of hiking trails up peaks and across valleys. After doing this hike, head over to nearby "Windy Peak" (Hike 15) and make it a two-peak day.

MILES AND DIRECTIONS

0.0   Start at the signed Blue Grouse Trailhead at the north side of the circular parking lot. Hike north on Blue Grouse Trail up a couple of switchbacks and then contour northwest across mountain slopes.

The summit of "North Ralston Peak" gives views west toward the Continental Divide.

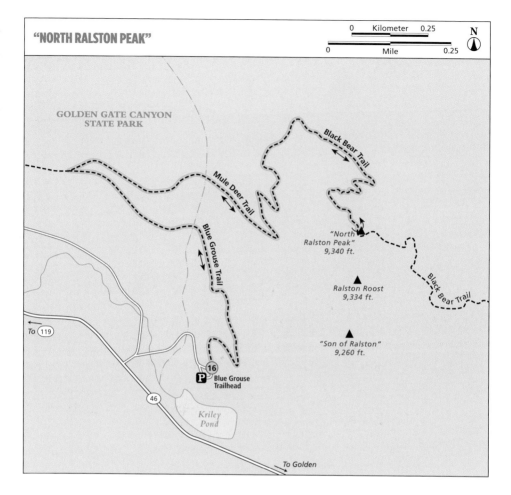

0.7 Reach a junction with Mule Deer Trail (GPS: 39.841211,-105.435116). Go right on it and gradually gain elevation through meadows and a mixed conifer forest. "North Ralston Peak" rises directly ahead, its summit left of Ralston Roost, a sheer rock pinnacle.

1.2 Start up three switchbacks, quickly rising to jumbled boulders left of the trail.

1.5 Reach a saddle behind the boulders (GPS: 39.841331,-105.427752). The trail heads northeast here, threading through quaking aspens on flat terrain.

1.6 Reach a junction with Black Bear Trail among aspens and a meadow (GPS: 39.842635,-105.426665). Following signs, keep right on Black Bear Trail and hike southeast across a meadow and then into thick spruce, fir, and lodgepole pine forest on the northeast flank of the mountain. The rocky trail climbs a series of switchbacks.

2.0 Reach a level spot surrounded by boulders on a ridge (GPS: 39.840654, -105.425200). From here to the summit, the trail passes among aspens and then twists through boulders along the high ridge. Look for strategically placed signs with arrows marking Black Bear Trail. Go left on the trail, scrambling over boulders and between trees.

Clouds swirl over Continental Divide peaks west of "North Ralston Peak's" rocky summit.

2.1   Arrive at the 9,340-foot summit of "North Ralston Peak" right of the trail (GPS: 39.839588,-105.424198). Find a seat among the summit boulders and enjoy a scenic panorama to the west. The ragged Continental Divide stretches across the western skyline with four 13,000-foot peaks—Mount Flora, Mount Eva, Parry Peak, and James Peak. After enjoying the view, return down the three trails.

4.2   Arrive back at the trailhead (GPS: 39.835561,-105.429738).

"North Ralston Peak," the bump on the left, Ralston Roost, and "Son of Ralston" rise above meadows in Golden Gate Canyon State Park.

17 MARYLAND MOUNTAIN

The summit of Maryland Mountain, towering north of Black Hawk and Central City, is reached by well-kept trails that steadily climb the peak's south slopes to its rocky top and wide views of the mining district and the Continental Divide.

Start: Hidden Treasure Trailhead, CO 119
Difficulty: Moderate
Trails: Historic Gilpin Tramway, Summit Trail
Hiking time: About 2 hours
Distance: 3.8 miles, out and back
Elevations trailhead to summit: 8,205 to 9,203 feet (+998 feet)
Rank status: Ranked
Restrictions: Open dawn to dusk; leashed dogs only; no water at trailhead; hikers only on Summit Trail

Amenities: Restrooms at trailhead; campgrounds in Golden Gate Canyon State Park; services in Black Hawk and Central City
County: Gilpin
Maps: *DeLorme*: p. 39, C7; Trails Illustrated #100: Boulder, Golden; USGS Central City
Land status/contact: Maryland Mountain-Quartz Valley Open Space Park; City of Black Hawk, (303) 582-2221

FINDING THE TRAILHEAD

From the junction of US 6, CO 93, and CO 58 on the west side of Golden, drive west on US 6 and then CO 119 for 20 miles up Clear Creek Canyon to the junction of CO 119 / Clear Creek Boulevard and Black Hawk Street in Black Hawk. Continue straight on CO 119 for 0.8 mile to a right turn to signed Hidden Treasure Trailhead and a parking lot (GPS: 39.811384,-105.496471).

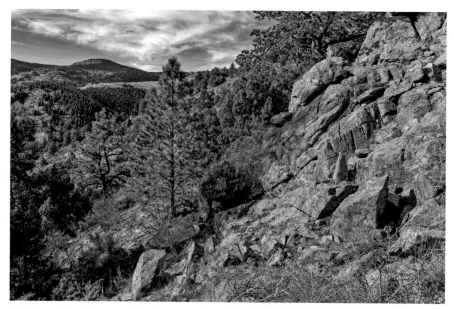

The Summit Trail passes rock outcrops on the south slope of Maryland Mountain.

An overlook on the Summit Trail provides views of Bald Mountain near Central City.

THE HIKE

Maryland Mountain, dominating the northern skyline of Black Hawk, lies on the northern edge of the Central City Mining District west of Denver. Dubbed "The Richest Square Mile on Earth," the district was mobbed by 1859 Pikes Peak or Bust Gold Rush miners who founded Central City and Black Hawk and dug gold from thousands of mines. Maryland Mountain, once bustling with prospectors, is now an open space park that offers hiking, mountain biking, picnicking, and nature study. The city of Black Hawk, a gambling destination today, opened the Hidden Treasure Trailhead in 2020 and built a network of hiking and biking trails that lace the mountain. Besides offering spectacular summit views, the mountain boasts historic sites including the Bonanza Mill, the Gilpin Tramway, and many closed mines.

The hike begins at an excellent trailhead off the highway north of Black Hawk. It crosses a bridge over the highway and follows the bed of the 1880s Gilpin Tramway, a narrow-gauge railroad that brought ore from Central City to a smelter in Black Hawk. The hike's second section twists up Maryland Mountain's south face on the Summit

Trees frame a view of the Continental Divide from Maryland Mountain's summit.

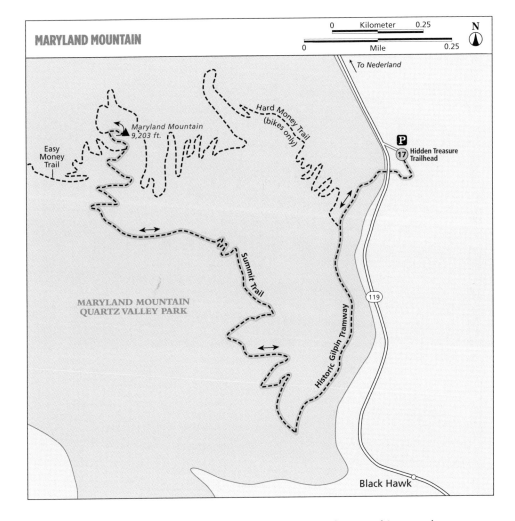

Trail, a hiker-only footpath. Most of the park's other trails are multi-use and some are designated only for mountain bikes.

MILES AND DIRECTIONS

0.0 Start at the Hidden Treasure Trailhead at the south end of the parking lot. Follow a concrete trail and cross a foot bridge over CO 119. At the west side of the bridge, go left on the Historic Gilpin Tramway trail. Follow the wide, flat trail southwest.

0.2 Pass a junction on the right with Hard Money, a bike-only, descent trail. Continue southwest on the main trail.

0.6 Reach a Y junction with the Summit Trail (GPS: 39.805113,-105.500114). Go right on it and follow the hiker-only trail up the south slopes of Maryland Mountain.

1.85 Reach a junction with Easy Money, a bike-hike trail. Go right on it and hike 150 feet to a junction. Go right on the marked Summit Trail. The left trail is Easy Money / Hard Money Trails (bikes only).

Maryland Mountain, rising on the northern edge of the Central City Mining District, is reached from a trailhead near Black Hawk.

1.9 After 200 feet, arrive at the rocky 9,203-foot Maryland Mountain summit (GPS: 39.812339,-105.505636). Admire views of Mount Evans, Parry Peak, and James Peak to the west, and then retrace the Summit Trail back down the mountain.

3.8 Arrive back at the trailhead (GPS: 39.811384,-105.496471).

18 COLORADO MINES PEAK

The Continental Divide National Scenic Trail offers access to many peaks east and west of 11,306-foot Berthoud Pass. Colorado Mines Peak, rising east of the pass, provides an easy introduction to this popular hiking, peakbagging, and backcountry skiing area.

Start: Berthoud Pass Trailhead, Berthoud Pass / US 40
Difficulty: Moderate
Trails: Mount Flora Trail #1978 (on the Continental Divide National Scenic Trail); FR 239.1
Hiking time: About 2 hours
Distance: 4.0 miles, out and back
Elevations trailhead to summit: 11,333 to 12,493 feet (+1,160 feet)
Rank status: Ranked
Restrictions: No winter sledding or snowmobiling on pass; avalanche danger in winter

Amenities: Seasonal warming hut with vault toilets; interpretive signs; Robbers Roost and Idlewild Campgrounds north of pass and Big Bend Campground to the south; services in Empire and Winter Park
Counties: Clear Creek and Grand
Maps: *DeLorme*: p. 38, C4; Trails Illustrated #103: Winter Park, Central City, Rollins Pass; USGS Berthoud Pass
Land status/contact: Arapaho National Forest, (970) 295-6600; Clear Creek Ranger District, (303) 567-3000

FINDING THE TRAILHEAD

From I-25 south of Denver, take US 6 W for about 10 miles. Bear right at signs to get onto I-70 W toward Grand Junction. Drive 28.6 miles and take exit 232 toward US 40 E / Empire / Granby, then continue onto US 40 W and drive about 15 miles to the top of Berthoud Pass and a large parking area on the right. The trailhead is located at the southeast corner of the lot, at a gated dirt road (GPS: 39.797817,-105.776714).

Colorado Mines Peak, topped with communications towers, rises above Berthoud Pass.

Engelmann Peak rises beyond windswept krummholz trees along the trail up Colorado Mines Peak.

The trail up Colorado Mines Peak edges along a snow-covered road on the Continental Divide.

COLORADO MINES PEAK

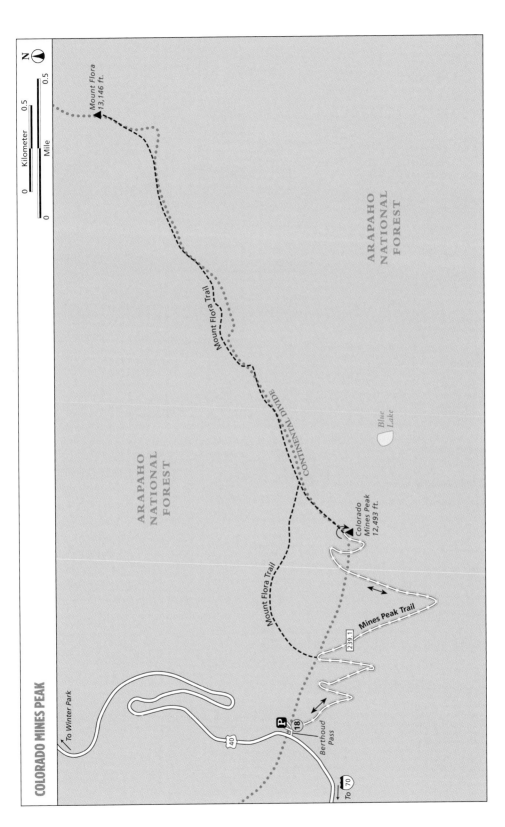

To Winter Park

40

P

18

Berthoud
Pass

70

To 70

ARAPAHO
NATIONAL
FOREST

Mount Flora Trail

239.1

Mines Peak Trail

Colorado
Mines Peak
12,493 ft.

CONTINENTAL DIVIDE

Blue
Lake

ARAPAHO
NATIONAL
FOREST

Mount Flora Trail

Mount Flora
13,146 ft.

N

Kilometer
0   0.5

Mile
0   0.5

Engelmann Peak towers beyond the final trail section which traverses slopes blanketed with alpine tundra.

THE HIKE

Colorado Mines Peak isn't the most difficult 12,000-foot mountain in Colorado, but the path to its summit provides a gateway to many more peaks along the Continental Divide east of Berthoud Pass and offers superb views of surrounding mountains and valleys. The entire hike follows a closed service road that leads to a complex of towers and buildings on the summit area, home to the Berthoud Pass Automated Weather Observing System (AWOS), a weather station. From the summit of Colorado Mines Peak, 13ers Mount Flora, Mount Eva, and Parry Peak, named for 1860s botanist Charles Christopher Parry, march north on the Continental Divide. The trail offers more spectacular alpine views above tree line, with 13,362-foot Engelmann Peak dominating the southern skyline and Stanley Mountain (Hike 19) on the long ridge directly west of Berthoud Pass.

MILES AND DIRECTIONS

0.0   From the Berthoud Pass Trailhead and parking lot, hike south up the gated service road. The trail switchbacks north and south seven times from the trailhead at roughly 0.2 mile (north); 0.4 mile (south); 0.6 mile (north); 0.8 mile (south); 1.3 miles (north); 1.8 miles (south); and 1.9 miles (north) to the summit, passing several side trails left of the route along the way.

The rocky summit of Colorado Mines Peak sits among tall communications towers.

2.0 Reach the summit of 12,493-foot Colorado Mines Peak, an obvious rock pile between buildings that is right of the road's end (39.794954,-105.763860). Enjoy the fresh mountain air and stunning views and then return the way you came.

4.0 Arrive back at the trailhead (GPS: 39.797817,-105.776714).

EXTRA CREDIT: MOUNT FLORA

For a longer hike to ranked 13er Mount Flora, after reaching the summit of Colorado Mines Peak backtrack down the road for two switchbacks. Depart the road and get on the Continental Divide Trail on the right side of the road at the switchback. Hike east and north for about 1.9 miles to the summit of Mount Flora (GPS: 39.807650,-105.735167). Return the way you came, or for a more scenic and direct hike to the trailhead, return down the trail for about 1.65 miles and bear right onto a secondary trail. Continue west for about 1 mile to the parking lot on Berthoud Pass.

19 STANLEY MOUNTAIN, "NO NAME," AND "RUSSELL PEAK"

West of Berthoud Pass, a steep initial ascent up the northeast flank of "Russell Peak" rewards the hiker with an easy stroll to three peaks that rise above 12,000 feet on the Continental Divide, the spine of North America.

Start: Berthoud Pass Trailhead, Berthoud Pass / US 40
Difficulty: Strenuous
Trails: Berthoud Pass West Trail (CDT_F), Mount Nystrom Trail; both trails lie on the Continental Divide National Scenic Trail
Hiking time: 4–5 hours
Distance: 7.4 miles, out and back
Elevations trailhead to summit: 11,300 to 12,300 feet at "Russell Peak" (+1,000 feet); to 12,424 feet at "No Name" (+1,124 feet); and to 12,521 feet at Stanley Mountain (+1,221 feet)
Rank status: Ranked (Stanley Mountain); Unranked ("No Name" and "Russell Peak")
Restrictions: Wilderness rules apply; group size limited to 12; dogs must be leashed or under voice control; camping and campfires prohibited

within 100 feet of trail and water sources; no motorized vehicles or equipment; no mountain bikes; avalanche danger in winter; no sledding or snowmobiles
Amenities: Seasonal warming hut with vault toilets; interpretive signs; Robbers Roost and Idlewild Campgrounds north of pass and Big Bend Campground to the south; services in Empire and Winter Park
Counties: Clear Creek and Grand
Maps: *DeLorme*: p. 38, C4; Trails Illustrated #103: Winter Park, Central City, Rollins Pass; USGS Berthoud Pass
Land status/contact: Vasquez Peak Wilderness Area; Arapaho National Forest, (970) 295-6600; Clear Creek Ranger District, (303) 567-3000

FINDING THE TRAILHEAD

From I-25 in downtown Denver, take US 6 W for about 10 miles. Bear right at signs to get onto I-70 W toward Grand Junction. Drive 28.6 miles and take exit 232 toward US 40 E / Empire / Granby, then continue onto US 40 W and drive about 15 miles to the top of Berthoud Pass and a large parking area on the right. Park in the lot at the Berthoud Pass Trailhead and cross to the west side of the highway to begin the hike (GPS: 39.798390,-105.777404).

THE HIKE

This enjoyable hike follows the Continental Divide Trail, a long-distance footpath that runs 3,028 miles from Mexico to Canada, over two unranked summits—"Russell Peak" and "No Name"—to the rocky knob of 12,521-foot Stanley Mountain. Gaining the summits of all three peaks requires a bit of up and down along the Continental Divide, a wide grassy ridge here, doubling the roughly 1,200 feet net gain of this hike to about 2,400 feet of elevation round trip. You will be above tree line for over 4 round-trip miles with no escape if the weather comes in, so do not attempt this hike if there is any chance of lightning or thunderstorms. Choose a good weather day, get an early start, and enjoy this glorious alpine hike.

"No Name," an unranked and unnamed peak, rises above a cliff-lined cirque.

"Russell Peak" and "No Name" loom above the Berthoud Pass West Trail.

The first part of the hike from Berthoud Pass to the summit of "Russell Peak" offers gorgeous views west to Colorado Mines Peak (Hike 18), Mount Flora, Mount Eva, and Parry Peak to the east. Once on the broad ridge to Stanley Mountain, enjoy views of myriad Front Range peaks including the long east ridge and summit of 12,947-foot Vasquez Peak, centerpiece of the Vasquez Peak Wilderness Area, to the west, and Mount Parnassus, Bard Peak, and bulky Engelmann Peak to the south.

MILES AND DIRECTIONS

- **0.0** Begin from the trailhead on the west side of the highway on Berthoud Pass. Hike west uphill on the Berthoud Pass West Trail (CDT_F).
- **0.1** Pass the Vasquez Peak Wilderness Area information sign to the right of the trail (GPS: 39.797927,-105.778976) and continue west.
- **0.8** Hike on the trail west and north to the top of the steep, treeless slopes used for skiing in winter. Continue along an open ridge at tree line toward switchbacks visible on the northeast slope of "Russell Peak" ahead (GPS: 39.802554,-105.785911).
- **1.1** Begin climbing southwest up a long series of switchbacks on a steep slope (GPS: 39.802745,-105.791878).
- **1.5** Reach the summit of 12,300-foot "Russell Peak" to the right of the trail (39.801977, -105.794258). Continue west-northwest on the rising trail.

STANLEY MOUNTAIN, "NO NAME," AND "RUSSELL PEAK"

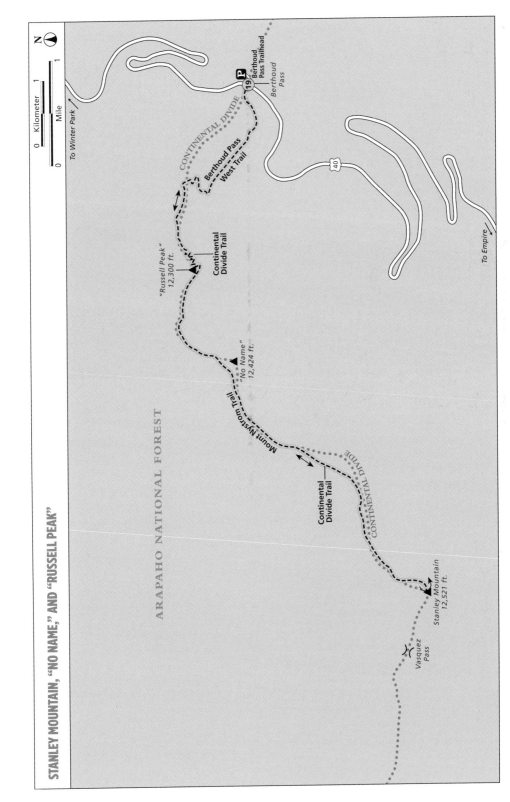

A hiker follows the Mount Nystrom Trail up the northwest flank of "No Name."

The Mount Nystrom Trail, part of the Continental Divide Trail, traverses over alpine meadows along the Continental Divide.

The trail climbs open meadows and snowfields to the pointed summit of Stanley Mountain.

1.8   Enter the signed Vasquez Peak Wilderness Area on the high ridge and continue southwest on the trail along the Continental Divide (GPS: 39.803161,-105.798883).

2.1   After dipping across a low point on the ridge, 12,424-foot "No Name" rises left of the trail which skirts its gentle west flank. To reach its summit, go left and follow a social trail to the top (GPS: 39.799592,-105.802965). Afterwards, return to the main trail and hike southwest on the wide, plateau-like ridge above a massive bowl.

3.7   The trail reaches the base of Stanley Mountain's final pyramid and bends right. Scramble up boulders to reach the summit of 12,521-foot Stanley Mountain (GPS:39.785802,-105.822807). Return the way you came.

7.4   Arrive back at the trailhead (GPS: 39.798390,-105.777404).

20 CHIEF MOUNTAIN

Chief Mountain south of Idaho Springs is a pleasant ranked 11er with a well-used trail and spacious views across the Front Range, including 14,265-foot Mount Evans to the west.

Start: Chief Mountain Trailhead, CO 103
Difficulty: Moderate
Trails: Chief Mountain Trail #58
Hiking time: About 2 hours
Distance: 3.0 miles, out and back
Elevations trailhead to summit: 10,720 to 11,709 feet (+989 feet)
Rank status: Ranked
Restrictions: Limited parking on highway shoulder; visit midweek for fewer hikers; no bicycles; leashed dogs only; no toilets at trailhead, no available water
Amenities: Echo Lake Campground nearby; services in Idaho Springs and Evergreen
County: Clear Creek
Maps: *DeLorme*: p. 39, D7; Trails Illustrated #104: Idaho Springs, Loveland Pass; USGS Idaho Springs
Land status/contact: Arapaho National Forest, (970) 295-6600; Clear Creek Ranger District, (303) 567-4382

FINDING THE TRAILHEAD

From I-70 west of Denver, take exit 252 toward Evergreen and bear right on CO 74 / Evergreen Parkway. Drive 2.8 miles and turn right on CO 103 (Squaw Pass Road) toward Mestaa'ehehe Pass. Go west for 12.2 miles to the trailhead, a pullout on the highway's right side between mile markers 18 and 19. From I-70 in Idaho Springs, take exit 240 toward Mount Evans and turn left on CO 103 S. Drive 18.7 miles to the pullout on the left (north). Parking is limited. Cross the highway to its south side. The trailhead sign is a short distance up the trail and may be difficult to spot, especially in snowy conditions (GPS: 39.682412,-105.521100).

The Continental Divide forms the skyline west of a lone snowdrift on Chief Mountain.

A hiker descends the Chief Mountain Trail below 14ers Grays Peak and Torreys Peak.

THE HIKE

Chief Mountain, the high point of a long ridge of peaks east of Mount Evans, is climbed by a wide, easy-to-follow trail that swings across the mountain's wooded north slopes to timberline. The bald, rocky summit yields panoramic, 360-degree views that stretch over 100 miles from bulky Pikes Peak to the south to flat-topped Longs Peak, the high point of Rocky Mountain National Park, to the north. The mountain's west slopes, but not the summit and trail, lie in the 74,401-acre Mount Evans Wilderness Area.

East of the mountain rise Papoose Mountain and Mestaa'ehehe Mountain (mess-taw-HAY), formerly named Squaw Mountain. It was renamed by the US Board of Geographic Names in late 2021 to honor Owl Woman, a Southern Cheyenne leader who negotiated trade with groups at Bent's Fort and maintained good relations between the Native people and Anglos. Squaw Pass was also renamed Mestaa'ehehe Pass.

The trailhead is popular on summer weekends so plan an early morning, evening, or weekday hike to avoid the crowds. Snow on the trail is usually packed down, making for a great winter adventure. The last hundred feet are steep and rocky and may be slippery under snow.

MILES AND DIRECTIONS

0.0 From the Chief Mountain Trailhead, hike south on Chief Mountain Trail, which switchbacks west then southeast through thick forest.

0.3 Cross a closed, narrow road and pick up the trail on the other side (GPS: 39.680867,-105.518750).

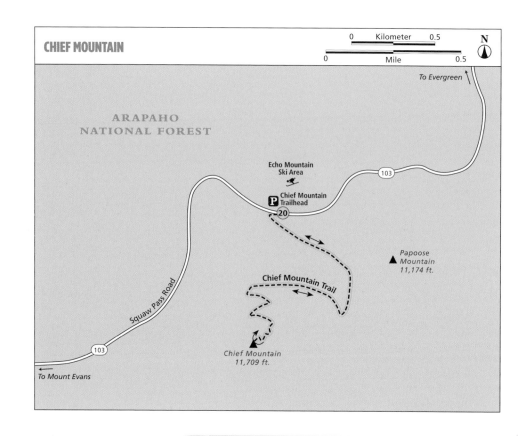

CHIEF MOUNTAIN

ARAPAHO
NATIONAL FOREST

To Evergreen

Echo Mountain
Ski Area

Chief Mountain
Trailhead

Chief Mountain Trail

Papoose
Mountain
11,174 ft.

Squaw Pass Road

To Mount Evans

Chief Mountain
11,709 ft.

Mount Evans, the fourteenth highest peak
in Colorado, lifts broad shoulders beyond
the rocky summit of Chief Mountain.

Late afternoon light catches the summit boulders on Chief Mountain.

0.5 Don't be fooled by social trails heading east toward Papoose Mountain. Instead, stay on the main trail and hike south and then west across the mountain's north flank (GPS: 39.679350,-105.516133).

1.1 The trail rises above the trees offering views north and west of peaks from Guanella Pass to Loveland Pass and the Continental Divide (GPS: 39.678617,-105.523150).

1.5 Arrive at the summit of 11,709-foot Chief Mountain (GPS: 39.675783,-105.522950). Return the way you came.

3.0 Arrive back at the trailhead (GPS: 39.682412,-105.521100).

21 BERGEN PEAK

Following two trails, this lengthy hike near Evergreen climbs to the rocky top of Bergen Peak and sweeping views across the Front Range that include three 14ers—Pikes Peak, Mount Evans, and Longs Peak.

Start: Stagecoach Trailhead, Stagecoach Boulevard
Difficulty: Strenuous
Trails: Meadow View Trail, Bergen Peak Trail
Hiking time: About 5 hours
Distance: 9.4 miles, out and back
Elevations trailhead to summit: 7,780 to 9,708 feet (+1,928 feet)
Rank status: Unranked
Restrictions: Open daily from 1 hour before sunrise to 1 hour after sunset; leashed dogs allowed; no open fires or camping; parking lot fills on weekends; alternative parking and trailhead is at Lewis Ridge Trailhead on CO 74; no nearby public campgrounds; no available water
Amenities: Toilets at trailhead; services in Evergreen
County: Jefferson
Maps: *DeLorme*: p. 39, D8; Trails Illustrated #100: Boulder, Golden; USGS Saddleback Mountain, Evergreen
Land status/contact: Elk Meadow Park; Jefferson County Open Space, (303) 271-5925; report violations to Jefferson County Dispatch, (303) 980-7300

FINDING THE TRAILHEAD

From I-70 west of Denver, take exit 252 and drive south on Evergreen Parkway / CO 74 for 5.8 miles to Stagecoach Boulevard. Turn right on Stagecoach and drive west for 1.3 miles to the Stagecoach Trailhead and parking lot on the right (GPS: 39.654572,-105.366480). Trailhead street address: 32281 Stagecoach Blvd., Evergreen.

The Bergen Peak Trail offers a view east to Mount Morrison on the edge of the Front Range.

Ponderosa Pines line hillsides above Elk Meadow below the Bergen Peak Trail.

A hiker passes beneath the shade of a tall ponderosa pine on the Bergen Peak Trail.

Mule deer graze high on Bergen Peak's East Ridge.

THE HIKE

Bergen Peak, towering northwest of Evergreen, is a prominent unranked summit reached by a challenging hike up two trails that begin in 1,658-acre Elk Meadow Park, a Jefferson County parkland. Higher, the hike passes through Bergen Peak State Wildlife Area and ends on Denver Mountain Park property at the top. The hike, gaining almost 2,000 feet of elevation, offers a mature forest of ponderosa pine, Douglas fir, spruce, and lodgepole pine, wildlife including elk and mule deer, and scenic views. The easy-to-follow trails have gradual grades, marked junctions, and long switchbacks, making it fine for novice hikers.

Beginning at the Stagecoach Trailhead, the hike follows Meadow View Trail to a marked junction at the start of the Bergen Peak Trail. This well-marked trail makes a long, uphill ascent on evergreen-shaded slopes, alternating between the mountain's wooded east face and the sunny south slopes. Higher, the trail leaves Elk Meadow Park and climbs through Bergen Peak Wildlife Management Area. Past a junction with Too Long Trail, the hike enters Denver Mountain Park land and finishes up the steep east face to a loop around the mountaintop to the boulder-strewn summit.

Evening light reddens Elephant Butte and other Front Range mountains south of Bergen Peak.

MILES AND DIRECTIONS

0.0 Start at the Stagecoach Trailhead and hike northeast past restrooms on Meadow View Trail.

0.3 Reach a junction with Sleepy S Trail on the right (GPS: 39.655327,-105.366377). Keep left on Meadow View Trail and hike northwest across wooded slopes.

1.0 Arrive at a junction on the left with Bergen Peak Trail (GPS: 39.656961,-105.362333). Go left on it and begin switchbacking up northeast-facing slopes.

1.9 Reach an open ridge at 8,311 feet and views south. The trail heads right here and continues up wooded slopes before climbing the peak's wide east ridge and passing through Bergen Peak Wildlife Management Area.

3.7 Reach a junction with Too Long Trail on the right at 9,211 feet (GPS: 39.666123, -105.391380). Go left on the Bergen Peak Trail for the final segment and switchback up the steep upper face.

4.4 After the trail's angle eases, reach a marked Scenic View on the right with views north to the Indian Peaks and Longs Peak (GPS: 39.667270,-105.395031). Continue up the trail and swing around the north and south sides of the summit area.

4.7 Arrive at the 9,708-foot summit of Bergen Peak marked by a wooden sign (GPS: 39.666182,-105.395192). Return back down the trails to the trailhead.

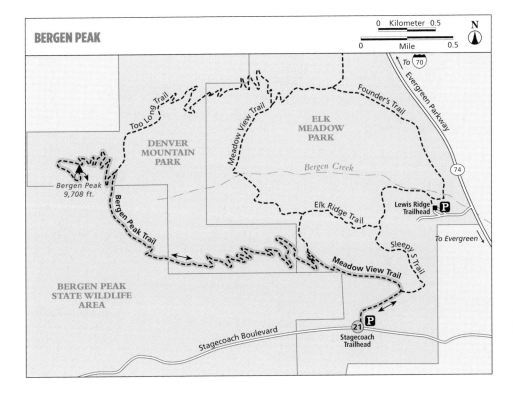

BERGEN PEAK

ELK MEADOW PARK

DENVER MOUNTAIN PARK

Too Long Trail

Meadow View Trail

Founder's Trail

Bergen Creek

Bergen Peak 9,708 ft.

Bergen Peak Trail

Elk Ridge Trail

Lewis Ridge Trailhead

Sleepy S Trail

Meadow View Trail

To Evergreen

Evergreen Parkway

To 70

74

BERGEN PEAK STATE WILDLIFE AREA

Stagecoach Boulevard

Stagecoach Trailhead

21

0 Kilometer 0.5
0 Mile 0.5

N

5.7 At the junction with Too Long Trail, go right on Bergen Peak Trail.

8.4 At the junction with Meadow View Trail, go right.

9.1 At the junction with Sleepy S Trail, keep right on Meadow View Trail.

9.4 Arrive back at the trailhead (GPS: 39.654572,-105.366480).

Option: An alternative descent route extends the hike by a mile by following aptly named Too Long Trail from the first junction below the summit down to Meadow View Trail, which is followed back to the trailhead.

Reach Evergreen Mountain's summit by following shady trails that twist up the peak's northeast flank to dazzling views of surrounding mountains including 14,265-foot Mount Evans, Mount Spalding, and Epaulet Mountain.

Start: Evergreen Mountain East Trailhead, Buffalo Park Road
Difficulty: Moderate
Trails: Evergreen Mountain East Trail, Summit Trail, Evergreen Mountain West Trail, Ranch View Trail
Hiking time: About 3 hours
Distance: 5.9 miles, lollipop
Elevations trailhead to summit: 7,486 to 8,536 feet (+1,050 feet)
Rank status: Ranked
Restrictions: Open daily from 1 hour before sunrise to 1 hour after sunset; leashed dogs allowed; no open fires or camping; park at West Trailhead

lot 0.5 mile to the west if the east lot is full; no public campgrounds nearby, no available water
Amenities: Toilets at parking lot; services in Evergreen
County: Jefferson
Maps: *DeLorme*: p. 39, D8; Trails Illustrated #100: Boulder, Golden; USGS Conifer
Land status/contact: Alderfer/Three Sisters Park, Jefferson County Open Space, (303) 271-5925; report violations to Jefferson County Dispatch, (303) 980-7300

FINDING THE TRAILHEAD

Drive to Evergreen from Denver on I-70 to CO 74 S / Evergreen Parkway or from C-470 on CO 74 through Morrison or US 285 to CO 74 N. From the junction of CO 73 and CO 74 in Evergreen, drive south on CO 74 for 0.7 mile and turn right on Buffalo Park Road. Drive 1.3 miles to a right turn into the signed parking lot for Alderfer/Three Sisters Park. Street address: 30357 Buffalo Park Rd. The East Evergreen Mountain Trailhead is on the south side of the road opposite the parking area by a power pole (GPS: 39.622826,-105.346747).

The Evergreen Mountain East Trail passes rocky overlooks on the peak's east flank.

Storm clouds wreath Mount Evans beyond the bedrock summit of Evergreen Mountain.

THE HIKE

Evergreen Mountain, towering west of its namesake town, is a bulky peak covered with thick stands of lodgepole pine on its northern slopes and ponderosa pines on its lower apron. The broad summit area, topped by a rocky knob, is reached by excellent trails that gain over 1,000 feet from trailhead to top. The trails offer gentle grades, making it a great family hike, and spacious views west to lofty Mount Evans. The mountain and trails are in 1,135-acre Alderfer/Three Sisters Park, a Jefferson County Open Space property with 15.6 miles of trails. Accessible year-round, the hike is perfect in summer with shade and cool temperatures as well as in winter with proper clothing and gear.

Start at the Evergreen Mountain East Trailhead on the south side of Buffalo Park Road and opposite the parking lot. The trail heads southwest through ponderosa pines and climbs wooded slopes to the Summit Trail and Evergreen Mountain West Trail. The Summit Trail, traversing steep slopes, makes a half-mile loop around the summit area. To tag the high point, go left from the trail and scramble up broken ledges to the rocky top, a perfect spot for a sandwich and view west to Mount Evans and south to distant Pikes Peak. The descent follows the Summit Trail back to Evergreen Mountain West Trail and descends the mountain's north slopes to the Wild Iris Loop and Ranch View Trail, which leads back to the trailhead.

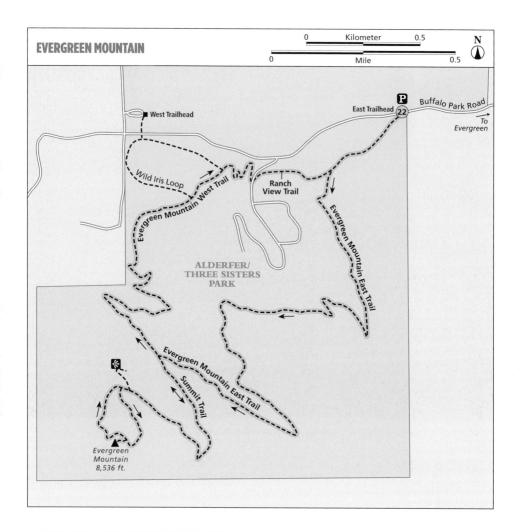

EVERGREEN MOUNTAIN

0 — Kilometer — 0.5
0 — Mile — 0.5
N

West Trailhead

East Trailhead 22

Buffalo Park Road

To
Evergreen

Wild Iris Loop

Ranch
View Trail

Evergreen Mountain West Trail

Evergreen Mountain East Trail

ALDERFER/
THREE SISTERS
PARK

Evergreen Mountain East Trail

Summit Trail

Evergreen
Mountain
8,536 ft.

MILES AND DIRECTIONS

0.0 Start at the signed Evergreen Mountain East Trailhead on the road's south side opposite the parking lot. Hike southwest on the wide trail.

0.3 Reach a Y junction with Ranch View Trail, the return trail, on the right (GPS: 39.620615,-105.350343). Keep left on the Evergreen Mountain East Trail.

0.8 Reach a switchback and junction with Lois Lane Trail on the left. Keep right on the main trail and begin hiking up the mountain's northeast slopes.

1.5 Arrive at a three-way junction and the end of Evergreen Mountain East Trail (GPS: 39.613747,-105.359248). Go left on the signed Summit Trail. The right trail is Evergreen Mountain West Trail (not your route). Hike southeast up wooded slopes then back onto the northeast slopes to a junction with 0.1-mile Scenic View Trail. Continue 100 feet to the next junction.

2.7 Reach a Y junction and the start of the 0.5-mile summit loop (GPS: 39.612324, -105.361000). Go left on the Summit Trail.

Elephant Butte rises beyond tawny meadows and the Evergreen Mountain West Trail.

3.0 Depart trail on the left (GPS: 39.610372,-105.360709) to reach summit. Scramble up rock slabs to Evergreen Mountain's 8,536-foot high point after 100 feet (GPS: 39.610356,-105.361060). Return to the main trail.

3.3 Return to the junction at the start of the loop. Return down Summit Trail.

4.0 Reach the junction at the start of the Summit Trail. Go straight on the Evergreen Mountain West Trail and descend the wooded northwest side of the mountain.

5.1 Arrive at a junction with 0.6-mile Wild Iris Loop on the left (GPS: 39.619638, -105.357473). Continue straight on the main trail along the edge of a meadow.

5.2 Reach the junction with the north branch of the Wild Iris Loop. Go straight on Ranch View Trail down a hill and across a road.

5.6 Reach the first junction with Evergreen Mountain East Trail at the end of Ranch View Trail. Go left on wide Evergreen Mountain East Trail.

5.9 Arrive back at the trailhead (GPS: 39.622826,-105.346747). The parking lot is across the road.

23 ELEPHANT BUTTE

The granite summit of Elephant Butte, rising above the town of Evergreen, is reached by a superb trail that twists through granite cliffs on the mountain's rugged south slopes.

Start: West Trailhead, Alderfer / Three Sisters Park
Difficulty: Moderate
Trails: Bluebird Meadow Trail, Homestead Trail, Mountain Muhly Trail, Elephant Butte Trail
Hiking time: About 3 hours
Distance: 5.0 miles, out and back
Elevations trailhead to summit: 7,710 to 8,405 feet (+695 feet)
Rank status: Ranked
Restrictions: Open daily from 1 hour before sunrise to 1 hour after sunset; follow trails, no shortcutting; leashed dogs allowed; pick up dog waste; no open fires or camping; no open carry or discharging of firearms; no motorized vehicles; no mountain biking on Elephant Butte Trail; no nearby public campgrounds; no available water
Amenities: Toilets at trailhead; services in Evergreen
County: Jefferson
Maps: *DeLorme*: p. 39, D8; Trails Illustrated #100: Boulder, Golden; USGS Evergreen, Conifer
Land status/contact: Alderfer / Three Sisters Park, Jefferson County Open Space, (303) 271-5925; report violations to Jefferson County Dispatch, (303) 980-7300; Elephant Butte Conservation Area, Denver Mountain Parks, (720) 865-0900

FINDING THE TRAILHEAD

Drive to Evergreen from Denver on I-70 to CO 74 S / Evergreen Parkway, or from C-470 on CO 74 through Morrison, or US 285 to CO 74 N. From the junction of CO 73 and CO 74 in Evergreen, drive south on CO 74 for 0.7 mile and turn right on Buffalo Park Road. Drive 2.2 miles, passing the East Trailhead, to South Le Masters Road. Turn right (north) on it and drive 275 feet to the signed parking lot on the right for the West Trailhead at Alderfer / Three Sisters Park. Street address: 5136 South Le Masters Rd., Evergreen. Start at the trailhead left of the toilets on the east side of the parking lot (GPS: 39.622878,-105.359808).

THE HIKE

Elephant Butte is a humpbacked mountain studded with granite cliffs in a formerly closed 665-acre Denver Mountain Park Conservation Area that abuts the western boundary of Alderfer / Three Sisters Park west of Evergreen. The rough peak, accessed from Alderfer / Three Sisters Park, is ascended by the Elephant Butte Trail which climbs the mountain's south slopes.

The hike begins at the West Trailhead in Alderfer / Three Sisters Park, a Jefferson County parkland, and follows three trails through the park to the Elephant Butte Trail. The trail threads through cliffs and tall ponderosa pines to a bedrock summit and views of 14,265-foot Mount Evans to the west, Bergen Peak (Hike 21) to the north, and nearby Evergreen Mountain (Hike 22) to the south. The upper slopes of Elephant Butte and part of its north slope were burned by a wildfire in July 2020. To avoid resource damage and injury from dead snags, hikers need to stay on the trail. The trail, mostly on south-facing slopes, dries quickly after snow, making it a good winter hike, though

The Elephant Butte Trail edges below abrupt cliffs on the mountain's south face.

Granite cliffs frame Mount Evans to the west of Elephant Butte.

The bedrock summit of Elephant Butte offers views west up Bendemeer Valley to Mount Evans.

MICROspikes and trekking poles are recommended for traction and balance on the shaded, icy trails leading to the summit.

MILES AND DIRECTIONS

0.0 Start at the West Trailhead on the east side of the parking lot. A kiosk at the trailhead offers a park map, park brochure, and regulations. Go left from the sign and follow the signed Bluebird Meadow Trail. Walk west along the north edge of the parking lot and then bend north on the wide trail. Elephant Butte, the hike's objective, rises directly ahead.

0.3 After crossing a boardwalk, reach a junction with Homestead Trail (GPS: 39.625395, -105.359145) at the base of a rocky knob. Go left on Homestead Trail and hike left around the knob, gently descending wooded slopes near the park's west boundary.

0.4 Reach a junction with Mountain Muhly Trail. Go left on it and continue north, descending the wide trail into a canyon. Reach a junction with Bearberry Trail on the right. Continue straight.

0.9 Reach the bottom of the canyon and cross Buffalo Creek on an old dam (GPS: 39.632031,-105.356845).

1.0 Climb out of the canyon and reach a junction with Coneflower Trail on the right. Continue straight on Mountain Muhly Trail, slowly climbing through a ponderosa pine forest.

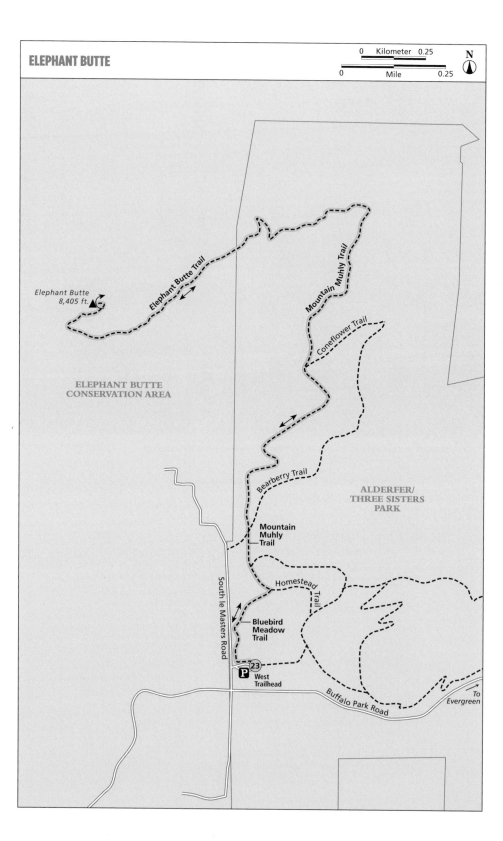

ELEPHANT BUTTE

0   Kilometer   0.25

0   Mile   0.25

N

Elephant Butte
8,405 ft.

Elephant Butte Trail

Mountain Muhly Trail

Coneflower Trail

ELEPHANT BUTTE
CONSERVATION AREA

Bearberry Trail

ALDERFER/
THREE SISTERS
PARK

Mountain
Muhly
Trail

Homestead Trail

South le Masters Road

Bluebird
Meadow
Trail

23

P West
Trailhead

Buffalo Park Road

To
Evergreen

Hikers cross a meadow in Alderfer / Three Sisters Park below rugged Elephant Butte.

1.5 At the top of a ridge, go left and reach a junction with Elephant Butte Trail at a log fence (GPS: 39.638266,-105.355449). Go left on Elephant Butte Trail and begin climbing through forest. Mountain Muhly Trail goes right at the junction and descends a hill (not your route).

1.9 Reach an old wire fence and enter Denver Mountain Park property on the east flank of Elephant Butte. Continue west on the singletrack trail, climbing through tall pines and scrambling up a short gully below a cliff. Follow the trail up the mountain's southern face and pass below a high granite cliff topped by overhangs.

2.4 Past the cliff the trail scrambles over boulders and bends right. Climb a rocky gully to the upper slopes burned by a 2020 wildfire.

2.5 Walk below a rock outcropping and then go left onto a rocky ridge that leads to the summit of 8,405-foot Elephant Butte (GPS: 39.634889,-105.366938). Sit on the granite bedrock for a snack, drink, and 360-degree views across the Front Range, and then follow the trails back down the mountain and across Alderfer / Three Sisters Park.

5.0 Arrive back at the trailhead (GPS: 39.622878,-105.359808).

24 GREEN MOUNTAIN (LAKEWOOD)

Green Mountain, a bulky peak in William F. Hayden Park west of Denver, is easily climbed by two trails on its southeastern side to a broad summit with expansive views across the Front Range.

Start: Green Mountain Trailhead, Florida parking lot at West Alameda Avenue
Difficulty: Moderate
Trails: Green Mountain Trail, Hayden Trail
Hiking time: 2–3 hours
Distance: 4.4 miles, lollipop
Elevations trailhead to summit: 6,141 to 6,855 feet (+714 feet)
Rank status: Ranked
Restrictions: Open 5 a.m. to 10 p.m. daily; lock vehicle and don't leave valuables inside; leashed dogs allowed; pick up pet waste; no shade; watch for rattlesnakes; no camping or fires; stay on designated trails; no nearby public campgrounds; no available water
Amenities: Porta-potty at trailhead; services in Lakewood
County: Jefferson
Maps: *DeLorme*: p. 40, D1 and D2; Trails Illustrated #100: Boulder, Golden; USGS Morrison
Land status/contact: William F. Hayden Park; Lakewood Parks and Recreation, (303) 987-7800; Bear Creek Lake Park Visitor Center, (303) 697-6159

FINDING THE TRAILHEAD

From Denver and I-25, drive west on either C-470 from the south or I-70 to C-470 from the north. Take the Alameda Parkway exit off C-470 and drive east for 8.8 miles to a left turn into the Florida parking lot and the Green Mountain Trailhead (GPS: 39.690646,-105.152115). The trailhead address is: 13851 W. Alameda Ave., Lakewood. Alternatively, start at the smaller Utah parking lot to the west.

The Green Mountain Trail offers stunning views of the Denver skyline.

Mount Morrison and Mount Evans etch the western horizon above yuccas and grasses near the summit of Green Mountain.

THE HIKE

Green Mountain, a sprawling mountain with rounded ridges, is the centerpiece of 2,325-acre William Frederick Hayden Park, a Lakewood city park named for an early rancher who acquired the mountain in 1912. Now the mountain, rising west of Denver, is a natural preserve with a network of hiking trails, wildlife, and a profusion of wildflowers in early summer. Following two trails, the hike climbs to Green Mountain's broad summit and expansive views that include 14ers Longs Peak, Mount Evans, and Pikes Peak as well as downtown Denver's skyline. The well-marked trails have gentle grades and gain 800 feet to the top.

The described hike climbs Hayden Trail to Green Mountain Trail to the summit and returns down Green Mountain Trail. Begin at Green Mountain Trailhead and follow the Hayden Trail up the southern slopes to the Green Mountain Trail. This trail becomes a service road that leads to the mountain's wide summit and excellent views of the Front Range and Denver.

MILES AND DIRECTIONS

0.0 Start at Green Mountain Trailhead on the north side of Florida parking lot. Hike 200 feet to a junction and go left on a connector trail to Hayden Trail. The right trail, the return loop, is Green Mountain Trail.

0.4 Reach a four-way junction north of Utah parking (GPS: 39.688075,-105.157010). Go right on Hayden Trail and ascend the southern slopes.

GREEN MOUNTAIN (LAKEWOOD)

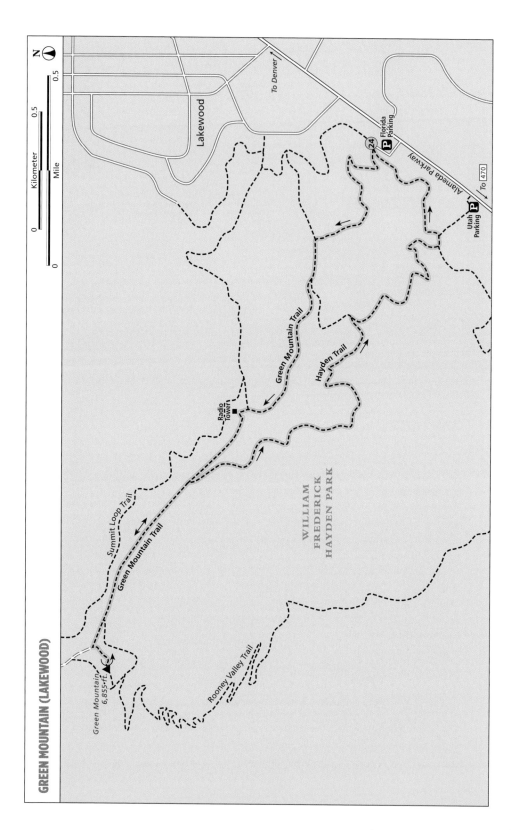

1.0   Reach a junction and go left on the marked Hayden Trail. The right trail is an 0.2-mile connector to Green Mountain Trail.

1.9   Reach a junction with Green Mountain Trail (GPS: 39.697715,-105.168826). Go left on Green Mountain Trail, a service road, and hike up a hill.

2.3   Meet a junction on the left with Rooney Valley Trail. Continue straight.

2.4   Go left on an unmarked trail and hike southeast to the summit.

A hiker traverses open slopes on the Hayden Trail below a mountain-filled horizon.

2.5   Arrive at the 6,855-foot summit of Green Mountain (GPS: 39.701036,-105.177843).

2.6   Return to Green Mountain Trail and go right on a service road.

3.1   Return to Hayden Trail junction on the right. Continue straight and hike southeast on the service road.

3.3   Reach the fenced radio tower (GPS: 39.695587,-105.165405). Go right on singletrack Green Mountain Trail and begin descending.

3.4   Junction with Summit Loop Trail. Continue straight on Green Mountain Trail.

3.8   Reach a junction on the right with 0.2-mile connector trail to Hayden Trail. Go straight on Green Mountain Trail.

3.9   Meet a junction on left with a trail. Continue straight and descend a blunt ridge.

4.4   Arrive back at the trailhead (GPS: 39.690646,-105.152115).

The Hayden Trail twists across ridges and shallow valleys on the southern flank of Green Mountain.

25 **MOUNT MORRISON**

Mount Morrison, reached by a tough hike up the South Ridge Trail, offers a rocky summit above Red Rocks Amphitheater with spacious views of Denver and the Front Range.

Start: Unmarked trailhead at Red Rocks Entrance 4
Difficulty: Strenuous
Trails: South Ridge Trail
Hiking time: About 3 hours
Distance: 3.6 miles, out and back
Elevations trailhead to summit: 5,850 to 7,881 feet (+2,031 feet)
Ranked status: Ranked
Restrictions: Open daily 1 hour before sunrise to 1 hour after sunset; leashed dogs allowed; no shade; watch for rattlesnakes; no fires or camping; hikers only; no nearby public campgrounds; no available water or toilets
Amenities: None at trailhead; services in Morrison
County: Jefferson
Maps: *DeLorme*: p. 40, D1; Trails Illustrated #100: Boulder, Golden; USGS Morrison
Land status/contact: Matthew/ Winters Park; Jefferson County Open Space, (303) 271-5925; report violations to Jefferson County Dispatch, (303) 980-7300; Red Rocks Park and Amphitheater; Denver Mountain Parks, (720) 865-0900

FINDING THE TRAILHEAD

From the junction of I-70 and C-470 west of Denver, drive south on C-470 and take the Morrison exit. This exit is also reached from south I-25 by following C-470 west. Drive 1.2 miles through Morrison on CO 74 / Bear Creek Road to Red Rocks Park Entrance 4 at Titans Road. Turn right at the signed junction and park in a lot to the left. The trailhead is at a gate on the north side of the parking area (GPS: 39.653706,-105.201913).

Mount Morrison rises above a scrubby forest of pine and juniper.

A rock buttress frames
Mount Evans near the
summit of Mount Morrison.

A runner dashes down the South Ridge Trail on Mount Morrison.

THE HIKE

Mount Morrison, a prominent peak towering above famed Red Rocks Amphitheater, is climbed by the South Ridge Trail, a footpath that gains over 2,000 feet or more than 100 feet every 0.1 mile. The trail starts in Denver's Red Rocks Park and quickly enters 2,461-acre Mathews/Winters Park, a Jefferson County natural park that includes 12 miles of trails on Mount Morrison and the Dakota Hogback east of Red Rocks. The difficult hike passes superb overlooks of the Denver skyline and the surrounding mountains. The trail is rough in many places with steep slopes that are slick when wet and talus slopes on the final section. Use careful route finding to avoid rock scrambling and to keep the grade at Class 1 on the upper slope.

The hike, beginning at Red Rocks Entrance 4 west of Morrison, steeply climbs the mountain's southeastern slope. It's an immediate butt-kicker as it heads directly up an old power line for 1,020 feet in the first mile to a saddle that offers views west into deep Bear Creek Canyon.

The next leg, gaining over 800 feet in 0.8 mile, climbs a rocky ridge to the final summit pyramid where it winds through rock outcroppings and talus fields to a rock step in a gully. Finish up on a better trail to the bedrock summit with expansive views that stretch from Longs Peak in the north to Pikes Peak in the south.

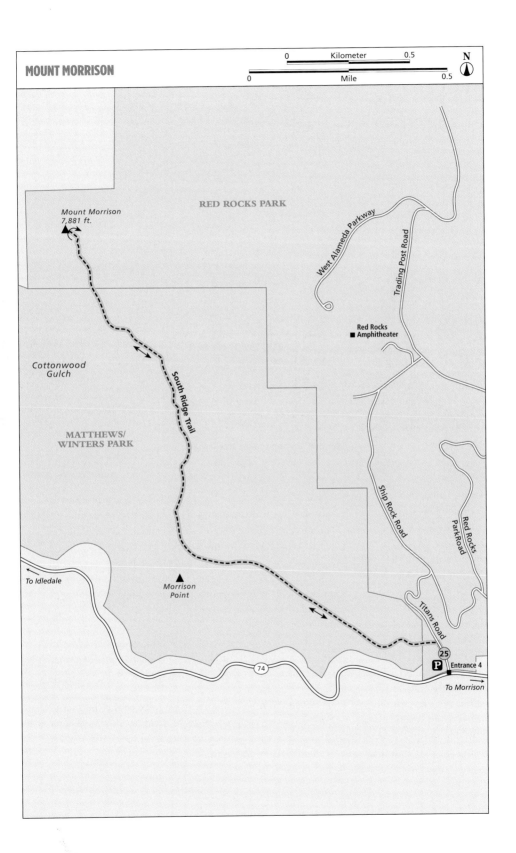

0   Kilometer   0.5

0   Mile   0.5

N

RED ROCKS PARK

Mount Morrison
7,881 ft.

West Alameda Parkway

Trading Post Road

Red Rocks
Amphitheater

Cottonwood
Gulch

South Ridge Trail

MATTHEWS/
WINTERS PARK

Ship Rock Road

Red Rocks
Park Road

To Idledale

Morrison
Point

Titans Road

74

25

P   Entrance 4

To Morrison

Hikers scramble up broken cliffs and talus on Mount Morrison's steep upper trail.

MILES AND DIRECTIONS

0.0 Start at the trailhead on the north side of a parking lot on gated Titans Road. Walk 180 feet up the road to the unmarked trailhead at a gate on the left (GPS: 39.654403,-105.202519). Hike uphill past the Red Rocks Park and Matthews/Winters Park boundary. Continue northwest up the steep trail alongside an old power line.

0.7 Reach the south side of a false summit at 6,620 feet. Continue west on a level ridge and then up a steep section.

0.9 Arrive at a 6,870-foot saddle on the south ridge with views west up Bear Creek Canyon (GPS: 39.657969,-105.214464). Turn north and hike up a ridge.

1.2 Follow the ridge north with gentle grades.

1.3 The trail ascends dry slopes on the ridge's left side.

1.5 Reach the start of the final steep climb up the wide south ridge (GPS: 39.666289,-105.218124).

1.7 Reach the base of a rock step that requires climbing moves. For an easier route, go left and traverse around a rock buttress and climb low angle talus slopes (GPS: 39.668313,-105.219178).

1.8 Arrive at the rocky summit of 7,881-foot Mount Morrison (GPS: 39.669238, -105.219743). Return down the trail.

3.6 Arrive back at the trailhead (GPS: 39.653706,-105.201913).

26 "INDEPENDENCE PEAK"

Reached by a rising trail on its north slope, "Independence Peak's" bedrock summit offers wide views of Front Range mountains, including Mount Falcon, Mount Morrison, Bergen Peak, and Chief Mountain.

Start: Independence Peak Trailhead, Pence Park parking lot on Parmalee Gulch Road
Difficulty: Moderate
Trails: Independence Peak Trail (called "Independence Mountain Trail" on a sign just past the trailhead)
Hiking time: About 1.5 hours
Distance: 2.2 miles, out and back
Elevations trailhead to summit: 7,465 to 8,220 feet (+755 feet)
Rank status: Unranked
Restrictions: Open daily year-round; area closed 1 hour after sunset to 1 hour before sunrise; hiker-only trail; no mountain bikes; leashed dogs only; pick up pet waste; stay on designated trails; no camping, shooting, fireworks, or littering; no alcoholic beverages; no nearby public campgrounds; no available water; no toilets at trailhead
Amenities: Information kiosk at trailhead; services in Evergreen
County: Jefferson
Maps: *DeLorme*: p. 40, D1 and p. 39, D8; Trails Illustrated #100: Boulder, Golden; USGS Evergreen
Land status/contact: Pence Park; Denver Mountain Parks, (720) 865-0900; Park Rangers, (720) 913-1311

FINDING THE TRAILHEAD

From C-470 on the west side of Denver and Lakewood, take exit 5 onto US 285 W toward Fairplay. Drive 4.5 miles west on the highway and turn right on Parmalee Gulch Road / CR 120. Follow it west for 3.8 miles and turn left into the Pence Park parking lot and the Independence Mountain Trailhead. Alternatively, take exit 4 onto Morrison Road / CO 8. Drive west on CO 8 / Bear Creek Road for 8.4 miles, passing through the town of Morrison, to Kittredge and turn left (south) on Myers Gulch Road. Follow it for 1.8 miles to a right turn into the Pence Park parking lot. Trailhead address: 4400 Parmalee Gulch Rd., Evergreen (GPS: 39.635336, -105.279375).

THE HIKE

"Independence Peak," an unranked subpeak of nearby 8,370-foot Independence Mountain, is reached by a trail in Pence Park, a Denver Mountain Park between Kittredge and Indian Hills west of Denver. The Independence Peak Trail, beginning at a trailhead on Myers Gulch Road, traverses up the mountain's north flank, passing through a mixed fir and spruce forest. The rocky summit, formed from granite bedrock, offers spectacular views of mountains above Evergreen and north to peaks in Golden Gate Canyon State Park. To the east rises Mount Falcon and Mount Morrison. "Independence Peak" is easily climbed with Mount Falcon for a two-peak day. Independence Mountain, a higher 8,370-foot point west of the peak, is inaccessible because of private property and a house beside the summit.

The view northwest from "Independence Peak's" summit includes Bergen Peak and other wooded mountains.

"Independence Peak," reached by a short, steep trail, rises in Pence Park, a Denver Mountain Park.

The Independence Peak Trail climbs above Myers Gulch and O'Fallon Park.

MILES AND DIRECTIONS

0.0   Start at Independence Peak Trailhead on the southwest corner of the parking lot. Hike southwest on marked trail.

0.05   Reach a junction with the North Loop on the right and the South Loop on the left (GPS: 39.635377,-105.280091). Continue straight on the North Loop Trail. The South Loop is the return trail. Contour across a hillside, then ascend the rocky trail on the west side of a blunt ridge.

0.5   Reach a junction with the South Loop (GPS: 39.634407,-105.283346). Go right on signed "Independence Mountain Trail" and climb across the mountain's wooded north slopes. The South Loop on the left is the return trail.

0.9   Cross a dry wash in trees and bend north across a northeast-facing slope.

1.1   Finish by scrambling up granite ribs to the rocky summit of 8,220-foot "Independence Peak" (GPS: 39.632497,-105.290552). Enjoy views east to Mount Falcon and northwest to Mount Evans and wooded mountains above Evergreen. Return down the trail.

1.8   Reach the junction with the South Loop on the right. Follow it and descend east.

2.1   Reach the first junction and the end of the South Loop. Go right on the main trail and hike east.

2.2   Arrive back at the trailhead (GPS: 39.635336,-105.279375).

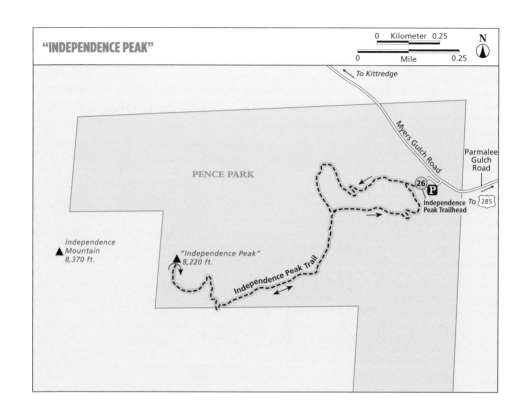

"INDEPENDENCE PEAK"

Kilometer 0.25
Mile 0.25

N

To Kittredge

Myers Gulch Road

Parmalee Gulch Road

PENCE PARK

26 P

Independence Peak Trailhead

To 285

Independence Mountain 8,370 ft.

"Independence Peak" 8,220 ft.

Independence Peak Trail

Distant peaks in Golden Gate Canyon State Park etch the horizon north of "Independence Peak."

27 MOUNT FALCON

Mount Falcon, a low peak in Mount Falcon Park, offers an excellent, easy hike to a lookout tower on its summit and marvelous views of Denver and the Front Range.

Start: West Trailhead, Mount Falcon Park
Difficulty: Very easy
Trails: Castle Trail, Meadow Trail, Tower Trail
Hiking time: About 1 hour
Distance: 1.6 miles, lollipop
Elevations trailhead to summit: 7,765 to 7,851 feet (+86 feet; 360 feet round-trip elevation gain)
Rank status: Ranked
Restrictions: Open 1 hour before sunrise to 1 hour after sunset; leashed dogs only; pick up dog waste; no water at trailhead; no open fires, camping, open carry or discharge of firearms, motor vehicles, or marijuana use allowed; no water availability; no nearby public campgrounds
Amenities: Toilets near the trailhead; picnic areas; historic sites; services in Evergreen
County: Jefferson
Maps: *DeLorme*: p. 40, D1; Trails Illustrated #100: Boulder, Golden; USGS Morrison
Land status/contact: Mount Falcon Park, Jefferson County Open Space, (303) 271-5925; report violations to Jefferson County Dispatch, (303) 980-7300

FINDING THE TRAILHEAD

From C-470 on the west side of Denver, turn west on US 285 and drive 4.2 miles to a signed right turn on Parmalee Gulch Road / CR 120. Follow it northwest for 2.7 miles to a right turn on Picutis Road, signed for Mount Falcon Park. Follow several roads for 1.9 miles from the junction, following signs for the park. The directions sound confusing, but the route is straightforward and well-signed. From the junction, drive 250 feet and go left on Comanche Road at a Y junction. Follow it to a right turn on Ohkay Road. Drive to a Y junction and keep right on Picutis Road, which becomes Nambe Road. Follow Nambe until it becomes Mount Falcon Road. Continue east to the Mount Falcon West Trailhead and parking lot (GPS: 39.636091,-105.239099). An overflow parking lot is on the left before the trailhead parking lot. Trailhead address: 21074 Mt. Falcon Rd., Indian Hills.

THE HIKE

Mount Falcon lifts its 7,851-foot summit above lower ridges in Mount Falcon Park, a 2,252-acre Jefferson County parkland in the Front Range west of Denver. The beloved park, offering 12.2 miles of trails, is popular with hikers who come for superb views, well-maintained trails, and historic sites including the lightning-burned ruins of John Brisben Walker's stone castle and the Colorado marble cornerstone of an unbuilt summer White House for presidents. Walker, who also staged the first concerts at today's Red Rocks Amphitheater from 1906 to 1910, proposed the twenty-two-room presidential castle in 1911 but was unable to raise funds to build it.

The hike to a lookout tower atop Mount Falcon begins at the park's West Trailhead and then follows three trails across meadows and through evergreen forest. The easy-to-follow trails, well-marked with signs, pass the Eagle Eye Shelter, a covered structure for

The view west from Mount Falcon's craggy summit includes "Independence Peak" and Mount Evans.

picnics and mountain views on the site of the Kirchoff family cabin, which they occupied from 1933 to 1972. A wooden tower with a roof and railings rises about Mount Falcon's rocky summit. It offers treetop views that include downtown Denver's skyscrapers to the east, Red Rocks and Mount Morrison to the north, and wooded Evergreen Mountain, Bergen Peak, and Chief Mountain to the west. After hiking up Falcon, take a walk on Castle Trail to Walker's home ruins and the Summer White House site with its stunning views.

MILES AND DIRECTIONS

0.0   Start at the West Trailhead on the east side of the parking lot. Hike southeast on Castle Trail, a closed dirt road shaded by ponderosa pines. Pass a park sign with maps and info.

0.1   Reach a junction with Parmalee Trail on the right and a trash bin and toilets on the left. Continue southeast on the wide trail. Falcon Peak is the rounded knob directly ahead.

0.4   Reach a junction and go straight on the signed Meadow Trail (GPS: 39.633074, -105.233446). The Castle Trail turns left here and goes to the Walker Home Ruins and Summer White House Site. Continue southeast on Meadow Trail across an open grassland.

The Tower Trail twists through piney woods to a lookout tower on Mount Falcon's summit.

An overlook on the Castle Trail gives views west across Mount Falcon Park to high mountains.

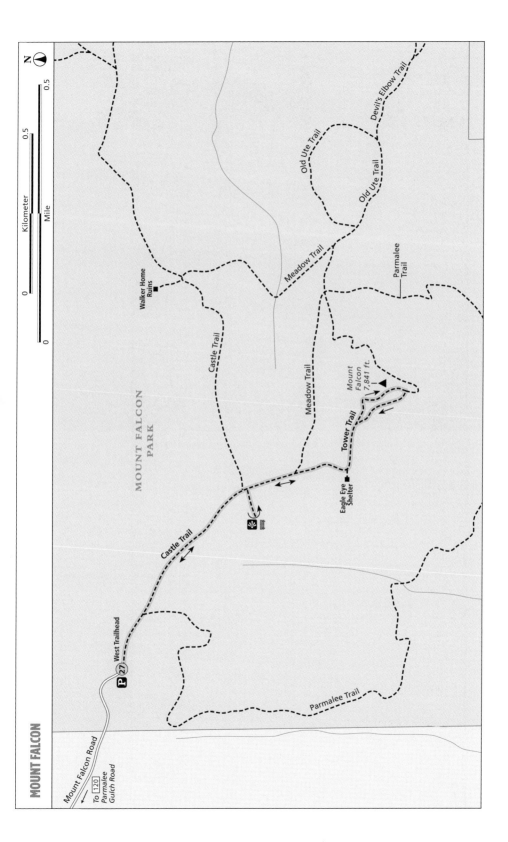

MOUNT FALCON

MOUNT FALCON PARK

N

0   0.5   Kilometer
0   0.5   Mile

To 120
Parmalee
Gulch Road

Mount Falcon Road

P 27 West Trailhead

Castle Trail

Castle Trail

Parmalee Trail

Parmalee Trail

Walker Home
Ruins

Meadow Trail

Meadow Trail

Old Ute Trail

Old Ute Trail

Devil's Elbow Trail

Parmalee
Trail

Tower Trail

Eagle Eye Shelter

Mount
Falcon
7,841 ft.

The west slope of Mount Falcon rears above a dry canyon in Mount Falcon Park.

0.5 Reach a junction and go straight on the signed Tower Trail. The Meadow Trail turns left here. The trail gently climbs south through open forest.

0.6 Reach a junction at Eagle's Eye Shelter, formerly the Kirchoff Cabin from 1933 to 1972, and go left on the singletrack Tower Trail (GPS: 39.630405,-105.232780). The trail bends southeast and gently climbs through woods. The shelter, reached by a short, laid-stone path, offers shade and scenic views of mountains to the west.

0.65 Reach a Y junction and the start of the Tower Trail loop. Go left on the trail, signed for hikers only, and hike 0.05 mile to a junction. Go right on cut marble steps and follow the arrow-marked trail to more steps and the mountain summit.

0.75 Arrive at the Mount Falcon summit tower at 7,851 feet (GPS: 39.629650, -105.230495). Climb twelve steps to a covered platform with 360-degree views of Denver, Mount Morrison, and the Front Range. After enjoying the view, descend back to the trail and hike south.

0.8 Reach a junction and go right on the Tower Trail. Hike northwest back to the start of the loop. Continue straight on Tower Trail and hike past Eagle's Eye Shelter, then turn north.

1.0 Return to the junction with Meadow Trail. Continue straight on it across the meadow.

1.2 Return to the junction with wide Castle Trail and continue northwest on it.

1.6 Arrive back at the trailhead (GPS: 39.636091,-105.239099).

28 LIONS HEAD

Lions Head, reached by a long day hike, is a prominent peak that lords over Staunton State Park, Elk Falls, and the village of Pine Junction on US 285 southwest of Denver.

Start: Lazy V Trailhead, Staunton State Park
Difficulty: Strenuous
Trails: Old Mill Trail, Staunton Ranch Trail, Bugling Elk Trail, Lions Back Trail, Lions Head Trail
Distance: 8.1 miles, out and back
Hiking time: 4–5 hours
Elevations trailhead to summit: 8,580 to 9,463 feet at summit (+883 feet)
Ranked status: Ranked
Restrictions: Fee area; day use hours from 6 a.m. to 10 p.m.; Lions Head Trail raptor closure is March 15 to July 31 (check with park for exact closure dates); Chimney Rock Trail is hikers only; leashed dogs allowed; stay on designated trails; mountain bikes only on park roads; ground fires prohibited; gathering of artifacts, vegetation, and timber prohibited
Amenities: Toilets at trailhead; visitor center; walk-in tent campsites; services in Conifer and Evergreen
Counties: Jefferson and Park
Maps: *DeLorme:* p. 39, E8; Trails Illustrated #100: Boulder, Golden; USGS Meridian Hill
Land status/contact: Staunton State Park (303) 816-0912

FINDING THE TRAILHEAD

From Denver, drive west on US 285 to Shaffers Crossing about 6 miles west of Conifer. Turn right (north) on Elk Creek Road / CR 83 and drive 1.3 miles to a signed right turn into Staunton State Park. Drive 0.4 mile north on the park road to the visitor center. Pay the entrance fee and continue northwest for 1.7 miles on Upper Ranch Drive, passing Staunton Ranch Trailhead on the right 0.3 mile north of the visitor center, to the Lazy V Trailhead and a circular parking lot (GPS: 39.510505,-105.393110). Park address: 12102 South Elk Creek Rd., Pine.

The hike up Lions Head passes Elk Falls Pond.

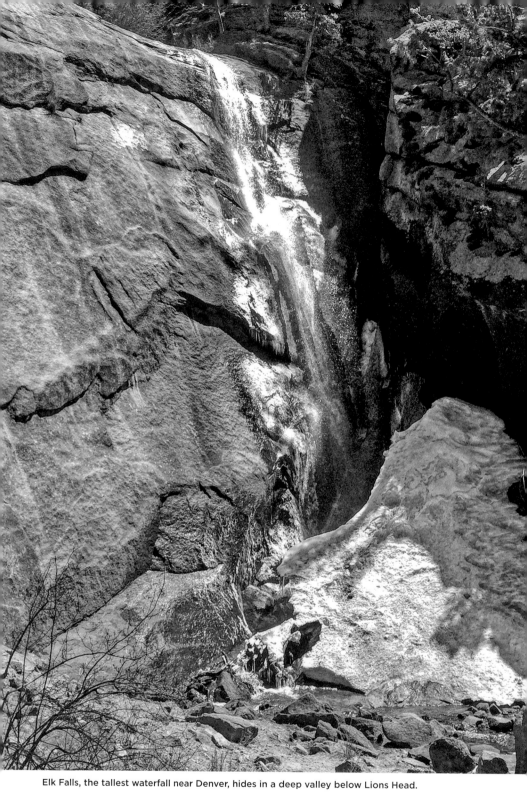

Elk Falls, the tallest waterfall near Denver, hides in a deep valley below Lions Head.

Lions Head rises above a deep canyon carved by Elk Creek.

THE HIKE

Lions Head lifts its cliff-lined crown high above Elk Creek and Elk Falls on the southern edge of 3,908-acre Staunton State Park in the Front Range southwest of Denver. The hike to Lions Head's 9,463-foot summit from the park's main trailhead follows well-maintained trails that cross easy and moderate terrain until the last half mile, which steeply climbs the peak's north slope. Park signs mark the trails and junctions, making route finding a snap.

The mountain's summit perches above a high cliff, an ideal nesting place for raptors. The Lions Head Trail, a summit loop, is closed from March 15 to July 31 to protect skittish peregrine falcons. Hikers on the summit above the nesting sites disturb the falcons, leading them to abandon nests. The closure begins at the Elk Falls Overlook trail junction. The Lions Back Trail below remains open to the overlook during the closure.

The hike begins at the Lazy V Parking Lot, the hub for many of Staunton's 30 miles of trails, and heads north on Old Mill Trail (OM) on Staunton Ranch Trail (SR). After traversing meadows and ponderosa pine woods, SR Trail reaches a service road and becomes Bugling Elk Trail (BE). This trail dips into a drainage that leads to North Elk Creek's wide valley and Elk Falls Pond at 8,846 feet. The final leg follows Lions Back Trail to Lions Head Trail and the summit.

Good side hikes follow Chimney Rock Trail (CR) to Elk Falls Trail (EF), which descends past towering Chimney Rock to a view of 75-foot Elk Falls spraying down a

Lions Head, surrounded by soaring cliffs, is the high point of Staunton State Park southwest of Denver.

LIONS HEAD

smooth stone slab. Also, check out a short trail at the start of Lions Head Trail to 9,150-foot Elk Falls Overlook and expansive views of the waterfall below and the park's rugged mountains.

MILES AND DIRECTIONS

0.0 Start at the Lazy V Trailhead on the northwest side of the circular parking lot and hike north on Old Mills Trail (OM) for 460 feet to a closed service road. Go left on it for 100 feet, and then continue north on OM Trail.

0.2 Reach a junction with Staunton Ranch Trail (SR) and go left on it (GPS: 39.512779, -105.392935).

0.4 Reach a junction on the right with Staunton Rocks climbing access trail, kiosk, and bike rack. Continue straight and gently climb the hillside.

1.3 Reach a service road and go right on SR Trail (GPS: 39.517767,-105.405433).

1.6 Arrive at a major junction with Borderline Trail (BL) on right and Marmot Passage Trail (MP) on left (GPS: 39.519333,-105.410133). This is the end of SR Trail. Go west on Bugling Elk Trail (BL) on a service road, passing out of the park and then reentering it. Descend the North Fork of North Elk Creek valley and bend east along North Elk Creek.

The summit of Lions Head provides wide views across rugged mountains in Staunton State Park.

2.6 Reach a junction with Marmot Passage Trail at the west end of Elk Falls Pond (GPS: 39.515632,-105.420698) and the end of BL Trail. Continue along the pond's edge on Lions Back Trail (LB), a service road.

2.7 Reach a building by the pond. Keep right on LB Trail and go uphill past a junction with Chimney Rock Trail (CR) on the left. Continue up and then follow the trail south along a wide ridge.

3.4 Reach a junction with the upper end of CR Trail (GPS: 39.506017,-105.421200). Continue straight on wide LB Trail through aspens and begin climbing Lions Head's northern slopes.

3.7 Reach a junction on the left signed "Elk Falls Overlook." Continue uphill on LB Trail. To visit the overlook, go left and hike a short distance to the 9,150-foot overlook on granite slabs, then return to LB Trail and go left.

3.9 Reach a Y junction and go left. The right trail is the return leg of the summit loop. Hike up left.

4.0 Arrive at the 9,463-foot Lions Head summit at the lip of a high south-facing cliff (GPS: 39.503111,-105.420720). Use caution on the cliff edge. This is a good lunch stop with spacious views across the park. Continue right on the loop trail and descend north.

4.2 Return to the Y junction and go straight on LB Trail. Follow the trail down to Elk Falls Pond and return to the trailhead on Bugling Elk Trail and Staunton Ranch Trail.

8.1 Arrive back at the trailhead (GPS: 39.510505,-105.393110).

29 NORTH TWIN CONE PEAK

A dirt road route and communication tower-topped peak may not seem like the most scenic way to spend a Colorado morning, but an off-trail extra credit option and wide-ranging views from the summit make this moderate hike worth the effort.

Start: Informal trailhead on FR 126, east of Kenosha Pass
Difficulty: Moderate
Trails: FR 126
Hiking time: About 2 hours
Distance: 3.6 miles, out and back
Elevations trailhead to summit: 11,100 to 12,323 feet (+1,223 feet)
Rank status: Ranked
Restrictions: Kenosha Pass is open year-round, with access to the trailhead limited in winter; high clearance 4WD vehicle is recommended but not always required, depending on snow and mud conditions
Amenities: Toilets, seasonal camping, and picnic area at Kenosha Pass Campground; primitive backcountry camping at signed, designated sites only; services in Fairplay and Bailey
County: Park
Maps: *DeLorme*: p. 49, A5; Trails Illustrated #105: Tarryall Mountains, Kenosha Pass; USGS Mount Logan
Land status/contact: Pike National Forest; South Platte Ranger District, (303) 275-5610

FINDING THE TRAILHEAD

From Denver, take US 285 S for 37 miles to Bailey, and continue another 32.3 miles and turn left onto unpaved CR 845, signed for Pike National Forest, Kenosha Pass, and the Colorado Trail. If traveling from Fairplay, go 20.3 miles north on US 285, through Jefferson, and turn right onto CR 845. Go 0.3 mile, past the Kenosha Pass (Colorado Trail) East Trailhead, toilets, and Kenosha Pass (East) Campground, and turn right onto FR 126. The trailhead is 5.5 miles from this point, and the road gets increasingly rougher. Pass through a gate and enter private property at 0.8 mile, pass through a second gate to enter the national forest at 2.1 miles, pass an Adopt-a-Trail sign at 3.3 miles, and reach a yellow Adopt-a-Road sign at 5.5 miles, where there is a pullout on the right side of the road. This is the informal trailhead, and the hike continues up the road (GPS: 39.414717,-105.701283).

THE HIKE

North Twin Cone Peak, the second highest point of the Platte River Mountains, hems in the east side of Kenosha Pass. Neighboring 12,340-foot South Twin Cone Peak is the high point of the range, the northernmost of the three subranges in Lost Creek Wilderness Area. North Twin Cone is easily hiked on foot on a rough four-wheel-drive road that accesses a tower on the summit. South Twin Cone and unranked 12,303-foot Mount Blaine between the cones can be added to the hike for a full-day adventure, although the extra credit peaks require cross-country travel, route-finding skills, and a good map.

Kenosha Pass, at 10,000 feet, serves as a base for campers and hikers on the Colorado Trail, a 567-mile footpath from Denver to Durango, which crosses the highway here. An interpretive center and a historic section of the Denver, South Park, and Pacific Railroad

The trail up North Twin Cone Peak follows a rough, four-wheel-drive road up the peak's south slopes.

North Twin Cone Peak offers wide views across South Park to the Mosquito Range.

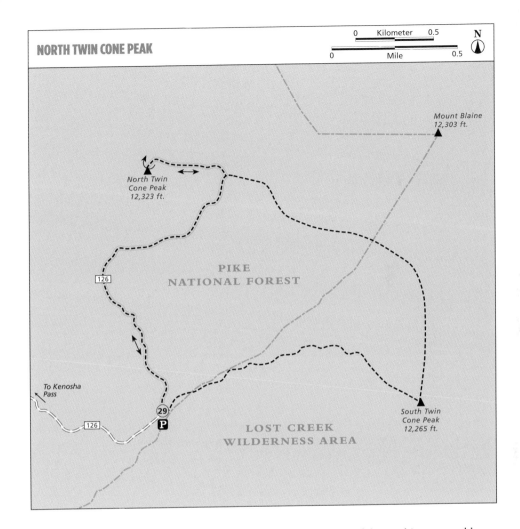

laid in a meadow by the US Forest Service, draws tourists, too. If the road is not passable to the trailhead, park here and enjoy a longer 14-mile roundtrip hike to North Twin Cone Peak. Otherwise, drive as close as possible to the trailhead, park in designated areas only, and enjoy an easy stroll to the high summit. This is a busy area during the summer. Consult the Pike National Forest website (fs.usda.gov/psicc) for the latest on fire restrictions and other regulations.

MILES AND DIRECTIONS

0.0   Begin at the unmarked trailhead on FR 126 and hike north up the rough dirt road. The road branches left and right multiple times, but always rejoins a short distance ahead.

1.4   Cross a saddle between North Twin Cone and Mount Blaine with views to Guanella Pass north, and continue west, past a post, and on to the high point beyond (GPS: 39.427898,-105.696503).

North Twin Cone Peak, viewed from South Twin Cone Peak, offers gentle slopes and easy grades to its rocky summit.

1.8 Arrive at ranked 12,328-foot North Twin Cone Peak, where a summit marker from 1981 denotes "Twin Cone" (GPS: 39.428433,-105.702217). Return the way you came.

3.6 Arrive back at the trailhead (GPS: 39.414717,-105.701283).

EXTRA CREDIT: SOUTH TWIN CONE PEAK

North Twin Cone Peak's obvious twin, ranked 12,340-foot South Twin Cone Peak, rises southeast of the north peak. There is no trail between the two peaks, but they are both above treeline and the route is obvious. From North Twin Cone, head east on the road to the North Twin Cone-Mount Blaine saddle. Note that this extra credit hike does not include directions to the unranked Mount Blaine, though if you are confident in your route-finding skills, you are welcome to add it to your hike. Depart the road at the saddle and hike east-southeast, staying high enough so you don't have to regain elevation, while descending gently to a point due north of South Twin Cone Peak. Then head south for the summit, crossing marshland. The distance from the saddle cutoff to the summit is about 1.4 miles. From South Twin Cone Peak, depart the summit and hike downslope west-northwest on talus, then curve west-southwest along the east side of Kenosha Creek and through the forest to a crossing near the trailhead, a distance of about 1.3 miles. A GPS unit is recommended to locate the trailhead. This hike enters the Lost Creek Wilderness Area and adds 1.3 miles to the overall hike distance, for a total of 4.9 miles for both peaks.

30 "PANORAMA POINT"

An easy, high-altitude trail leads from Boreas Pass west along the Continental Divide to a boulder-strewn summit with unfettered views.

Start: Boreas Pass Trailhead, Boreas Pass
Difficulty: Easy
Trails: Unofficial Boreas Pass Trail
Hiking time: About 1 hour
Distance: 1.4 miles, out and back
Elevations trailhead to summit: 11,481 to 12,029 feet (+548 feet)
Rank status: Unranked
Restrictions: Boreas Pass Road is closed at winter gates from Nov through mid-June, adding many miles to the hike; no bicycles allowed on trail
Amenities: Toilet at trailhead (east side of road); backcountry camping east side of pass; overnight accommodations by reservation only at nearby Roberts Cabin, Selkirk Campground, Ken's Cabin, and Boreas Pass Section House; services in Fairplay and Breckenridge
Counties: Park and Summit
Maps: *DeLorme*: p. 48, A3 and B3; Trails Illustrated #109: Breckenridge, Tennessee Pass; USGS Boreas Pass
Land status/contact: Pike National Forest, (719) 553-1400; South Park Ranger District, (719) 836-2031

FINDING THE TRAILHEAD

From the intersection of CO 9 and US 285 in Fairplay, take US 285 N for 9.3 miles and turn left (west) onto CR 33 / Boreas Pass Road to Boreas Pass and pullout parking on the left (west) side of the road. On the way, you'll drive through the town of Como. The road becomes unpaved at about 0.9 mile, switches back to the right at 3.8 miles, passes through a winter gate, and becomes increasingly steep, rocky, and exposed for a mile. If driving to the trailhead from Breckenridge, take Boreas Pass Road for 9 miles to the top of the pass (GPS: 39.410241,-105.968554).

The summits of "Panorama Point" on the right and "Madonna Dome" are easily reached from Boreas Pass.

Bald Mountain rises sharply to the north of "Panorama Point's" rocky summit.

A cairn and wooden post mark "Madonna Dome's" rounded summit.

THE HIKE

There's no better way to begin a hike than with a scenic drive to a lofty Rocky Mountain pass. This hike starts at the top of 11,481-foot Boreas Pass astride the Continental Divide with Summit County spreading north of the pass and Park County lying south of the pass. While numerous 13,000-foot peaks rise above the pass, all reached by steep slopes and faint trails, day hikers enjoy a more leisurely stroll along a defined trail up gentle slopes to "Panorama Point." The summit is visible from the trailhead. From the top of "Panorama Point," hikers find views east to Boreas Mountain, north to Bald Mountain, and west to the cloud-scraping Tenmile Range, including high point 14,271-foot Quandary Peak. The Mosquito Range, with its four 14ers, stretches south from Hoosier Pass to the twin Buffalo Peaks.

South of the point is "Madonna Dome," an extra credit peak. Long-distance hikers and peakbaggers with good route-finding skills can continue west from "Panorama Point" along the Continental Divide toward Hoosier Pass, tagging Red Peak, Red Mountain, and long Hoosier Ridge.

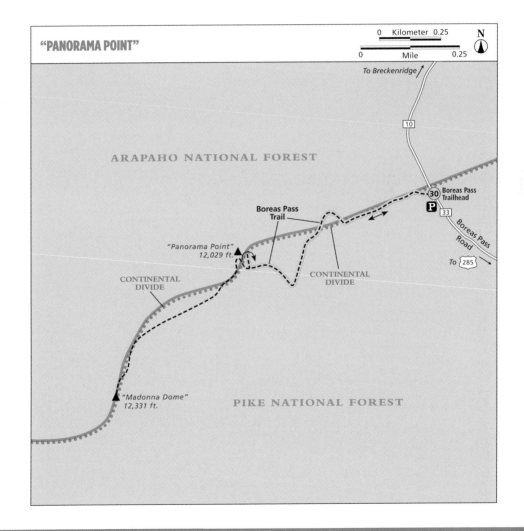

"Madonna Dome's" summit offers views north of high peaks, including Boreas and Bald Mountains.

MILES AND DIRECTIONS

0.0 From the Boreas Pass Trailhead, hike west-southwest on unsigned Boreas Pass Trail with the destination, "Panorama Point," in view ahead. The trail climbs gently through trees and across tundra along the Continental Divide.

0.65 When the rocky summit appears directly to the right, leave the main trail, skirt the right side of the summit area, and climb to the obvious highpoint (GPS: 39.407760,-105.977374).

0.7 Arrive at the summit of 12,029-foot "Panorama Point" (GPS: 39.408271,-105.977243). Return the way you came.

1.4 Arrive back at the trailhead (GPS: 39.410241,-105.968554).

EXTRA CREDIT: "MADONNA DOME"

From the summit of "Panorama Point" you're just half a mile from ranked 12er "Madonna Dome." There is no established trail between the two summits, but the route finding is simple. From "Panorama Point," hike southwest downslope, losing about 150 feet of elevation. Continue southwest, now upslope, to gain the ridge ahead. Follow the ridge, staying climber's left, to the cairned summit of 12,331-foot "Madonna Dome." The high peaks of Hoosier Pass appear west of the summit. Hiking both "Panorama Point" and "Madonna Dome" makes for a 2.4-mile, 1,000-feet of elevation gain, round-trip hike.

31 PLYMOUTH MOUNTAIN AND BILL COUCH MOUNTAIN

Hikers climb these two mountains in Deer Creek Canyon Park on several excellent trails that twist through a mixed conifer and Gambel oak woodland to high, rocky summits offering wide views across the Front Range and the Denver metropolitan area.

Start: Deer Creek Canyon Park Trailhead, Deer Creek Canyon Park
Difficulty: Strenuous
Trails: Meadowlark Trail, Plymouth Creek Trail, Plymouth Mountain Trail, Scenic View Trail, Red Mesa Loop, Golden Eagle Trail
Hiking time: About 3 hours
Distance: 7.8 miles, reverse lollipop, out and back
Elevations trailhead to summit: 6,090 to 7,295 feet at Plymouth Mountain (+1,205 feet); to 7,082 feet at Bill Couch Mountain (+992 feet)
Rank status: Both unranked
Restrictions: Open 1 hour before sunrise to 1 hour after sunset; Meadowlark and Golden Eagle Trails are hiker and equestrian only; muddy trails may be closed in early spring; leashed dogs only; pick up dog waste; no open fires, camping, open carry or discharge of firearms, motor vehicles, or marijuana use; nearby Black Bear Trail seasonally closed; watch for rattlesnakes; no nearby public campgrounds
Amenities: Toilets, water, picnic pavilion, and informational signs at trailhead; services in Littleton
County: Jefferson
Maps: *DeLorme* p. 40, E2; Trails Illustrated #100: Boulder, Golden; USGS Indian Hills
Land status/contact: Deer Creek Canyon Park, Jefferson County Open Space, (303) 271-5925; report park violations to Jefferson County Dispatch, (303) 980-7300

FINDING THE TRAILHEAD

From I-25 and I-70, take C-470 to the southwest side of the Denver metro area and exit onto Kipling Avenue. Drive south for one block and turn right on West Ute Avenue. Follow it for 0.8 mile west, bending south onto South Owens Street, and reach a T junction with Deer Creek Canyon Road. Go right on it and drive 1.9 miles to Grizzly Drive, then turn left on Grizzly and drive south for 0.4 mile to a large parking lot and trailhead at signed Deer Creek Canyon Park. The trailhead is at the southwest corner of the parking lot (GPS: 39.543225,-105.152080). Trailhead street address: 13388 Grizzly Dr., Littleton.

THE HIKE

Plymouth Mountain and Bill Couch Mountain, named for a nineteenth-century homesteader, lord over 1,637-acre Deer Creek Canyon Park, a Jefferson County Open Space area on the southwestern edge of Littleton. Hikers reach the summits of the two peaks on a series of well-maintained and easy-to-follow trails that cross slopes covered with Gambel oak, thread up wooded canyons, and traverse high ridges to summit overlooks. The trails are quiet except on busy weekends, so go during the week for solitude and wildlife. Look for mule deer, black bear, and occasional mountain lions. Be alert for rattlesnakes on warm days since the area boasts a high concentration of the venomous reptiles. The

Bill Couch Mountain towers above meadows along the Meadowlark Trail.

The summit of Plymouth Mountain is a boulder pile accessed by rock scrambling.

hike's Meadowlark and Golden Eagle Trails are for hikers and equestrians only, with no mountain bikers allowed.

The hike begins at Deer Creek Canyon Park Trailhead and follows Meadowlark Trail to a junction with Plymouth Creek Trail in a canyon. This trail climbs the canyon to a junction with Plymouth Mountain Trail, which is followed to Scenic View Trail and an overlook. The trail swings past several large boulders that form Plymouth Mountain's 7,295-foot high point. This summit is reached by rock scrambling so only experienced climbers should attempt the final ascent. The hike returns to the junction with Plymouth Creek Trail, which climbs to Red Mesa Loop and Golden Eagle Trail. This final trail leads to the summit of 7,082-foot Bob Couch Mountain and expansive views of Front Range peaks to the north, long hogbacks below the mountain front, and distant skyscrapers in downtown Denver.

MILES AND DIRECTIONS

0.0 Start at the Deer Creek Canyon Park Trailhead right of the restrooms. Go straight on the Meadowlark Trail and hike west through a meadow. Switchback up scrub oak-covered slopes and then contour south and southwest below Bill Couch Mountain into Plymouth Creek canyon.

1.5 Reach a junction with signed Plymouth Creek Trail in a canyon (GPS: 39.535032, -105.156573). Go right on it and follow the trail west up the bottom of the canyon.

1.95 Reach a junction with Plymouth Mountain Trail on the left. Continue straight on Plymouth Creek Trail. Do not go left on the Plymouth Mountain Trail here. To reach

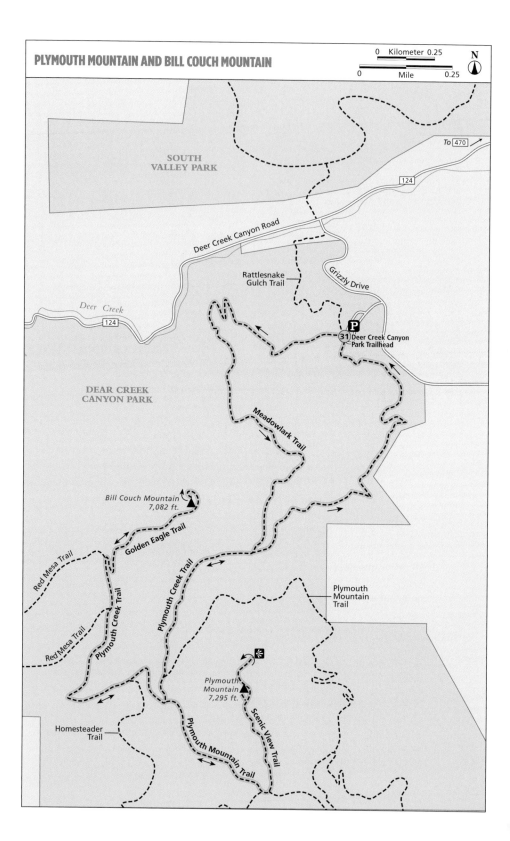

0   Kilometer 0.25

N

0   Mile   0.25

To [470]

[124]

SOUTH
VALLEY PARK

Deer Creek Canyon Road

Rattlesnake
Gulch Trail

Grizzly Drive

Deer Creek

[124]

P

(31) Deer Creek Canyon
Park Trailhead

DEAR CREEK
CANYON PARK

Meadowlark Trail

Bill Couch Mountain
7,082 ft.

Golden Eagle Trail

Red Mesa Trail

Plymouth Creek Trail

Plymouth Creek Trail

Red Mesa Trail

Plymouth
Mountain
Trail

Plymouth
Mountain
7,295 ft.

Scenic View Trail

Homesteader
Trail

Plymouth Mountain Trail

Bill Couch Mountain rises above the western edge of the Denver suburbs.

the summit of Plymouth Mountain, the correct trail to take is at the next junction a few hundred feet up the trail.

2.0 Reach the junction with the upper section of Plymouth Mountain Trail on the left (GPS: 39.529340,-105.160540). Keep left on it and hike up a wooded ravine. Continue past the signed Homesteader Trail junction on the right.

2.4 Just after the Homestead Trail, reach a junction on the left with Scenic View Trail (GPS: 39.525967,-105.155744). Go left on it and hike north up a wide wooded ridge.

2.7 Reach a jumble of big boulders on the left (GPS: 39.529583,-105.156942). This is the 7,295-foot high point of Plymouth Mountain. To reach the summit, experienced climbers can scramble up boulders (Class 3) to the top of the biggest boulder. Return to the trail and continue north through piney woods.

2.8 Arrive at a scenic overlook at the trail's end (GPS: 39.531011,-105.156554). After enjoying views northeast to hogbacks and the Denver skyline in the distance, retrace your steps south on Scenic View Trail.

3.2 Return to Plymouth Mountain Trail and go right on it, descending northwest back down the ravine.

3.6 Arrive back at the junction with Plymouth Creek Trail. Go left on signed Plymouth Creek Trail to climb Bill Couch Mountain. You will return to this junction on the descent to return to the trailhead.

3.8 Pass a junction with Homesteader Trail on the left. Continue up the wide trail and cross a dry creek. Continue northeast across sunny slopes.

4.3 Reach a junction with the start of Red Mesa Loop at the end of Plymouth Creek Trail (GPS: 39.533038,-105.163578). Keep right on Red Mesa Loop and hike north through scrub oaks across a mountain slope.

Plymouth Mountain lifts bulky shoulders above Plymouth Creek's deep canyon.

The rocky summit of Bill Couch Mountain yields scenic views across the foothills below.

4.4 Reach a junction on the right with signed Golden Eagle Trail (GPS: 39.534830,-105.163826). Go right on it and descend northeast to a saddle. Follow the trail across the south slope of Bill Couch Mountain, then spiral around the east side.

4.9 Arrive at the rocky summit of 7,082-foot Bill Couch Mountain and great views across the Front Range (GPS: 39.536983,-105.159800). After a snack, return west on Golden Eagle Trail.

5.4 Reach the Red Mesa Loop junction and go left on the trail.

5.5 Return to the junction with Plymouth Creek Trail and descend south on it.

6.2 Return to the junction on the canyon floor with Plymouth Mountain Trail on the right. Go left on Plymouth Creek Trail, following the trail down the canyon.

6.7 Return to the junction with Meadowlark Trail on the left. The last leg of the hike continues straight on Plymouth Creek Trail down the canyon. Just before reaching houses on the right, the trail leaves the canyon and threads along a rim above the deepening canyon to the left. Past the second house, the trail bends left and descends into the canyon, then climbs out the opposite site. Finish by heading northwest across open slopes and meadows.

7.8 Arrive back at the trailhead (GPS: 39.543225,-105.152080).

A hiker follows Scenic View Trail to the wooded summit of Plymouth Mountain.

32 CARPENTER PEAK

An excellent trail climbs the east flank of Carpenter Peak, the high point of Roxborough State Park, to a stony summit with spacious views of the park's red-rock formations, the tawny prairie, Denver's skyline, and the wooded Front Range.

Start: Roxborough State Park Trailhead west of the visitor center, Roxborough State Park
Difficulty: Strenuous
Trails: Willow Creek Trail, Carpenter Peak Trail
Hiking time: 3–4 hours
Distance: 6.2 miles, out and back
Elevations trailhead to summit: 6,195 to 7,180 feet (+985 feet)
Rank status: Unranked
Restrictions: Fee area; open daily but hours change seasonally; summer hours: 8 a.m. to 7 p.m., winter hours: 8 a.m. to 6 p.m.; stay on designated trails; no rock climbing; trails are closed to pets, horses, and bicycles
Amenities: Restrooms at visitor center; drinking water; interpretive signs; services in Littleton
County: Douglas
Maps: *DeLorme*: p. 50, A2; Trails Illustrated #135 Deckers, Rampart Range; USGS Kassler
Land status/contact: Roxborough State Park, (303) 973-3959

FINDING THE TRAILHEAD

From C-470 on Denver's south side, drive south on US 85 / South Santa Fe Drive for 4.2 miles to Titan Road. From I-25 in Castle Rock, take exit 184 onto Meadows Parkway and drive 0.2 mile south to US 85. Follow US 85 northwest to Titan Road. Drive west on Titan Road for 3 miles until it bends south and becomes North Rampart Range Road. Drive south on North Rampart Range Road for 3.5 miles to its intersection with Roxborough Park Road. Turn left (east) and drive 325 feet and turn right (south) on Roxborough Drive. Drive 0.3 mile to the Roxborough State Park entrance station. Continue south on the dirt and paved road to a parking lot at its end (GPS: 39.428936,-105.067921). From the north side of the parking lot, hike 0.1 mile up a paved path to the park visitor center and the trailhead to the west (GPS: 39.429490,-105.069503). Visitor center address: 4751 E Roxborough Dr., Littleton.

THE HIKE

Carpenter Peak, the 7,180-foot high point of Roxborough State Park southwest of Denver, lifts rounded ridges to a rockpile summit overlooking the park's iconic sandstone hogbacks, slabs, and pinnacles. The hike up the well-traveled Willow Creek and Carpenter Peak Trails, beginning at the park visitor center, offers gentle grades and spectacular views across the Front Range. The trail passes meadows and scrub oak copses among towering rock formations and then steadily ascends the mountain's wooded east flank.

The hike is popular on weekends, so visit on weekdays for solitude. The trail is a designated segment of the American Discovery Trail, a coast-to-coast footpath that stretches over 6,800 miles from Delaware to California. When hiking in summer, bring water, a hat, and sunscreen, and be alert for rattlesnakes on the lower trail. The trail makes a fun winter hike with appropriate clothing and gear.

Looking north from the granite summit of Carpenter Peak to Waterton Canyon.

Evening light warms a tall grass meadow and sandstone hogback along the Carpenter Peak Trail.

Sandstone fins, hogbacks, and pinnacles lie below Carpenter Peak in Roxborough State Park.

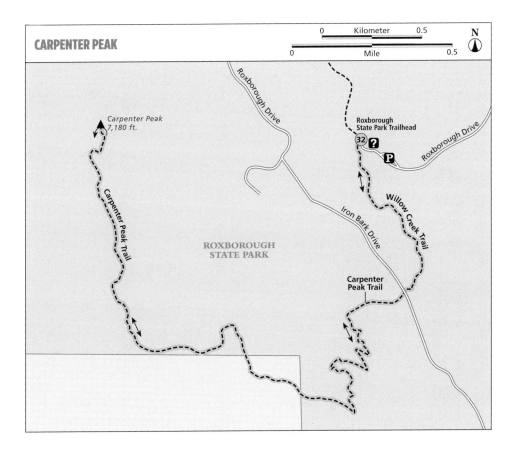

0   Kilometer   0.5

0   Mile   0.5

N

Carpenter Peak
7,180 ft.

Roxborough Drive

Roxborough
State Park Trailhead

32

P

Carpenter Peak Trail

Willow Creek Trail

Iron Bark Drive

Roxborough Drive

ROXBOROUGH
STATE PARK

Carpenter
Peak Trail

Roxborough State Park protects a series of long hogbacks composed of tilted sandstone layers below the Front Range. Roxborough offers quiet natural experiences including hiking, nature study, photography, and wildlife watching. The park, boasting nine distinct plant communities, is a meeting place for plants and animals from both the prairie to the east and the mountains to the west. The Carpenter Peak Trail climbs through these ecological zones, crossing meadows tangled with wildflowers and grasses, threading through dense Gambel oak thickets, climbing past ponderosa pines and Douglas firs on moist slopes, and groves of quaking aspen below their usual elevation. Botanists say the aspens are a relict species left from the last ice age when the climate was cooler.

MILES AND DIRECTIONS

0.0 Start at the Roxborough State Park Trailhead for Carpenter Peak, Willow Creek, and South Rim Trails on the west side of a service road west of the park visitor center. Hike south on signed Willow Creek Trail.

0.4 Reach a junction with the Willow Creek Trail going left (GPS: 39.424646, -105.066101). Continue straight on Carpenter Peak Trail.

0.5 Reach a junction with the South Rim Trail on the left (GPS: 39.423634,-105.066105). Continue straight on Carpenter Peak Trail.

Denver's skyscraper skyline rises beyond serene sandstone ridges at Roxborough State Park.

0.55 Cross a closed dirt road and hike west on the trail, steadily climbing uphill through scrub oak, pine, and firs.

1.75 Reach a junction in dense woods with the Elk Valley Loop Trail on the left (GPS: 39.418971,-105.074315). Continue straight across forested slopes to an open ridge.

2.2 Reach a bench on the ridgetop with views to the east. Continue west to a shallow valley, then traverse north across wooded slopes.

3.0 Reach a Y junction with the trail to Waterton Canyon on the left (GPS: 39.429212, -105.085252). Go right and follow the trail through boulders to the summit boulders.

3.1 Reach Carpenter Peak's 7,180-foot summit (GPS: 39.430194,-105.084765). The actual high point is on top of a rock pile. After enjoying views of the sandstone fins below, follow the trail back down.

6.2 Arrive back at the trailhead (GPS: 39.429490,-105.069503).

33 DEVILS HEAD

Devils Head is a towering clump of granite accessed by an easy hike and a 143-step open metal staircase. A fire tower sits on top, offering views for more than 100 miles in all directions.

Start: Devils Head Trailhead, Rampart Range Road
Difficulty: Easy
Trails: Devils Head National Recreation Trail #611
Hiking time: About 2 hours
Distance: 2.8 miles, out and back
Elevations trailhead to summit: 8,808 to 9,748 feet (+940 feet)
Rank status: Ranked
Restrictions: Rampart Range Road closes by Dec 1 and reopens between Apr 1 and May 31, depending on snow and mud conditions; overflow parking at junction of FR 300 and entrance to the trailhead may be gated 0.5 mile back, adding 1 mile round trip to the hike; trail closed to bicycles and motorized vehicles; dogs must be leashed
Amenities: Toilets near the trailhead and near ranger's area; seasonal campgrounds; seasonal, first-come first-served camping at Devils Head Campground and Picnic Area; services in Sedalia
County: Douglas
Maps: *DeLorme*: p. 50, C2; Trails Illustrated #135: Deckers, Rampart Range; USGS Devils Head
Land status/contact: Pike National Forest; South Platte Ranger District, (303) 275-5610

FINDING THE TRAILHEAD

From I-25 in Castle Rock, about 28 miles south of Denver and 40 miles north of Colorado Springs, take exit 184 for Founders Parkway toward US 85 N / CO 86 E / Meadows Parkway. Go 0.3 mile and turn left onto US 85 N / CO 86 E / Meadows Parkway, then go 0.5 mile and turn right onto US 85 N / Santa Fe Drive. Drive 5.3 miles and turn left onto CO 67 S / Manhart Street, then go 9.9 miles and turn left onto unpaved Rampart Range Road / FR 300.

Continue for 9.3 miles on the dirt Rampart Range Road, following signs for Devils Head Campground, and keep left on FR 180.

Drive past the campground and picnic area and turn right, then continue 0.2 mile to parking for twenty-five cars and the trailhead.

If you're coming from Sedalia, take CO 67 S / Manhart Avenue for 9.8 miles. Turn left on Rampart Range Road and drive 9.3 miles, then turn left on FR 180 and go 0.1 mile to the trailhead on the left (GPS: 39.269367,-105.105167).

If the parking area is full, park in a signed overflow parking lot located at the junction of FR 300 and FR 180 before the Devils Head Campground (GPS: 39.275754, -105.107651) and walk about 0.5 mile to the trailhead. Do not park along the road, which restricts access to the area by emergency vehicles.

THE HIKE

Devils Head is the high point of the Rampart Range, and home to the Devils Head Fire Lookout Tower, one of the original Front Range lookout towers. The Devils Head area is laced with recreational trails popular with off-highway vehicles (OHVs), and the cliffs beyond nearby Zinn Overlook are popular with rock climbers.

Devils Head lifts a rugged profile above Jackson Creek's lush valley.

The Devils Head Lookout Tower, established in 1912, is reached by climbing 143 stairs to the peak's summit.

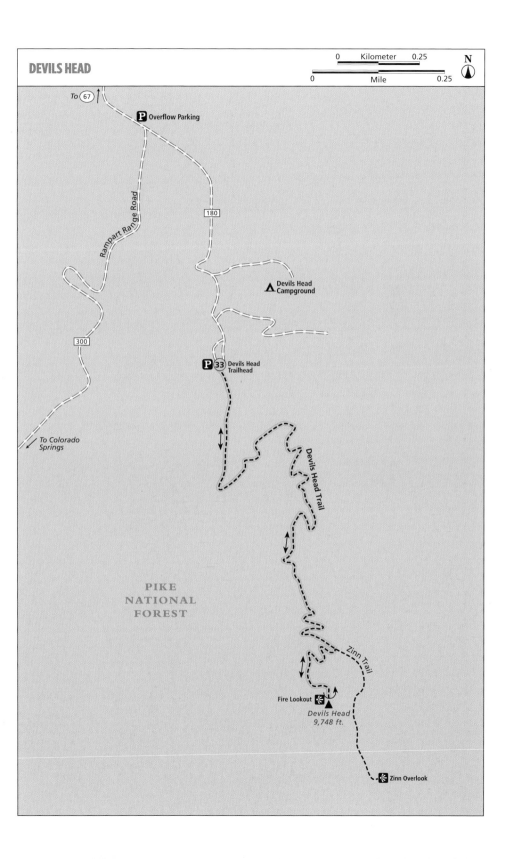

Pikes Peak rises beyond Starcastle, one of Devils Head's lower summits.

Pikes Peak scrapes the southern horizon beyond granite faces and spires on Devils Head.

MILES AND DIRECTIONS

0.0 Begin at the Devils Head Trailhead, hike up steps, and follow the trail as it gradually ascends south, through groves of aspen, fir, and spruce trees, and past piles of pink and gray granite.

1.2 Pass the signed Zinn Overlook cutoff to the left (GPS: 39.261700,-105.101017) and continue straight, south-southeast on the trail. Descend past the ranger's cabin on left, and toilet on right, to the stairs ahead.

1.4 Reach the bottom of the staircase (GPS: 39.260733,-105.101533). Ascend the stairs to the top (GPS: 39.260317,-105.101183). Take in the views, then head back down the stairs and return the way you came.

2.8 Arrive back at the trailhead (GPS: 39.269367,-105.105167).

EXTRA CREDIT: ZINN OVERLOOK

For more views, take a side trip to Zinn Overlook. After departing Devils Head, hike back toward the trailhead for 0.2 mile and turn right onto Zinn Trail #615 (GPS: 39.261700,-105.101017). Hike south for 0.1 mile to a rocky outcrop at 9,482 feet (GPS: 39.258182,-105.099388). This side trip adds 0.2 mile to your hike.

34 LINCOLN MOUNTAIN

Hike Lincoln Mountain, a flat-topped mesa on the north side of the Palmer Divide between Colorado Springs and Denver, on a trail that switchbacks up its eastern slope and then circumnavigates the mountain's wide, grassy summit.

Start: Lincoln Mountain Trailhead, Lincoln Mountain Open Space
Difficulty: Easy
Trails: Palmer Divide Ranch Trail, Lincoln Mountain Trail, Lincoln Mountain Loop
Hiking time: About 2 hours
Distance: 4.2 miles, lollipop
Elevations trailhead to summit: 7,040 to 7,394 feet (+354 feet)
Rank status: Unranked
Restrictions: Open 1 hour before sunrise to 1 hour after sunset; leashed dogs only; no water at trailhead; no motorized vehicles; no nearby public campgrounds
Amenities: Toilets and info kiosk at trailhead; services in Monument and Franktown
County: Douglas
Maps: *DeLorme*: p. 51, D5; Trails Illustrated, none; USGS Greenland; Douglas County Lincoln Mountain Open Space Map
Land status/contact: Lincoln Mountain Open Space; Douglas County Open Space and Natural Resources, (303) 660-7495

FINDING THE TRAILHEAD

Lincoln Mountain Trailhead is west of CO 83 between Denver and Colorado Springs. Reach it by driving south on CO 83 from Parker and Franktown on the southeast side of Denver or north from Colorado Springs on CO 83 to Jones Road. Turn west on the dirt road and drive 0.6 mile to a parking lot and the trailhead on the right (north) side of the road (GPS: 39.174465,-104.750227). Trailhead address: 7333 Jones Rd., Larkspur.

The Lincoln Mountain Trail encircles the broad summit, offering spectacular views southwest to 14,115-foot Pikes Peak.

Lined with wavering grass, the Lincoln Mountain Trail crosses open terrain with far-reaching views of distant Front Range mountains.

THE HIKE

The Lincoln Mountain Trail climbs from the trailhead to the mountain's broad 7,394-foot summit in 876-acre Lincoln Mountain Open Space, a Douglas County parkland that preserves a couple high mesas above West Cherry Creek. The easy hike, following wide trails, threads through grassy meadows, a ponderosa pine and Gambel oak woodland, and broken cliff bands. Through conservation easements and land acquisitions, Douglas County has protected over 35,000 acres of undeveloped land, including Lincoln Mountain Open Space, keeping a swathe of Colorado's historic ranches, crucial wildlife habitat, and unspoiled views protected for future generations.

The Lincoln Mountain Trail is easy to follow, well signed, and has gentle grades. Hikers share the trail with mountain bikers and equestrians. Winter offers fine hiking with light snowfall but bring MICROspikes and trekking poles for icy trail sections. Lincoln Mountain's spacious summit yields spectacular views southwest across ranchland to 14,115-foot Pikes Peak, one of America's most famous high mountains.

The mountain's highest point hides in tall grass near the summit plateau's eastern edge but there is no trail, markers, or cairns identifying the location. If you are a peakbagger, load the summit coordinates (GPS: 39.174591,-104.759699) into a GPS unit to find the actual high point.

Pikes Peak and Almagre Mountain fill the sky beyond Lincoln Mountain's summit.

Hikers follow the Lincoln Mountain Trail along the northern edge of the summit plateau.

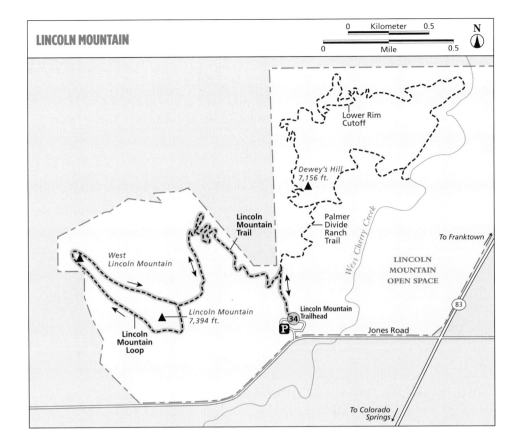

MILES AND DIRECTIONS

0.0 Start at the Lincoln Mountain Trailhead at the northwest corner of the parking lot. Go through a wooden fence past toilets and an info kiosk, and hike north on wide Palmer Divide Ranch Trail.

0.2 Reach the junction of Lincoln Mountain Trail and Palmer Divide Ranch Trail (GPS: 39.177013,-104.750786). Go left on signed Lincoln Mountain Trail and hike through meadows and Gambel oak groves on the east slope of a mesa.

1.5 Reach a trail junction on the northeast side of the broad Lincoln Mountain summit (GPS: 39.175030,-104.758209). Go left on the Lincoln Mountain Loop Trail and hike along the east and then the southwest edge of mountain's summit. The mountain's 7,394-foot high point is in the summit meadow but not marked.

2.2 Reach the west end of the summit mesa and bend right at the top of West Lincoln Mountain. Follow the trail east along the mesa's north edge.

2.7 Reach the trail junction on the east side of Lincoln Mountain's summit. Go left on the trail and descend the east slopes to the start of the trail at the first junction.

4.0 Reach the junction with the Palmer Divide Ranch Trail. Go right on it and hike south toward the parking lot.

4.2 Arrive back at the trailhead (GPS: 39.174465,-104.750227).

35 SPRUCE MOUNTAIN

A trail climbs to the northeast end of Spruce Mountain's flat summit and follows a loop trail through piney woods to Windy Point, the mountain high point, and scenic views of Pikes Peak and the wooded Rampart Range.

Start: Spruce Mountain Trailhead, Spruce Mountain Open Space
Difficulty: Moderate
Trails: Spruce Meadows Trail, Oak Shortcut Trail, Spruce Mountain Trail, Upper Loop Trail
Hiking time: About 2.5 hours
Distance: 4.7 miles, lollipop
Elevations trailhead to summit: 7,130 to 7,605 feet (+475 feet)
Rank status: Unranked
Restrictions: Open 1 hour before sunrise to 1 hour after sunset; leashed dogs only; no fires; mountain bikers and equestrians
Amenities: Portable toilets at trailhead; drinking water at nearby Greenland Open Space Trailhead; interpretive sign; services in Palmer Lake and Larkspur
County: Douglas
Maps: *DeLorme*: p. 50, D4; Trails Illustrated, none; USGS Larkspur
Land status/contact: Spruce Mountain Open Space; Douglas County Open Space and Natural Resources, (303) 660-7495

FINDING THE TRAILHEAD

From Denver, drive I-25 south to exit 173 to Larkspur. Drive south on Spruce Mountain Road / CR 53 for 5.6 miles to trailhead on right. From Colorado Springs, drive I-25 north to exit 163. Turn left and drive west on County Line Road for 2.6 miles to Palmer Lake. Go right on Spruce Mountain Road / CR 53. Drive 3.6 miles north to the parking lot on the left. Spruce Mountain Open Space address: 13415 Spruce Mountain Rd., Larkspur. Trailhead is at the parking lot's west side (GPS: 39.167942,-104.875063).

Sandstone shelves offer views from Greenland Overlook on Spruce Mountain.

Bluffs, cliffs, and woods line Spruce Mountain's southern edge above Carpenter Creek's wide valley.

THE HIKE

Spruce Mountain, the centerpiece of 1,390-acre Spruce Mountain Open Space, is a long mesa rimmed with sandstone cliffs that sits at the base of the Rampart Range between Denver and Colorado Springs. Windy Point, the mountain's 7,605-foot high point, is reached by a good trail that climbs to the mesa top and then loops around its rimrock. The well-signed trail offers gradual grades, open ponderosa pine and Gambel oak woods, and scenic views that stretch from Pikes Peak to the south to Longs Peak to the north. The open space, a Douglas County parkland, has 8.5 miles of trails, including Spruce Mountain Trail to the summit and Eagle Pass Trail.

From the trailhead and parking lot, the hike follows Spruce Meadows Trail to Oak Shortcut Trail, which meets Spruce Mountain Trail at Pine Junction. Continue up Spruce Mountain Trail on the rocky northwest flank to Greenland Overlook and views across the high prairie. The trail heads west to a junction and the start of its loop section. Go left along the southern rim to Windy Point, a marvelous viewpoint that looks south to Palmer Lake and Pikes Peak. Use caution at the unfenced overlook above cliffs and keep children under control. The last leg heads northeast on the loop trail to the last junction and then descends Spruce Mountain Trail to the parking lot.

A rocky promontory overlooks Carpenter Creek and distant Mount Herman.

SPRUCE MOUNTAIN

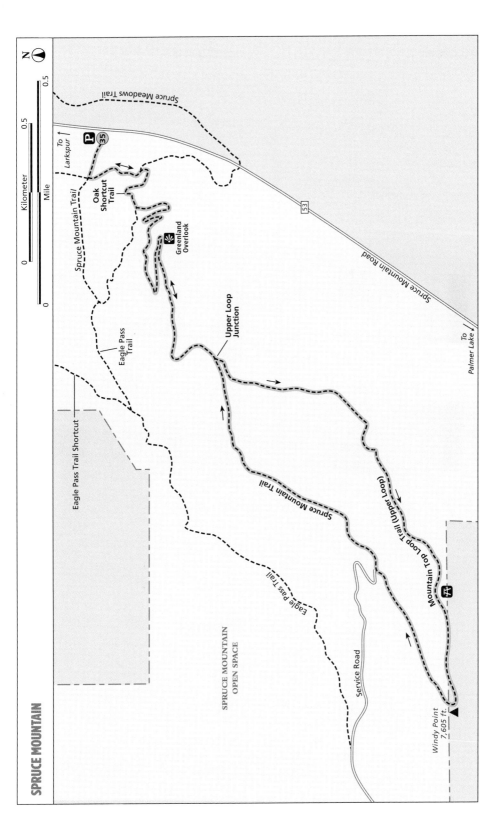

N

To
Larkspur

P 35

Spruce Mountain Trail

Oak
Shortcut
Trail

Spruce Meadows Trail

Greenland
Overlook

Upper Loop
Junction

Eagle Pass
Trail

Eagle Pass Trail Shortcut

Spruce Mountain Trail

Mountain Top Loop Trail (Upper Loop)

SPRUCE MOUNTAIN
OPEN SPACE

Eagle Pass Trail

Service Road

Windy Point
7,605 ft.

To
Palmer Lake

Spruce Mountain Road

53

Kilometer

Mile

0   0.5   0.5

0   0.5   0.5

Mount Herman and the Rampart Range march south from Windy Point, Spruce Mountain's high point.

Cliffs at Windy Point, the high point of Spruce Mountain, frame Mount Herman and Pikes Peak.

MILES AND DIRECTIONS

0.0 Start at the Spruce Mountain Trailhead on the west side of the parking lot. Walk 350 feet to a junction with Spruce Meadows Trail. Go left on it and hike south.

0.1 Reach a junction with Oak Shortcut Trail. Go right on Oak Shortcut and hike uphill through Gambel oak.

0.3 Meet the Spruce Mountain Trail on the right at Pine Junction (GPS: 39.166513, -104.877033). Go left on Spruce Mountain Trail and continue up the mountain's northeast flank.

0.8 Arrive at Greenland Overlook (GPS: 39.165660,-104.879439). Walk left for 100 feet on a side trail for the best views. Return to Spruce Mountain Trail and continue west.

1.2 Junction with Spruce Mountain Upper Loop Trail (GPS 39.163626,-104.883723). Go left on the doubletrack trail and follow it along the mountain's south rim.

2.4 Reach 7,605-foot Windy Point—Spruce Mountain's high point (GPS: 39.15516, -104.898723). A short spur trail goes left from the main trail to an overlook. Return to the main trail and go left (north).

3.5 Return to the Y junction at the end of the loop trail. Keep left and hike northeast on Spruce Mountain Trail.

3.9 Hike past Greenland Overlook and descend trails to return to the trailhead.

4.7 Arrive back at the trailhead (GPS: 39.167942,-104.875063).

36 SUNDANCE MOUNTAIN AND "UPPER SUNDANCE MOUNTAIN"

Sundance Mountain and neighboring "Upper Sundance Mountain" rise above the town of Palmer Lake, offering views of surrounding Front Range peaks including Mount Herman and Chautauqua Mountain to the south and the tawny prairie to the east.

Start: Palmer Lake Reservoir Trailhead, Old Carriage Road
Difficulty: Moderate
Trails: Palmer Reservoir Trail, Sundance Valley Trail, Sundance Connector Trail, Sundance Mountain Trail, Swank Trail, Ice Cave Creek Trail
Hiking time: 2–3 hours
Distance: 5.3 miles, lollipop
Elevations trailhead to summit: 7,227 to 8,255 feet at Sundance Mountain (+1,028 feet); to 8,320 feet at "Upper Sundance Mountain" (+1,093 feet)
Rank status: Both unranked
Restrictions: Fee area, self-serve debit/credit card kiosk; hiker use only; area is Palmer Lake water supply; no dogs allowed on lake trails at any time (strictly enforced); no firearms, horses, motor vehicles, or camping; no swimming or wading in lakes or streams; no nearby public campgrounds
Amenities: Porta-potty at trailhead; services in Palmer Lake
County: El Paso
Maps: *DeLorme*: p. 50, D3 and D4; Trails Illustrated #137: Pikes Peak, Cañon City; USGS Palmer Lake
Land status/contact: City of Palmer Lake watershed, (719) 481-2953; Pike National Forest, (719) 553-1400; Pikes Peak Ranger District, (719) 636-1602

FINDING THE TRAILHEAD

From Colorado Springs and Denver, drive either north or south on I-25 to Monument and take exit 161. Drive west on CO 105 for 3.5 miles to Palmer Lake. Turn left (west) on South Valley Road in Palmer Lake and drive west for 0.35 mile. Turn left (south) on Old Carriage Road and drive 0.2 mile to a large roadside parking lot and the trailhead in a valley (GPS: 39.118669,-104.921208).

THE HIKE

Sundance Mountain forms the western skyline of Palmer Lake, a charming town straddling a low point of the Palmer Divide east of the Front Range. The hike reaches the named summit of rounded 8,255-foot Sundance Mountain, passing the Lower Reservoir, part of Palmer Lake's water supply, and climbing a shallow valley to the mountain crest. A higher summit, unofficially named "Upper Sundance Mountain," rises just north of lower Sundance Mountain. While the hike is easily done as an out–and–back adventure, follow the described hike which explores Ice Cave Creek's spectacular canyon on the descent.

The hike's lower section follows Palmer Reservoir Trail alongside North Monument Creek to two reservoirs which form the town of Palmer Lake's water supply. The trails and junctions are not signed or marked. Pay attention to the hike directions and map to stay on course.

The Sundance Valley Trail climbs through pines and firs to a high saddle.

Palmer Lake and grassy valleys spread below "Upper Sundance Mountain's" high ridges.

The Sundance Mountain Trail offers views across wooded valleys to its rounded namesake peak.

MILES AND DIRECTIONS

0.0 Start at the Palmer Lake Reservoir Trailhead on the parking lot's west side. Pass an information sign and hike west on Palmer Reservoir Trail.

0.3 Past a metal culvert, reach a closed service road and go left on Palmer Reservoir Trail (GPS: 39.118680,-104.926140). Pass through a gate and hike west to Lower Reservoir. Follow the road to an unmarked junction on the right.

0.6 Reach a junction with unsigned Sundance Valley Trail (GPS: 39.117119,-104.931593). Go right and hike up the singletrack trail on slopes right of a dry creek bed.

0.9 Clamber over a large boulder that blocks the trail and continue up the valley through a mixed conifer woodland.

1.2 Reach a junction with the unsigned Sundance Connector Trail on the right (GPS: 39.124527,-104.931671). Go right on the obvious narrow trail and contour south across west-facing slopes.

1.3 Reach a saddle and a junction with the unsigned Sundance Mountain Trail (GPS: 39.123702,-104.929683). Turn right and head up north-facing slopes on the trail.

1.4 Arrive at a cairn on the rounded top of 8,255-foot Sundance Mountain (GPS: 39.122012,-104.929276). For better views, hike south for 0.1 mile on the trail onto open slopes on the south side of the mountain. After enjoying the summit, return down the trail to the saddle.

A jumble of granite blocks and boulders covers the mountainside above Ice Cave Creek.

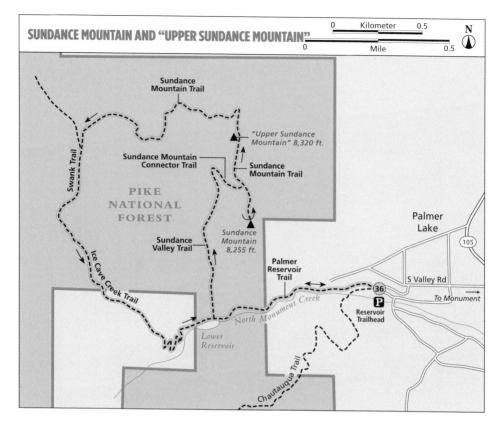

0   Kilometer   0.5

0   Mile   0.5

N

Sundance Mountain Trail

"Upper Sundance Mountain" 8,320 ft.

Sundance Mountain Connector Trail

Sundance Mountain Trail

Swank Trail

PIKE NATIONAL FOREST

Palmer Lake

105

Sundance Mountain 8,255 ft.

Sundance Valley Trail

Ice Cave Creek Trail

Palmer Reservoir Trail

S Valley Rd

36

To Monument

Reservoir Trailhead

North Monument Creek

Lower Reservoir

Chautauqua Trail

1.5   Reach the saddle and the junction with the ascent trail. From here you can retrace your steps back down the ascent trails to the trailhead for a 2.8-mile hike. For full value, continue the hike with the description below. Hike north from the saddle on the Sundance Mountain Trail.

1.7   Arrive at boulders on the summit of 8,320-foot "Upper Sundance Mountain" just left of the trail (GPS: 39.125943,-104.930111). Follow the trail north down open slopes with views of Palmer Lake to a junction (GPS: 9.127448,-104.930059). Go left on unmarked Sundance Mountain Trail and hike southwest onto a wide ridge. Pass a junction with the eroded upper part of Sundance Valley Trail on the left that drops down a steep slope. Continue straight.

2.1   Reach a rounded bump on the left, a ridge high point unofficially named "Middle Sundance Mountain" (GPS: 39.126931,-104.931969). Continue west on the trail, which begins descending the ridge to steep west-facing slopes. Look left for good views of wooded Sundance Mountain. The trail descends sharply down braided gravel slopes. Watch your footing and continue to the bottom of a valley.

2.7   Reach a junction in the valley with Swank Trail (GPS: 39.125700,-104.940307). Go left on Swank Trail and hike south down the valley.

3.0   Reach a Y junction with Ice Cave Creek Trail as the valley widens (GPS: 39.121960, -104.941724). Keep left on Ice Cave Creek Trail and cross a trickling creek. The next leg of the hike, following Ice Cave Creek's valley southeast, is lovely with dark woods and fields of granite boulders. Follow the trail as it dips and weaves through boulders on slopes south of the creek. The trail finally pulls away from the valley, passes an overlook of the Lower Reservoir and Sundance Mountain, and then switchbacks down slopes.

Ice Cave Creek Trail offers dramatic views of Sundance Mountain and the Lower Reservoir.

3.9   Meet Palmer Reservoir Trail, a wide service road, above the Lower Reservoir (GPS: 39.116020,-104.933718). Go left on the road and hike to the reservoir's east end.

4.1   Return to the junction with Sundance Mountain Trail on the left and the end of the hike's loop portion. Continue east on the main trail, descending the steep road to the right turn on the trail that leads to the trailhead.

5.3   Arrive back at the trailhead (GPS: 39.118669,-104.921208).

37 CHAUTAUQUA MOUNTAIN

This loop hike west of Palmer Lake starts with a steep, pulse-pounding ascent and pays off with a rolling descent and an easy, scenic stroll past Upper and Lower Palmer Lake Reservoirs.

Start: Palmer Lake Reservoir Trailhead, Old Carriage Road
Difficulty: Moderate
Trails: Chautauqua Mountain Trail, Balanced Rock Road, Palmer Lake Reservoir Trail
Hiking time: About 3 hours
Distance: 4.7-mile loop
Elevations trailhead to summit: 7,227 to 8,352 feet (+1,125 feet)
Rank status: Unranked
Restrictions: Fee area, self-serve debit/credit card kiosk; year-round access depending on road conditions; no camping and no campfires; no smoking on trails; no swimming or wading; no dogs allowed: The reservoirs supply the town of Palmer Lake with drinking water and a town ordinance prevents dogs on trails or near the reservoirs, which is strictly enforced and punishable by fine; no nearby public campgrounds
Amenities: Porta-potty at trailhead; services in Palmer Lake
County: El Paso
Maps: *DeLorme*: p. 50, D4; Trails Illustrated #137: Pikes Peak, Cañon City; USGS Palmer Lake
Land status/contact: Pike National Forest, (719) 553-1400; Pikes Peak Ranger District, (719) 636-1602

FINDING THE TRAILHEAD

From Colorado Springs and Denver, drive either north or south on I-25 to Monument and take exit 161. Drive west on CO 105 for 3.5 miles to Palmer Lake. Turn left (west) on South Valley Road in Palmer Lake and drive west for 0.35 mile. Turn left (south) on Old Carriage Road and drive 0.2 mile to a large roadside parking lot and the trailhead in a valley (GPS: 39.118669,-104.921208).

Mount Herman rises south from a viewpoint near Chautauqua Mountain's summit on the edge of the Rampart Range.

Wildflowers add sparkling color to the rising trail on Chautauqua Mountain.

THE HIKE

This forested loop hike up Chautauqua Mountain is best done clockwise to avoid a very steep and slippery descent on the northeast ridge of the peak. From the summit, you'll have views of Sundance Mountain to the north, the town of Palmer Lake to the east, and the Upper and Lower Palmer Lake Reservoirs tucked in the valley below. Though this hike leads to the USGS high point of the peak, the trail reaches several higher points on the southern "descent," and the true high point is likely on top of a boulder at about 8,400 feet.

MILES AND DIRECTIONS

0.0   From the Palmer Lake Reservoir Trailhead, hike west on Reservoir Trail and take an immediate left off the main trail and onto a secondary trail.

0.1   Go left again on a trail and hike southwest toward North Monument Creek (GPS: 39.118717,-104.922333). After about 200 feet, cross the creek on rocks and hike up steep switchbacks.

0.2   The trail eases and heads southeast.

0.3   Reach a ridgeline. From this point, the trail becomes more rugged, steadily climbing up the mountain's steep northeast ridge with occasional views east (GPS: 39.116402,-104.922070).

0.9   Reach the first rocky outcrop on the left of the trail, which is a false summit.

1.0   A second false summit on the trail's left side is the best opportunity for photos, as the summit views are blocked by trees (GPS: 39.112767,-104.927800).

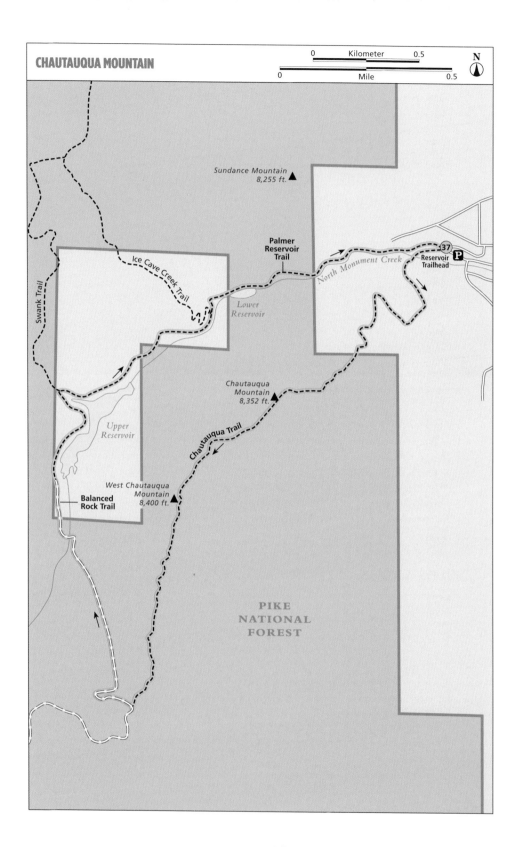

CHAUTAUQUA MOUNTAIN

0   Kilometer   0.5

0   Mile   0.5

N

Sundance Mountain
8,255 ft.

Palmer
Reservoir
Trail

37

Reservoir
Trailhead

P

North Monument Creek

Ice Cave Creek Trail

Swank Trail

Lower
Reservoir

Chautauqua
Mountain
8,352 ft.

Chautauqua Trail

Upper
Reservoir

West Chautauqua
Mountain
8,400 ft.

Balanced
Rock Trail

PIKE
NATIONAL
FOREST

The descent off the south side of Chautauqua Mountain follows an old road shaded by tall pines.

1.1   Arrive at the summit of 8,352-foot Chautauqua Mountain on the left side of the trail and up a short path (GPS: 39.112550,-104.930133). After tagging the top, continue southwest on Chautauqua Mountain Trail.

2.2   The trail descends, rising, falling, and weaving through boulders to the dirt road below. Turn right on Balanced Rock Road (GPS: 39.100067,-104.938067).

2.8   At a Y in the road/trail, bear left toward the west side of the Upper Reservoir (GPS: 39.107000,-104.941233). Hike past a gate and continue northeast along the north side of the Upper and Lower Reservoirs.

4.4   After descending the closed road, pass a gate and then leave the road and descend a narrow trail down a wash to the right (GPS: 39.118695,-104.926129). Follow the trail east down the valley.

4.7   Arrive back at the trailhead (GPS: 39.118669,-104.921208).

38 MOUNT HERMAN

The summit of Mount Herman, a prominent peak on the eastern edge of the Rampart Range, is reached by a short trail that climbs through shady evergreens to magnificent views of deep valleys, wooded mountains, and Pikes Peak.

Start: Mount Herman Trailhead, Mount Herman Road / FR 320
Difficulty: Easy
Trails: Mount Herman Trail #716
Hiking time: About 1.5 hours
Distance: 2.2 miles, out and back
Elevations trailhead to summit: 8,150 to 9,063 feet (+913 feet)
Rank status: Ranked
Restrictions: Leashed dogs only; snow closes access road in winter; no available water; no toilets; no nearby public campgrounds
Amenities: Services in Monument and Palmer Lake
County: El Paso
Maps: *DeLorme*: p. 50, D3 and D4; Trails Illustrated #137: Pikes Peak, Cañon City; USGS Palmer Lake
Land status/contact: Pike National Forest, (719) 553-1400; Pikes Peak Ranger District, (719) 636-1602

FINDING THE TRAILHEAD

From I-25 between Denver and Colorado Springs, take exit 161 at Monument. Drive west on 2nd Street for 0.7 mile, passing through downtown Monument, and turn left on Mitchell Avenue. Drive 0.7 mile south and, following signs for Mount Herman, turn right on Mount Herman Road, which becomes FR 320. Drive west for 5 miles past a junction with Red Rocks Drive at 2.3 miles to a small parking area, which holds about eight vehicles, and the Mount Herman Trailhead on the right (north) side of the road (GPS: 39.071171,-104.932114). After the junction with Red Rocks Drive, the dirt road becomes rough in places and traverses an exposed mountainside. Snow sometimes closes the road in winter. The winter trailhead is at a large parking lot on Red Rock Drive just right of the Mount Herman Road.

When you are driving on the first section of the Mount Herman Road west of Mitchell Avenue, do not park at another Forest Service trailhead that is also called "Mount Herman Trailhead." This trailhead, located 0.8 mile west of Mitchell Avenue, is located just south of the Mount Herman Road on the right side of Nursery Road. This trailhead accesses a network of mountain bike and hiking trails east of Mount Herman and does not provide access to the described Mount Herman hike.

THE HIKE

The Mount Herman Trail twists up the southwest flank of 9,063-foot Mount Herman, a handsome mountain in the Rampart Range north of Colorado Springs. The well-used trail is popular and scenic, passing through a mixed conifer forest and gleaming granite formations. The trail is easy to follow, but social paths can lead you astray, especially on the mountain's upper slopes. Stick to the well-traveled trail to reach Herman's summit. The spacious rooftop offers spectacular views of surrounding peaks in the Rampart Range, including Chautauqua and Sundance Mountains, and 14,115-foot Pikes Peak scraping the sky to the southwest. The mountain is likely named for Herman Schwanbeck, a local nineteenth-century German settler.

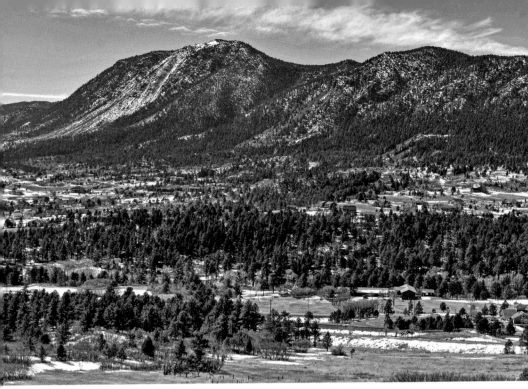

Mount Herman rears over wooded foothills on the eastern edge of the Rampart Range.

The Mount Herman Trailhead, located on the dirt Mount Herman Road between Monument and Woodland Park, is often inaccessible in winter because of snow and ice. Four-wheel-drive vehicles can usually reach the trailhead, but do not drive low-clearance, two-wheel-drive cars in winter. The small trailhead parking lot holds eight cars at the most, so arrive early on weekends.

An alternative hike follows Broken Ankle Trail up Mount Herman's steep, northeastern slopes. The parking lot and trailhead on Red Rocks Drive for this trail are open in winter. However, the trail is for experienced hikers only, with steep slopes and icy sections. Wear MICROspikes for traction and use trekking poles for balance and safety.

MILES AND DIRECTIONS

0.0   Start from the Mount Herman Trailhead and parking area at a switchback on the Mount Herman Road. Go north on the obvious trail on the east side of the parking lot.

0.1   Go right on the trail up a steep draw.

0.4   Reach a grassy pocket meadow in a forked valley on the west side of Mount Herman. Go right and begin climbing wooded slopes.

0.8   Reach gentle wooded slopes studded with granite outcrops on the mountain's broad south ridge. Watch for social paths deviating from the main trail (not your route) and stick to the main trail.

1.1   Arrive at the summit of 9,063-foot Mount Herman, with wide views, a windsock, and ammo box register (GPS: 39.081798,-104.926395). Return back down the trail.

2.2   Arrive back at the trailhead (GPS: 39.071171,-104.932114).

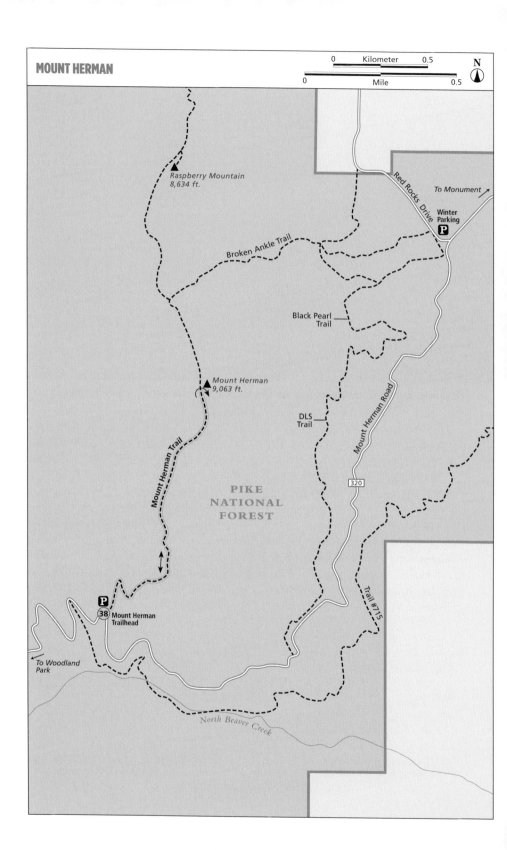

MOUNT HERMAN

Kilometer   0.5

Mile   0.5

N

Raspberry Mountain
8,634 ft.

Red Rocks Drive

To Monument

Winter
Parking

Broken Ankle Trail

Black Pearl
Trail

Mount Herman
9,063 ft.

DLS
Trail

Mount Herman Trail

Mount Herman Road

320

PIKE
NATIONAL
FOREST

Trail #715

P
38 Mount Herman
Trailhead

To Woodland
Park

North Beaver Creek

The Mount Herman Trail climbs through a mature conifer forest on the peak's south slopes.

WINTER OPTION

If the designated Mount Herman Trailhead is inaccessible in winter, an alternative trailhead is on Red Rocks Drive on the east side of Mount Herman. A trail, locally called Broken Ankle Trail, climbs 1.5 miles up a steep ravine to a saddle between Mount Herman and Raspberry Mountain, and then finishes on the north flank of Mount Herman. This trail is steep and only for experienced hikers. Footwear traction such as EXOspikes or MICROspikes, along with trekking poles for balance, are highly recommended for safety. The shaded trail holds ice from November to April. It is also dangerous as a descent route, with slick gravel when dry and ice in winter. A recommended alternative is to climb Mount Herman on Broken Ankle Trail, then descend south on the easier regular route, and hike 2.6 miles down the Mount Herman Road to the trailhead. Allow 4 hours to hike round-trip. Elevation gain from trailhead to summit is 1,693 feet.

FINDING THE WINTER OPTION TRAILHEAD

Approach Mount Herman using the directions above but go right on Red Rocks Drive at its junction of Mount Herman Road at 2.3 miles from Mitchell Avenue. Drive a couple hundred feet to a large parking area on the right and an unmarked trailhead on the west side of the road (GPS: 39.088984,-104.912335).

WINTER OPTION MILES AND DIRECTIONS

0.0 Start at the unnamed trailhead for Broken Ankle Trail on the west side of the road, opposite the parking lot, at 7,370 feet. Hike west through a meadow and ponderosa pine grove. Continue west along a creek bed and bend right through woods.

Mount Herman's rocky summit
yields views north across
Limbaugh Canyon to Cap Rock.

Ridges and canyons crease the Rampart Range northwest of Mount Herman.

0.4 Reach a four-way trail junction at a large cairn in a clearing (GPS: 39.088322, -104.919073). Take the unmarked middle trail and hike west up the wooded skirt below the mountain.

0.55 Reach a sharp left turn (GPS: 39.088056,-104.921607) and hike south across the mountainside. Do not take a social trail which continues straight at the turn.

0.6 Reach a trail junction (GPS: 39.087723,-104.921493) with a social trail continuing south. Go hard right and start a long series of switchbacks up steep, wooded slopes on the northeast flank of Mount Herman. After eleven switchbacks the trail heads up right across a steep slope and continues up more steep slopes left of a usually dry creek bed. This trail section is narrow and has steep sections with insecure footing and clambering over boulders. Continue up the trail until it begins to level out in aspens.

1.15 Reach a trail junction at a wide saddle (GPS: 39.085794,-104.928110). Go left here and hike up the broad north ridge of Mount Herman, threading through trees and scrambling over boulders. After 0.05 mile from the saddle, go left 30 feet to an overlook at a boulder, then return to the main trail and continue uphill.

1.2 Reach an overlook with views across Monument to the Palmer Divide and Black Forest. Continue up the trail.

1.4 Pass a rocky false summit on the right, keeping south on the trail below the east side of a rough ridge.

1.5 Arrive at Mount Herman's summit (GPS:39.081798,-104.926395). After enjoying the 360-degree views, return down Broken Ankle Trail (or descend via alternate route, below).

3.0 Arrive back at the trailhead on Red Rocks Drive (GPS: 39.088984,-104.912335).

Alternate Descent Route: From the summit, hike south on the Mount Herman Trail to the trailhead on Mount Herman Road (GPS: 39.071171,-104.932114) for a 2.5-mile hike. Use a car shuttle (use two cars, one at each trailhead) to return to the trailhead on Red Rocks Drive from here or hike 2.6 miles down the dirt road to Red Rocks Drive and the trailhead for Broken Ankle Trail.

39 GROUSE MOUNTAIN

A short trail climbs to spectacular views from the summit of Grouse Mountain, the highest peak in Mueller State Park, to the west of Colorado Springs and Pikes Peak.

Start: Grouse Mountain Trailhead, Mueller State Park
Difficulty: Very easy
Trails: Cheesman Ranch Trail #17, Grouse Mountain Overlook Trail #16
Hiking time: About half an hour
Distance: 1.0 mile, out and back
Elevations trailhead to summit: 9,665 feet to 9,843 feet (+178 feet)
Rank status: Ranked
Restrictions: Fee to enter park; trail closed June 1–20 for elk calving; last road section through Grouse Mountain Campground closes from mid-October to mid-May, requiring a 0.5-mile hike on road to trailhead
Amenities: Restrooms near trailhead; drinking water; visitor center; park campgrounds
County: Teller
Maps: *DeLorme*: p. 62, A1; Trails Illustrated #137: Pikes Peak, Cañon City; USGS Divide
Land status/contact: Mueller State Park, (719) 687-2366

FINDING THE TRAILHEAD

From Colorado Springs and I-25, take the Cimarron Street / US 24 exit (exit 141) from I-25. Drive west on US 24 up Ute Pass and through Woodland Park. Continue west on US 24 to the town of Divide. Turn left (south) on CO 67 toward Cripple Creek. Drive 3.8 miles to the park entrance and turn right (west) into the park. After the entrance booth, follow Wapiti Road past the visitor center and through the campgrounds to the Grouse Mountain Trailhead and parking lot at the road's end. Begin at the trailhead at the north end of the lot (GPS: 38.902413, -105.183248).

Rough boulders on Grouse Mountain look south across Mueller State Park to conical Mount Pisgah.

Grouse Mountain yields views east across meadows and woodlands to Raspberry Mountain and Pikes Peak's stormy north flank.

A mule deer stands watch in a meadow along the Cheesman Ranch Trail.

THE HIKE

Grouse Mountain, the high point of Mueller State Park, is reached by an easy hike to a rocky summit with dramatic 360-degree vistas of 14,115-foot Pikes Peak, wooded hills and valleys in the state park, and distant views of the Sangre de Cristo Mountains and the Sawatch Range. The Grouse Mountain Overlook Trail is perfect for kids wanting to summit a peak, with gradual grades and trail markers at every intersection. A wooden kiosk at the trailhead offers trail maps, park regulations, and information about black bears, which are common in the park. The last 0.5 mile of the road to the trailhead, passing through Grouse Mountain Campground, is closed from mid-October until mid-May. Park by the closed road and follow it to the trailhead, adding an extra mile to the round-trip distance.

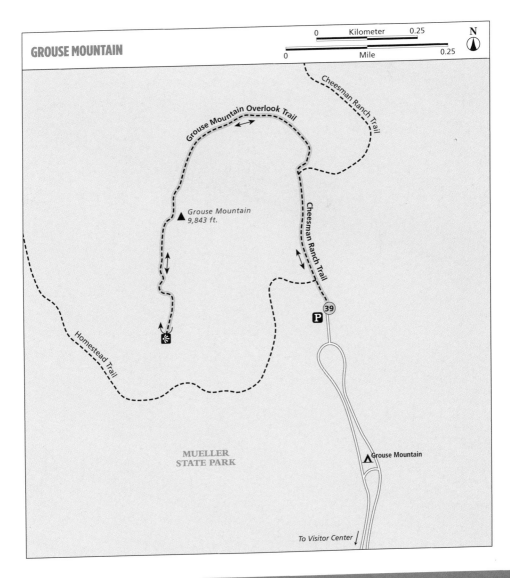

The doubletrack trails up Grouse Mountain pass through quaking aspen glades and open meadows that spill down the peak's eastern slope. The upper trail climbs through thick spruce, fir, and limber pine forest to the marked mountain high point, a couple of small boulders beside the trail. Continue south on the trail to an overlook on the summit's south side and marvelous views across the southern Front Range, including towering Pikes Peak, pointed Sentinel Point, pyramid-shaped Mount Pisgah rising above the old mining town of Cripple Creek, and the sawtoothed Sangre de Cristo Mountains, which harbors nine of Colorado's 14,000-foot peaks.

MILES AND DIRECTIONS

0.0 Start at the Grouse Mountain Trailhead at the end of the park road in Grouse Mountain Campground. Hike north on wide Cheesman Ranch Trail (#17) and after 100 feet reach a junction with the Homestead Trail (#12). Go straight on Trail #17.

0.2 Go left at a trail junction on Grouse Mountain Overlook Trail (#16) and hike up north-facing slopes.

0.4 Reach the marked summit of 9,843-foot Grouse Mountain (GPS: 38.903715, -105.186052). Continue south on the trail through boulders on the summit area.

0.5 Reach a rocky overlook on the south side of the Grouse Mountain summit. Retrace your steps back over the summit and down Grouse Mountain Trail.

1.0 Arrive back at the trailhead (GPS: 38.902413,-105.183248).

40 RASPBERRY MOUNTAIN

The unmistakable rambling forested massif of Raspberry Mountain rises south of US 24 in Divide, northwest of another familiar massif, 14,115-foot Pikes Peak. The hike to Raspberry's summit is popular year-round by boot or snowshoe.

Start: Raspberry Mountain Trailhead, CR 62 / FR 383
Difficulty: Moderate
Trails: Ring the Peak Trail, Catamount Trail / CR 621 / FR 385, Raspberry Mountain Trail (#785)
Hiking time: 2–3 hours
Distance: 5.0 miles, out and back
Elevations trailhead to summit: 9,902 to 10,605 feet (+703 feet)
Rank status: Ranked
Restrictions: CR 62 is closed seasonally, depending on snowfall, at the winter gate located just past the Rocky Mountain Mennonite Camp and 0.8 mile before the trailhead, adding 1.6 round-trip miles to the hike; no toilets at trailhead; no campfires allowed; dogs must be leashed; no available water
Amenities: Camping and toilets at nearby Crags Campground located 0.6 mile past the trailhead on CR 62 from late May to late Sept, with tent sites available on a first-come basis; dispersed camping allowed in the national forest but not within 0.25 mile of CR 62; services in Divide and Woodland Park
County: Teller
Maps: *DeLorme*: p. 62, A2 and B2; Trails Illustrated #137: Pikes Peak, Cañon City; USGS Woodland Park
Land status/contact: Pike National Forest, (719) 553-1400; Pikes Peak Ranger District, (719) 636-1602

FINDING THE TRAILHEAD

From the stoplight at US 24 in Divide, go south on CO 67. Drive 4.3 miles, just past Mueller State Park, and turn left onto unpaved Teller CR 62 / FR 383. Drive 1.6 miles, bear right at the Mennonite Camp, then continue another 0.9 mile to a large dirt parking area on the left side of the road. The trailhead is located at the south end of the parking lot, where a wooden footbridge crosses Fourmile Creek (GPS: 38.880682,-105.125299).

THE HIKE

Raspberry Mountain is a year-round local favorite, with gentle slopes and summit views that make for a fine hike any time of year. The Raspberry Mountain Trailhead is located on the same forest road as the Crags Trailhead, the starting point for hikers heading up the Devils Playground Trail to the summit of Pikes Peak. The road and nearby Crags Campground are busy during the summer, especially on weekends and holidays. Hikers enjoy shade in a thick forest for most of the hike, a welcome respite from the sun's rays in summer. Snow lingers from late fall to late spring, so Raspberry Mountain hikers during this time should bring traction such as EXOspikes, MICROspikes, or snowshoes, and use trekking poles for balance. Take extreme care on the exposed summit boulders, as a fall could be fatal.

On top of the treeless summit, hikers have unobstructed views of North Catamount Reservoir to the east; Pikes Peak to the southeast; the Sangre de Cristo Range on the

Broad-shouldered Raspberry Mountain towers above wooded valleys on the north slope of Pikes Peak.

Expansive views from the rocky top of Raspberry Mountain include the distant Sangre de Cristo Mountains and the Sawatch Range.

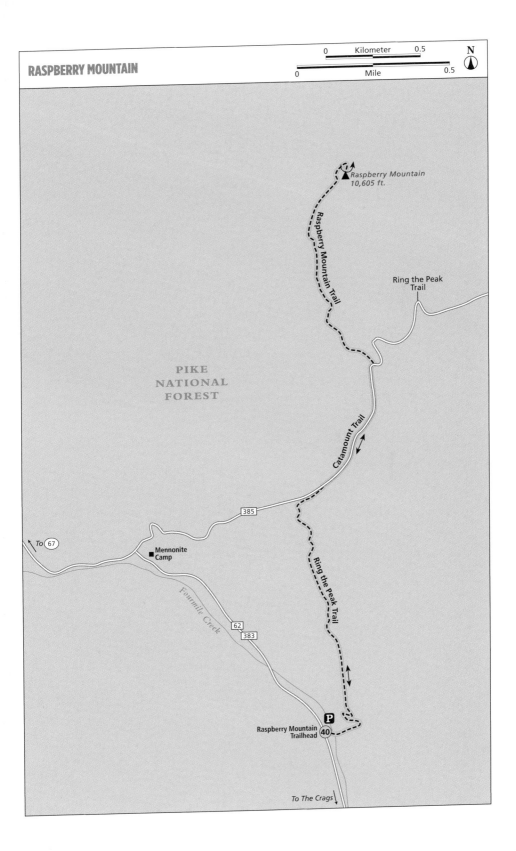

0   Kilometer   0.5

0   Mile   0.5

N

Raspberry Mountain
10,605 ft.

Ring the Peak
Trail

Raspberry Mountain Trail

PIKE
NATIONAL
FOREST

Catamount Trail

385

To 67

Mennonite
Camp

Ring the Peak Trail

Fourmile Creek

62

383

P

Raspberry Mountain
Trailhead   40

To The Crags

Pointed Mount Pisgah and the snowy Sangre de Cristos line the horizon south of Raspberry Mountain.

southern horizon; the Sawatch Range to the west; and the wooded Rampart Range to the northeast.

MILES AND DIRECTIONS

0.0 From the Raspberry Mountain Trailhead, cross a footbridge over Fourmile Creek and hike east into the forest. The trail switchbacks west and east before heading north.

1.0 Just past a minor creek, turn right onto Catamount Trail / FR 385 (GPS: 38.891391,-105.127387).

1.1 The trail trends northeast, then leaves the forest and crosses an open area (GPS: 38.891938,-105.126245).

1.3 The trail trends north and back into the forest (GPS: 38.893882,-105.124110).

1.6 Turn left onto Raspberry Mountain Trail and hike northwest (GPS: 38.897965, -105.122576). A small sign notes that the peak is 0.9 mile ahead.

2.4 The rocky summit area appears ahead. Do not attempt to climb straight up. Instead, stay on the trail and contour around the left (west) side of the boulders (GPS: 38.906391,-105.124773).

2.49 At an obvious break in the rocks, turn right off the trail and scramble between the rocks up a crude trail, then up and right toward the summit (GPS: 38.907182,-105.124087).

2.5 Reach the bedrock summit of 10,605-foot Raspberry Mountain (GPS: 38.907033, -105.124125), staying clear of the exposed south edge. Return back down the trail.

5.0 Arrive back at the trailhead (GPS: 38.880682,-105.125299).

41 "BABOON ROCK"

A short trail climbs to the bedrock summit of "Baboon Rock" and an exposed overlook perched above sheer cliffs in upper Elevenmile Canyon.

Start: Overlook Trailhead, Elevenmile Canyon Recreation Area
Difficulty: Easy
Trails: Overlook Trail (#691)
Hiking time: About 45 minutes
Distance: 1.0 mile, out and back
Elevations trailhead to summit: 8,475 to 8,940 feet (+465 feet)
Rank status: Unranked
Restrictions: Fee area; stay on designated trails; do not park in Spillway Campground unless camping there; no available water

Amenities: Toilets at nearby Idlewild Picnic Area; Spillway and Cove Campgrounds; services in Lake George and Florissant
County: Park
Maps: *DeLorme*: p. 61, A7; Trails Illustrated #152: Elevenmile Canyon, South Park; USGS Elevenmile Canyon
Land status/contact: Elevenmile Canyon Recreation Area; Pike National Forest, (719) 553-1400; South Platte Ranger District, (719) 836-2031

FINDING THE TRAILHEAD

Elevenmile Canyon is 45 miles west of Colorado Springs and I-25. From I-25, drive west on US 24 through Woodland Park and Divide to Lake George. Turn left (south) on CR 96 and drive 1 mile to a marked junction with CR 244. Turn right on dirt CR 96 into Elevenmile Canyon. Pass the entrance/fee station and drive 8.5 miles up the canyon to a U-shaped parking lot before a river bridge at the turnoff to Spillway Campground near the end of the canyon (GPS: 38.905293,-105.465330). The Overlook Trailhead is opposite the parking lot and right of Camp Rock on the road's north side.

A steep trail climbs to an airy overlook on top of "Baboon Rock" in Elevenmile Canyon.

Named by rock climbers, "Baboon Rock" dominates the skyline in Elevenmile Canyon.

The top of the Overlook Trail offers views west across Eleven Mile Canyon Reservoir to the Buffalo Peaks.

THE HIKE

The Overlook Trail scrambles steeply to the rocky summit of 8,940-foot "Baboon Rock," a lofty viewpoint perched above upper Elevenmile Canyon and shining Eleven Mile Canyon Reservoir at the southeast corner of South Park. The jutting granite formation, unofficially named by rock climbers, anchors the southern end of the Puma Hills, a low range on the west side of the Front Range. Elevenmile Canyon, a steep-walled canyon carved by the South Platte River, is popular with hikers, campers, climbers, and anglers. A dirt road twists up the scenic canyon, following the abandoned railbed of the Colorado Midland Railroad, which opened in 1887 as the first broad-gauged railroad in the Colorado Rockies.

The trail to the top, beginning by Camp Rock, crosses a meadow to tall ponderosa pines and then climbs a boulder-choked gully below the towering east face of "Baboon Rock." Scramble up stone steps and squeeze through a gap between a boulder and cliff to a narrow corridor, and continue up a wooded ramp and gully to the overlook with twisted trees growing from bedrock atop a granite buttress. The summit offers views of the South Platte River below the 135-foot-high dam, Thirtynine Mile Mountain to the southwest, and the Buffalo Peaks and Sawatch Range rubbing the western horizon.

MILES AND DIRECTIONS

- 0.0 Start at the signed Overlook Trailhead on the north side of CR 96 and opposite the parking lot. Hike north on the right side of Camp Rock.
- 0.2 Reach a junction with a trail from the campground on the left. Go right on the Overlook Trail up a rocky gully.

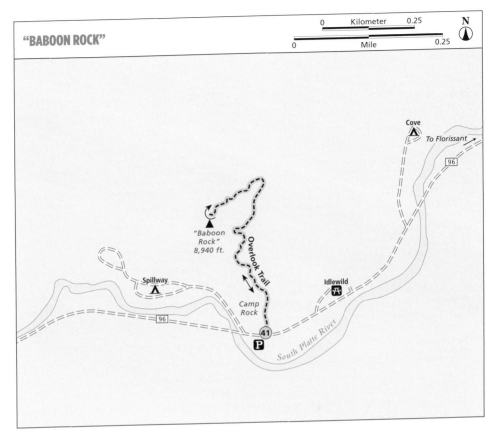

"BABOON ROCK"

Cove

To Florissant

96

"Baboon Rock" 8,940 ft.

Overlook Trail

Spillway

Idlewild

Camp Rock

96

41

P

South Platte River

0.5 Reach the exposed summit of 8,940-foot "Baboon Rock" and an overlook with views of the canyon and Eleven Mile Canyon Reservoir to the west (GPS: 38.908168, -105.466979). Use caution on the summit because of cliffs and drop-offs.

1.0 Return to the trailhead (GPS: 38.905293,-105.465330).

A twisted pine atop "Baboon Rock" marks the end of the Overlook Trail.

42 RED MOUNTAIN

The gravel summit of Red Mountain, topped by historic incline railway ruins, is reached by a short hike up wooded slopes to scenic views across Manitou Springs to Pikes Peak, Ute Pass, and the Garden of the Gods.

Start: Iron Spring Trailhead, Red Mountain Open Space
Difficulty: Easy
Trails: Paul Intemann Memorial Nature Trail, Red Mountain Trail
Hiking time: About 1.5 hours
Distance: 2.4 miles, out and back
Elevations trailhead to summit: 6,465 to 7,361 feet (+896 feet)
Rank status: Unranked
Restrictions: Leashed dogs only; clean up dog waste; no fires, smoking, or fireworks; no camping; alcohol and marijuana prohibited; motor vehicles prohibited; no toilets; no available water; no nearby public campgrounds
Amenities: Services in Manitou Springs
County: El Paso
Maps: *DeLorme*: p. 62, B4; Trails Illustrated #137: Pikes Peak, Cañon City; USGS Manitou Springs
Land status/contact: Red Mountain Open Space; Manitou Springs Public Services Department, (719) 685-4398

FINDING THE TRAILHEAD

From I-25 and downtown Colorado Springs, drive west on US 24 and take the first exit for Manitou Avenue. Drive west on Manitou Avenue to a roundabout and turn left on Ruxton Avenue, following signs for the Pikes Peak Cog Railway. Follow Ruxton until it splits into a one-way road to the cog railway depot and a one-way street back to Manitou Avenue. Go right and follow the road to the depot; make a U-turn left onto the return one-way street. Find a paid parking place to park here or along the right side of Ruxton Avenue. Parking is a big problem in summer. It is best to park at a lot at 10 Old Man's Trail on Manitou's east side and take a free shuttle between 6 a.m. and 6 p.m. to the trailhead. The Iron Spring Trailhead for the Paul Intemann Memorial Nature Trail, the hike's first leg, is on the south side of a bridge on Spring Street before Ruxton becomes a one-way loop (GPS: 38.857148,-104.927290). Iron Spring and an alternative trailhead are about 400 feet west of here.

THE HIKE

Rising above the southern edge of Manitou Springs in a 101-acre open space parkland, Red Mountain offers superlative views and a surprise ending—the summit house ruins of an incline railway built in the early twentieth century. The Red Mountain Incline Railway ferried riders up the mountain's steep northeast face. Look around the top for the concrete footings where the railway ended and the crumbling foundations of a restaurant and dance hall, where live music and whiskey flowed.

Before the railway, the summit was the gravesite of Emma Crawford, a tubercular patient who came to Manitou at age 18 in 1889 for dry air and sunshine. Before dying in 1891, young Emma hiked to Red Mountain's summit where she had a vision and marked her chosen burial plot with a scarf. Her coffin was moved south in 1912 for the construction of the summit house. Heavy rain in August 1929 washed the coffin

The summit of Red Mountain offers spectacular views of snowcapped Pikes Peak.

Mount Manitou looms behind Red Mountain above Manitou Springs.

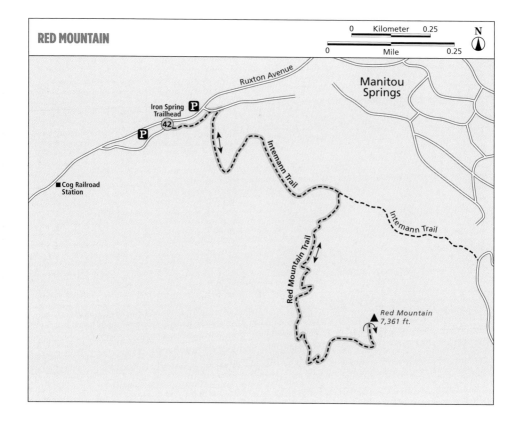

down the mountain, spilling her remains. Her bones were collected and reinterred in the Manitou cemetery, but locals say that Emma's ghost stalks Red Mountain and some hikers have spotted her Victorian-clad specter. Every October, Manitou Springs hosts a coffin race in her honor.

The hike follows maintained trails with gradual grades through Gambel oak thickets and mountain slopes shaded with pine and fir. Parking is the main obstacle to hike Red Mountain, especially in summer when street parking fills with Pikes Peak cog riders and Manitou Incline hikers. It is best to park at Old Man's Trail on the east side of town and take the free shuttle to the cog and incline area. Red Mountain can be combined with a hike up Iron Mountain on the Intemann Trail for a two-peak day.

MILES AND DIRECTIONS

0.0 Start at the Iron Spring Trailhead for the Paul Intemann Memorial Nature Trail on the south side of a bridge on Spring Street. Go left on the road. Follow the street, which makes a sharp right turn and continue up it.

0.1 Reach a junction with a road on the right (GPS: 38.856503,-104.927128). Continue straight and pass through a gate. Go right on the Intemann Trail.

0.5 Reach a junction with Red Mountain Trail (GPS: 38.854909,-104.922557). Go right on it and hike up the northwest flank of the mountain.

Foundations of the railway and buildings scatter across Red Mountain's summit.

1.2   Arrive at the summit of 7,361-foot Red Mountain, the turnaround point (GPS: 38.851318,-104.921443). After enjoying the views, descend the trail.

1.9   Return to the junction with the Intemann Trail. Go left.

2.4   Arrive back at the trailhead (GPS: 38.857148,-104.927290).

43 IRON MOUNTAIN

Rising east of Red Mountain, Iron Mountain forms the southern skyline of Manitou Springs. Traversed by the Intemann and Iron Mountain Trails, the peak offers a rocky summit and broad views across Manitou Springs to Pikes Peak, Garden of the Gods, and Colorado Springs.

Start: Intemann Trailhead, Crystal Park Road
Difficulty: Easy
Trails: Paul Intemann Memorial Nature Trail, Iron Mountain Trail
Hiking time: About 1.5 hours
Distance: 2.7 miles, out and back
Elevations trailhead to summit: 6,605 to 7,131 feet (+526 feet)
Rank status: Unranked
Restrictions: Park only in designated pull-off on south side of road; do not park at turn-around at Crystal Park entrance; leashed dogs only; clean up dog waste; no fires, smoking, or fireworks; no camping or littering; alcohol and marijuana prohibited; motor vehicles prohibited; no toilets; no available water; no nearby public campgrounds
Amenities: Services in Manitou Springs
County: El Paso
Maps: *DeLorme:* p. 62, B4; Trails Illustrated #137: Pikes Peak, Cañon City; USGS Manitou Springs
Land status/contact: Iron Mountain Open Space, Lee Open Space; Manitou Springs Public Services Department, (719) 685-5481

FINDING THE TRAILHEAD

From I-25 and downtown Colorado Springs, drive west on US 24 and take the first exit for Manitou Avenue. Drive west on Manitou Avenue for 0.3 mile to the first traffic light and turn left on Crystal Park Road. Follow the twisting road for 1.5 miles to a turn-around pull-off on the right just before the guard shack for Crystal Park. Make a U-turn and park on the right (south) side of the road opposite the trailhead (GPS: 38.842832,-104.903263). Note that part of the parking strip is posted "No Parking" on Mon, Thurs, and Fri from 7 a.m. to 5 p.m. as a drop-off zone during school days.

The hike up Iron Mountain climbs through open meadows studded with piñon pines.

The town of Manitou Springs fills the valley below Iron Mountain.

THE HIKE

Manitou Springs pushes against the wooded north flank of Iron Mountain, an unranked 7,131-foot peak that overlooks the town's quaint, twisting streets. Protected from development in 98-acre Red Mountain Open Space and Lee Open Space, the mountain forms an essential part of the town's natural backdrop and provides excellent hiking and scenic views. Until the City of Manitou Springs was able to acquire the open space in three parcels between 2010 and 2013, a landowner was developing the mountain, carving several now-closed roads, and eventually building a house, since removed, atop Iron Mountain. The city, however, was unable to provide services, including utilities, and the owner eventually sold the property, allowing beloved Iron Mountain to again be open to public access. The closed roads and damage to the mountain summit remain as marks of the ill-advised development.

Iron Mountain's summit can be reached by two trails: Paul Intemann Memorial Nature Trail (usually called the Intemann Trail) and Iron Mountain Trail (which Intemann Trail follows). This description describes the best route, climbing the Intemann Trail from Crystal Park Road to the top. The Iron Mountain Trail, beginning on Pawnee Avenue on Manitou's south side, is a 1-mile hike up the mountain's north side. It is not included here due to limited parking in the neighborhood at the trailhead.

For a full-value 4.7-mile hike, combine the two trails and the Red Mountain Trail to climb both Iron and Red Mountains between the Intemann Trailhead on Crystal Park Road and the Iron Spring Trailhead on Ruxton Avenue. This longer hike requires a car shuttle. See the Extra Credit option below and the Red Mountain chapter (Hike 42) for more details on the hike.

A medicine wheel offers meditative views across Manitou Springs to Garden of the Gods.

MILES AND DIRECTIONS

0.0   Start at the Intemann Trailhead on Crystal Park Road. Climb wooden steps to a trail-head sign and hike northwest through scrub oak trees on the Intemann Trail, part of the Ring the Peak Trail.

0.05 Dip down to a dry creek bed and climb a steep slope on more wooden steps. Continue up the rising singletrack trail, swinging around the east flank of Sheep Mountain.

0.65 The trail, now an old, closed road (formerly named Oak Ridge Road), bends west, and reaches a medicine wheel on the right (GPS: 38.847754,-104.907465). Go right on a short trail to the wheel and a bench. Continue west on the trail along the north side of Sheep Mountain.

The Iron Mountain Trail swings across the dry south slope of Iron Mountain.

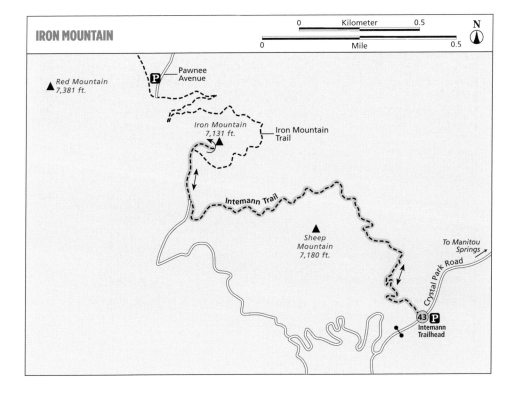

IRON MOUNTAIN

Red Mountain
7,381 ft.

Pawnee
Avenue

Iron Mountain
7,131 ft.

Iron Mountain
Trail

Intemann Trail

Sheep
Mountain
7,180 ft.

To Manitou
Springs

Crystal Park Road

Intemann
Trailhead

1.15 Reach a Y junction with the left fork of closed Oak Ridge Road (GPS: 38.847072, -104.914495). Continue straight on the old road and hike north along a wide ridge.

1.3 Reach another junction with Iron Mountain Trail on the right (GPS: 38.848968, -104.914284). Continue straight on the closed road, which becomes Iron Mountain Trail at the junction, and climb steeply up the south side of Iron Mountain.

1.35 Arrive at 7,131-foot Iron Mountain's granite summit (GPS: 38.849144,-104.913386) and enjoy views of Manitou Springs, Pikes Peak, and Garden of the Gods. Use caution on the summit since a broken cliff drops below the northern edge. Return back down to the trail.

2.7 Arrive back at the trailhead (GPS: 38.842832,-104.903263).

EXTRA CREDIT: IRON MOUNTAIN AND RED MOUNTAIN HIKE

To descend the Iron Mountain Trail to Manitou Springs or to climb Red Mountain for a two-peak hike, return to the junction of the Intemann and Iron Mountain Trails just below the summit. Follow the Iron Mountain Trail east, spiraling 0.9 mile around the east flank of the mountain and down its wooded north face to Pawnee Avenue.

After reaching the road, go right and walk 100 feet down Pawnee Avenue and go left on signed Intemann Trail, which leads a half mile to the Red Mountain Trail. Climb it for 0.6 mile to the Red Mountain summit, then reverse back to the Intemann Trail, which is followed for another 0.5 mile to Iron Spring Trailhead on Ruxton Avenue near the cog railway station for a 4.7-mile one-way hike.

44 MOUNT CUTLER

A wide trail climbs through a ponderosa pine and Douglas fir forest in North Cheyenne Cañon Park to the broad summit of 7,220-foot Mount Cutler and panoramic views of Colorado Springs and North Cheyenne Cañon.

Start: Mount Cutler / Mount Muscoco Trailhead, North Cheyenne Cañon Park
Difficulty: Easy
Trails: Mount Cutler Trail
Hiking time: About 1 hour
Distance: 2 miles, out and back
Elevations trailhead to summit: 6,741 to 7,220 feet (+479 feet)
Rank status: Unranked
Restrictions: Open daily; park and road closed from 9 p.m. to 5 a.m.; gates at canyon entrance and Gold Camp Road are locked nightly; limited trailhead parking; leashed dogs only; exposure on trail so keep children and pets close at hand; no toilets; no available water
Amenities: Toilets at Starsmore Discovery Center and portable toilets at Helen Hunt Falls; nearest camping at Cheyenne Mountain State Park; services in Colorado Springs
County: El Paso
Maps: *DeLorme*: p. 62, C4; Trails Illustrated #137: Pikes Peak, Cañon City; USGS Manitou Springs
Land status/contact: North Cheyenne Cañon Park; Colorado Springs Parks, Recreation, and Cultural Services (719) 385-5940

FINDING THE TRAILHEAD

From I-25 take Nevada Avenue / CO 115 exit (exit 140 B). Drive south on South Nevada Avenue / CO 115 for a mile and turn right (west) on Cheyenne Road. Follow Cheyenne Road for 2.6 miles to its end at Cheyenne Boulevard. (If you approach on Cheyenne Boulevard, stay right at this intersection.) Go left (west) on Cheyenne Boulevard for 0.1 mile to a Y intersection. Go right into North Cheyenne Cañon Park. Drive 1.4 miles up North Cheyenne Cañon Road to the trailhead on the left (GPS: 38.791810,-104.887147).

A hiker follows the Mount Cutler Trail around the mountain's steep southern slopes.

Cliff-lined Mount Cutler looms over North Cheyenne Cañon on the southwest edge of Colorado Springs.

THE HIKE

Mount Cutler, a low peak between North and South Cheyenne Cañons in North Cheyenne Cañon Park, is one of the easiest and most popular summit hikes in the Pikes Peak region. The wide trail offers a gentle uphill grade, airy exposure on the last section, and a view of Seven Falls in South Cheyenne Cañon. The wooded summit yields 360-degree views of the surrounding mountains, forests spilling down steep slopes, towering granite formations, and vistas of Colorado Springs and the tawny prairie beyond. After climbing Cutler's high point, follow a short trail out to the east summit, a rocky knob that yields more views (see Extra Credit: Mount Cutler's Lower East Summit and Overlook). This summit perches above vertical cliffs so hike with caution and control pets and children. The hike can be combined with the Mount Muscoco Trail, which begins at the same trailhead, for a 5.6-mile, two-summit day. See Hike 45 for more information.

MILES AND DIRECTIONS

0.0 Start at the Mount Cutler / Mount Muscoco Trailhead on the south side of North Cheyenne Cañon Road. Hike east up the rising trail.

0.4 Arrive at an overlook above the canyon.

0.5 Reach a saddle between Mount Cutler and Mount Muscoco (GPS: 38.788101,-104.879245). Continue straight. The Mount Muscoco Trail goes right here (not your route). The Mount Cutler Trail edges around the southwest side of the mountain, then goes left and climbs to the rounded summit.

1.0 Arrive at the summit of 7,220-foot Mount Cutler (GPS: 38.787892,-104.877828). Retrace your steps back down the trail.

2.0 Arrive back at the trailhead (GPS: 38.791810,-104.887147).

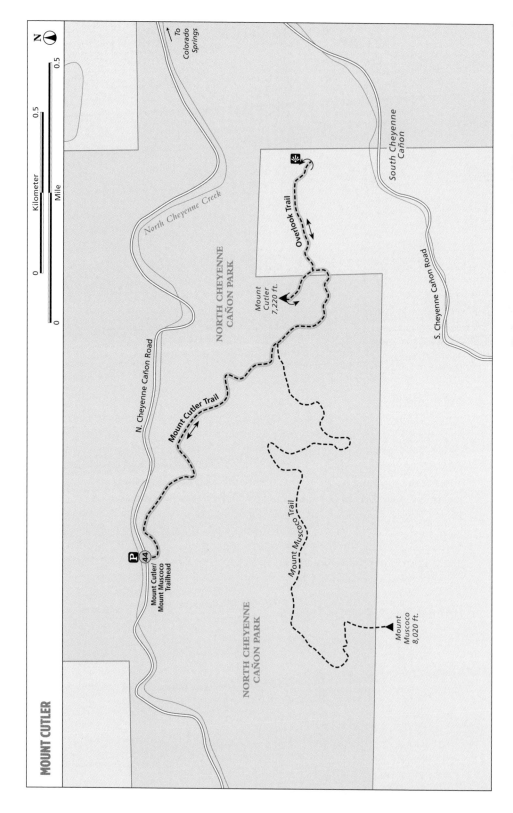

MOUNT CUTLER

N

Kilometer
0   0.5   0.5
Mile
0   0.5

To
Colorado
Springs

North Cheyenne Creek

N. Cheyenne Cañon Road

NORTH CHEYENNE
CAÑON PARK

Mount Cutler Trail

Mount
Cutler
7,220 ft.

Overlook Trail

South Cheyenne
Cañon

S. Cheyenne Cañon Road

P

44

Mount Cutler/
Mount Muscoco Trailhead

NORTH CHEYENNE
CAÑON PARK

Mount Muscoco Trail

Mount
Muscoco
8,020 ft.

The Mount Cutler Trail edges above South Cheyenne Cañon before climbing to a rounded summit.

EXTRA CREDIT: MOUNT CUTLER'S LOWER EAST SUMMIT AND OVERLOOK

To reach Mount Cutler's lower east summit, descend from the summit on the main trail to a junction. Go left (east) on one of two rough trails which join together just east of the main trail. Follow the trail another 0.25 mile east to Cutler's lower summit on the mountain's eastern edge. Some of the footing on the trail crosses loose gravel scattered across bedrock. Use caution on the hike and at the lofty overlook which sits above vertical cliffs. Keep children close at hand and pets leashed; gullies at the overlook's edge are steep, slippery gravel and a fall would likely be fatal. After enjoying the view, return to the main Mount Cutler Trail and descend to the trailhead.

45 MOUNT MUSCOCO

Mount Muscoco, the high point of North Cheyenne Cañon Park, is climbed on a good trail to the peak's isolated summit and scenic views across the southern Front Range.

Start: Mount Cutler / Mount Muscoco Trailhead, North Cheyenne Cañon Park
Difficulty: Moderate
Trails: Mount Cutler Trail, Mount Muscoco Trail
Hiking time: About 3 hours
Distance: 4.6 miles, out and back
Elevations trailhead to summit: 6,741 to 8,020 feet (+1,279 feet)
Ranked status: Ranked
Restrictions: Open daily; park and road closed from 9 p.m. to 5 a.m.; gates at canyon entrance and Gold Camp Road are locked nightly; limited trailhead parking; leashed dogs only; exposure exists near summit area so keep children and pets close at hand; no trailhead toilets; no available water
Amenities: Toilets at Starsmore Discovery Center and portable toilets at Helen Hunt Falls; nearest camping at Cheyenne Mountain State Park; services in Colorado Springs
County: El Paso
Maps: *DeLorme:* p. 62, C4; Trails Illustrated #137: Pikes Peak, Cañon City; USGS Manitou Springs
Land status/contact: North Cheyenne Cañon Park; Colorado Springs Parks, Recreation, and Cultural Services (719) 385-5940

FINDING THE TRAILHEAD

From I-25 take Nevada Avenue / CO 115 exit (exit 140B). Drive south on South Nevada Avenue / CO 115 for a mile and turn right (west) on Cheyenne Road. Follow Cheyenne Road for 2.6 miles to its end at Cheyenne Boulevard. (If you approach on Cheyenne Boulevard, stay right at this intersection.) Go left (west) on Cheyenne Boulevard for 0.1 mile to a Y intersection. Go right into North Cheyenne Cañon Park. Drive 1.4 miles up North Cheyenne Cañon Road to the marked trailhead on the left (GPS: 38.791810,-104.887147).

THE HIKE

The Mount Muscoco Trail is an excellent hike to a rocky summit with 360-degree views across North and South Cheyenne Cañons and Colorado Springs on the plains to the east. The trail is easy to follow with gentle grades except for the last rocky half-mile section. Mount Muscoco, the highest point in the Colorado Springs park system, is in 1,855-acre North Cheyenne Cañon Park on the city's southwest side. The trail was constructed in 2015, rerouting an old social path to create a sustainable summit hike with timber steps and water bars.

Begin at the Mount Cutler / Mount Muscoco Trailhead on North Cheyenne Cañon Road. The hike follows the Mount Cutler Trail for a half mile to a saddle and a tall ponderosa pine. Turn right here on the marked Mount Muscoco Trail and ascend sunny slopes to a ridgeline between canyons. Continue west, traversing the mountain's wooded north slope to the northwest flank. Finish up the steep trail to the twin summit blocks. The south summit is the highest point.

Mount Muscoco lifts wooded
shoulders above North
Cheyenne Cañon.

The trail passes through open woods below cliff-rimmed Mount Muscoco.

The Colorado Springs skyline lies beyond the east ridge of Mount Muscoco.

A hardy limber pine grows from granite bedrock below Muscoco's summit.

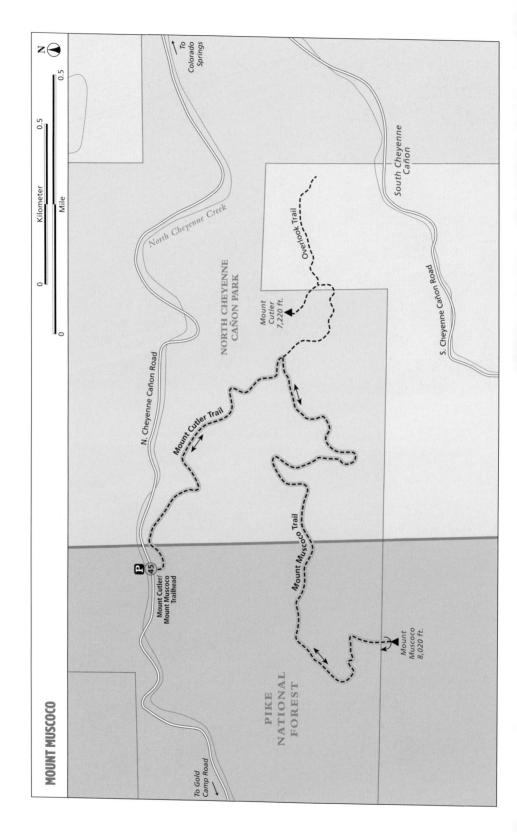

MOUNT MUSCOCO

North Cheyenne Creek

To Colorado Springs

N. Cheyenne Cañon Road

Mount Cutler Trail

NORTH CHEYENNE CAÑON PARK

Mount Cutler 7,220 ft.

Overlook Trail

South Cheyenne Cañon

S. Cheyenne Cañon Road

Mount Cutler/ Mount Muscoco Trailhead

P

45

Mount Muscoco Trail

PIKE NATIONAL FOREST

Mount Muscoco 8,020 ft.

To Gold Camp Road

N

Kilometer

Mile

0   0.5   0.5

Cheyenne Mountain and Saint Peters Dome rise above the rocky south ridge of Mount Muscoco.

From the summit, look west to Mount Rosa and rounded 12,367-foot Almagre Mountain, the second highest mountain in the Pikes Peak region, while to the south rises Saint Peters Dome and Cheyenne Mountain. Look for Helen Hunt Falls and Silver Cascade Falls tucked west in upper North Cheyenne Cañon.

MILES AND DIRECTIONS

0.0   Start at the Mount Cutler / Mount Muscoco Trailhead on the south side of North Cheyenne Cañon Road. Hike east up rising Mount Cutler Trail.

0.4   Stop at an overlook above the canyon.

0.5   Reach a saddle between Mount Cutler and Mount Muscoco (GPS: 38.788101, -104.879245). Go right (west) on the marked Mount Muscoco Trail. The Mount Cutler Trail (not your route) continues straight.

1.5   The trail reaches a level ridge.

1.55 Reach a saddle and hike across the peak's northern slopes.

2.0   Reach a signed junction with Daniels Pass Trail at 7,760 feet (GPS: 38.786284, -104.890923). Go left on Mount Muscoco Trail toward the summit and hike up steep slopes on the mountain's northwest flank.

2.3   Arrive at the south summit of 8,020-foot Mount Muscoco (GPS: 38.785094, -104.889666). Return back down the trails.

4.6   Arrive back at the trailhead (GPS: 38.791810,-104.887147).

46 **MAYS PEAK**

Rising between North Cheyenne Cañon and Bear Creek Canyon, Mays Peak is a rambling mountain with a pointed summit cone that yields forever views across the southern Front Range and Colorado Springs.

Start: High Drive Trailhead, junction of North Cheyenne Cañon Road / Gold Camp Road / High Drive
Difficulty: Easy
Trails: High Drive, Mays Peak Trail
Hiking time: About 2 hours
Distance: 3.2 miles, out and back
Elevations trailhead to summit: 7,506 to 8,283 feet (+777 feet)
Rank status: Ranked
Restrictions: Day use area; leashed dogs only; multi-use trail; no available water

Amenities: Porta-potties at trailhead; nearest camping at Cheyenne Mountain State Park; services in Colorado Springs
County: El Paso
Maps: *DeLorme*: p. 62, C4 and B4; Trails Illustrated #137: Pikes Peak, Cañon City; USGS Manitou Springs
Land status/contact: Colorado Springs Department of Parks & Recreation, (719) 385-5940; Pike National Forest, (719) 553-1400, Pikes Peak Ranger District, (719) 636-1602

FINDING THE TRAILHEAD

From I-25 in Colorado Springs, take Cimarron Street exit 141 and go west on US 24. Drive 1.5 miles and turn left onto S 21st Street, which becomes Cresta Road. Drive 3 miles and turn right on Cheyenne Boulevard, then go 1 mile and bear right on North Cheyenne Cañon Road. Drive 3.2 miles and park in the paved lot where the paved road meets Gold Camp Road. The lot also serves the Powell Trailhead. Start at a closed gate on the east side of the parking lot left of Gold Camp Road (GPS: 38.790283,-104.903500).

THE HIKE

Mays Peak rises north of Gold Camp Road and North Cheyenne Cañon southwest of Colorado Springs. The summit is reached by High Drive, a closed road that once connected North Cheyenne Cañon with Bear Creek Canyon to the north, and a trail which spirals around the south and east flanks of the mountain. The hike is easy to follow, has amenable grades, and reaches a large summit area with 360-degree views of the Pikes Peak massif, sprawling Colorado Springs, and the distant prairie.

Pay attention at a couple confusing trail sections so that you stay on course. To find the trail to the summit at a flat clearing at the top of High Drive, look to the southeast corner of the clearing for the unsigned trail. Do not go on signed Captain Jack's Trail, which comes into the clearing on its northeast side, crosses High Drive, and continues west. Also, pay attention on the upper part of the trail below the summit so that you don't take one of the many social trails created by rogue mountain bikers. Stick to the steep main trail to the summit.

A saddle on High Drive between Mays Peak and 8,380-foot Mount Buckhorn to the west was once home to English-born Ellen Elliott, dubbed Captain Jack, one of the most colorful historic characters in the Pikes Peak region. After running a café in Gunnison,

The Mays Peak Trail spirals around the peak from the High Drive above North Cheyenne Cañon.

The view from Mays Peak's summit includes Stove Mountain and Mount Rosa.

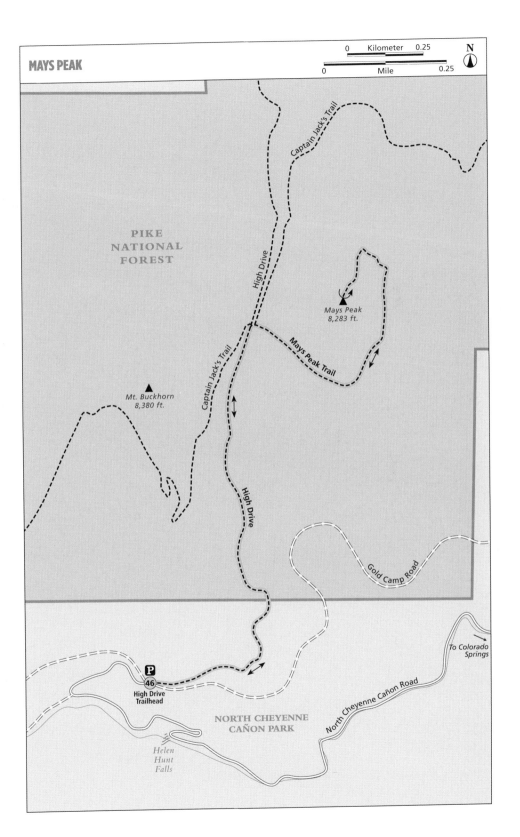

0   Kilometer   0.25

0   Mile   0.25

N

PIKE
NATIONAL
FOREST

Captain Jack's Trail

High Drive

Mays Peak
8,283 ft.

Mays Peak Trail

Captain Jack's Trail

Mt. Buckhorn
8,380 ft.

High Drive

Gold Camp Road

To Colorado
Springs

P
46
High Drive
Trailhead

NORTH CHEYENNE
CAÑON PARK

North Cheyenne Cañon Road

Helen
Hunt
Falls

Fresh snow and yucca adorn the rounded summit of Mays Peak.

owning the Black Queen Mine in Gilpin County, and keeping a Cripple Creek boarding house, Captain Jack moved to the High Drive saddle in 1900. A true eccentric, Captain Jack rented cabins to tourists, led burro rides, cooked fried chicken dinners, posed for photos with a loaded six-shooter tucked into her belt, and lived with burros, parrots, and cats. Little remains of the Captain's domain except a few foundation stones left after the buildings were torn down in the 1960s. She died in 1921 and was buried in Evergreen Cemetery with her head facing west toward Mays Peak.

MILES AND DIRECTIONS

0.0 Start at the High Drive Trailhead on the east side of the parking lot at a closed gate left of Gold Camp Road. Hike northeast up closed and gated High Drive, contouring the wooded eastern slopes of Mount Buckhorn.

1.0 Reach a large clearing at a saddle between Mount Buckhorn on the left and Mays Peak on the right (GPS: 38.800467,-104.899600). Several trails depart from the saddle. Do not take Captain Jack's Trail, which is on the northeast and northwest corners of the lot. That trail traverses the north side of Mays Peak and does not reach the summit but descends east to Gold Camp Road. Instead, find the unsigned trail at the southeast corner of the lot on the right side of a fence post. Go right of the fence post by a tall pine and follow a singletrack trail that steadily swings up the southern slopes of the peak. Stay on the main trail and do not take any social trails that branch off.

1.5 Arrive at a wooded area on low-angle slopes on the northeast side of the mountain. Keep left and climb steeply up the eroded trail. Avoid taking any social trails.

1.6 Arrive at the open summit of 8,283-foot Mays Peak (GPS: 38.801237,-104.896242). After a snack, follow the trail back down to the saddle on High Drive.

2.2 Go left on High Drive and descend the closed road back down to the trailhead.

3.2 Arrive back at the trailhead (GPS: 38.790283,-104.903500).

47 MOUNT ROSA

Mount Rosa's distinct pyramid-shaped summit rises on the western horizon above Colorado Springs. This all-day hike travels from dirt road and over forested trail before rewarding the hiker with a stunning summit backdrop of Pikes Peak.

Start: Powell Trailhead, junction of North Cheyenne Cañon Road / Gold Camp Road / High Drive
Difficulty: Very strenuous
Trails: Gold Camp Road / FR 370, Gold Camp Road Trail, Saint Marys Falls Trail #624, Mount Rosa Road / FR 381, Nelson's Trail #672, Mount Rosa Trail #673
Hiking time: 7–8 hours
Distance: 13.4 miles, out and back
Elevations trailhead to summit: 7,511 to 11,499 feet (+3,988 feet)
Rank status: Ranked

Restrictions: Day use only; no ground fires, camping, or alcoholic beverages; dogs must be leashed
Amenities: Porta-potties at trailhead; services in Colorado Springs
Counties: El Paso and Teller
Maps: *DeLorme:* p. 62, C3 and C4; Trails Illustrated #137: Pikes Peak, Cañon City; USGS Manitou Springs
Land status/contact: Colorado Springs Department of Parks, Recreation, and Cultural Services, (719) 385-5940; Pike National Forest, (719) 553-1400; Pikes Peak Ranger District, (719) 636-1602

FINDING THE TRAILHEAD

From I-25 in Colorado Springs, take Cimarron Street exit 141 and go west on US 24. Drive 1.5 miles and turn left onto S 21st Street, which becomes Cresta Road. Drive 3 miles and turn right onto Cheyenne Boulevard, then go 1 mile and bear right onto North Cheyenne Cañon Road. Drive 3.2 miles and park at the large, paved lot at the top of the hill, where the road meets Gold Camp Road. Powell Trailhead is located at the closed gate at the northwest end of the parking lot (GPS: 38.790891,-104.904224).

Pikes Peak and Almagre Mountain fill the sky above Mount Rosa.

Mount Rosa's bouldery summit offers spectacular views of 14,115-foot Pikes Peak.

THE HIKE

Mount Rosa's summit is reached by several routes, but this hike through Buffalo Canyon and up Rosa's northeast slopes is the most scenic. Round-trip elevation gain, due to losing and regaining altitude, is roughly 4,500 feet. There is no water along the trail, so be sure to carry enough for a full day and allow plenty of time to finish the hike before dark.

The first part of the hike along Gold Camp Road is fully exposed to the sun, but you'll be in the shade of the forest on and off through the central section of the hike, until climbing the eastern slopes of Rosa and gaining the north ridge of the peak. On your return, consider a short detour to Saint Marys Falls, which is well-signed and on a short side path off the main trail.

MILES AND DIRECTIONS

0.0 From the Powell Trailhead at the northwest side of the parking lot, hike west on the closed Gold Camp Road / FR 370. Kineo Mountain appears straight ahead.

0.7 Continue past North Cheyenne Creek and the cutoff to Seven Bridges Trailhead #622, on the right, and continue hiking on the road as it bends southeast (GPS: 38.786508,-104.914645).

1.1 Pass a closed railroad tunnel right of the trail and bear right up narrow Gold Camp Road Trail (GPS: 38.786911,-104.907547). Pause at a viewpoint just ahead looking

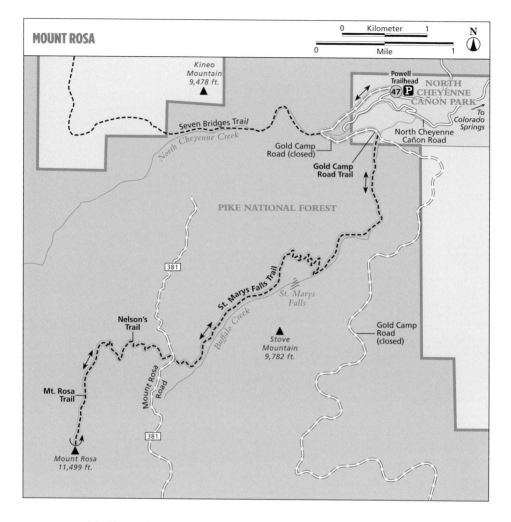

MOUNT ROSA

0   Kilometer   1

0   Mile   1

N

Kineo Mountain 9,478 ft.

Powell Trailhead
47 P
NORTH CHEYÉNNE CAÑON PARK

To Colorado Springs

Seven Bridges Trail

North Cheyenne Creek

North Cheyenne Cañon Road

Gold Camp Road (closed)

Gold Camp Road Trail

PIKE NATIONAL FOREST

381

St. Marys Falls Trail

St. Marys Falls

Nelson's Trail

Buffalo Creek

Stove Mountain 9,782 ft.

Gold Camp Road (closed)

Mt. Rosa Trail

Mount Rosa Road

381

Mount Rosa 11,499 ft.

east to Mount Muscoco, Mount Cutler, and southwest Colorado Springs before continuing up the trail.

1.2   At a signed junction, bear right on Saint Marys Falls Trail #624 and hike south on the trail along Buffalo Creek (GPS: 38.786340,-104.907014).

2.5   Pass a sign for Saint Marys Falls and switchback right and uphill (GPS: 38.771658, -104.915779). **Note:** This is not the cutoff to the falls.

2.8   At a sign for the cutoff trail to Saint Marys Falls, again switchback right and go uphill (GPS: 38.772816,-104.916123). The trail continues to switchback across the steep slope, then turns south.

3.5   The trail climbs steeply past a rocky section, levels off, and contours above Buffalo Creek and across from the north slopes of Stove Mountain (GPS: 38.772021,-104.920233).

3.9   Follow the trail as it curves west then south, with Mount Rosa appearing in the southwest sky (GPS: 38.769391,-104.924873).

4.7   Follow the trail as it turns west and passes through a cowboy gate and past a large cairn (GPS: 38.763021,-104.934344) to a junction. Turn right on the Mount Rosa Road / FR 381 and hike north.

Saint Marys Falls plunges off a granite bench below Mount Rosa.

Mount Rosa rises above Nelson's Trail on the peak's east flank.

4.75 Leave the dirt road and turn left on Nelson's Trail #672 (GPS: 38.763465, -104.934774). The trail switchbacks up west, rising above the shady forest and gaining about 1,000 feet in a mile.

5.8 The trail curves south toward Mount Rosa, with excellent views northwest of Pikes Peak (GPS: 38.764649,-104.944438).

5.95 At a signed junction of Nelson's Trail and Mount Rosa Trail, turn left onto the Mount Rosa Trail (GPS: 38.762911,-104.945525). The trail climbs about 500 feet up the north ridge of Mount Rosa.

6.7 Reach the rocky summit of 11,499-foot Mount Rosa (GPS: 38.754131,-104.948016). Return the way you came.

13.4 Arrive back at the trailhead (GPS: 38.790891,-104.904224).

48 GRAY BACK PEAK

The Gray Back Peak Trail follows a gravel ridge and then climbs through aspen and evergreen woods to the summit of Gray Back Peak and marvelous views of the eastern prairie and the Pikes Peak massif.

Start: Gray Back Peak Trailhead, Forest Road #371 off Old Stage Road
Difficulty: Moderate
Trails: Gray Back Peak Trail #649
Hiking time: About 2 hours
Distance: 3.8 miles, out and back
Elevations trailhead to summit: 8,736 to 9,348 feet (+612 feet)
Rank status: Unranked
Restrictions: Open daily year-round; Old Stage Road is steep and can be muddy, icy, and slippery; limited parking at trailhead; equestrians and mountain bikers share trail; no toilets; no available water
Amenities: Nearest campground at Cheyenne Mountain State Park; services in Colorado Springs
County: El Paso
Maps: *DeLorme*: p. 52, C4; Trails Illustrated #137: Pikes Peak, Cañon City; USGS Mount Big Chief
Land status/contact: Pike National Forest, (719) 553-1400; Pikes Peak Ranger District, (719) 636-1602

FINDING THE TRAILHEAD

From I-25 take Circle Drive exit (exit 138) and drive west on Circle Drive, which becomes Lake Avenue at junction with CO 115. Continue west on Lake to The Broadmoor Hotel. Turn right on Lake Circle and drive 0.25 mile to a circular roundabout. Turn left at the roundabout on Mesa Avenue and follow it around the west side of The Broadmoor. At a four-way intersection, go left on El Pomar Road and drive to an angling right turn on Old Stage Road. Follow the paved road until it becomes gravel. Continue up the gravel road for about 6 miles to FR 371 at a sign for Emerald Valley Ranch. Turn left on FR 371 and drive 0.3 mile on the narrow road to a saddle. Park on the left in a sloping lot at the trailhead (GPS: 38.731404,-104.906671).

The rocky summit ridge of Gray Back Peak offers expansive views across the southern Front Range.

The Wicked Cliffs rise above wooded slopes on Gray Back Peak's west flank.

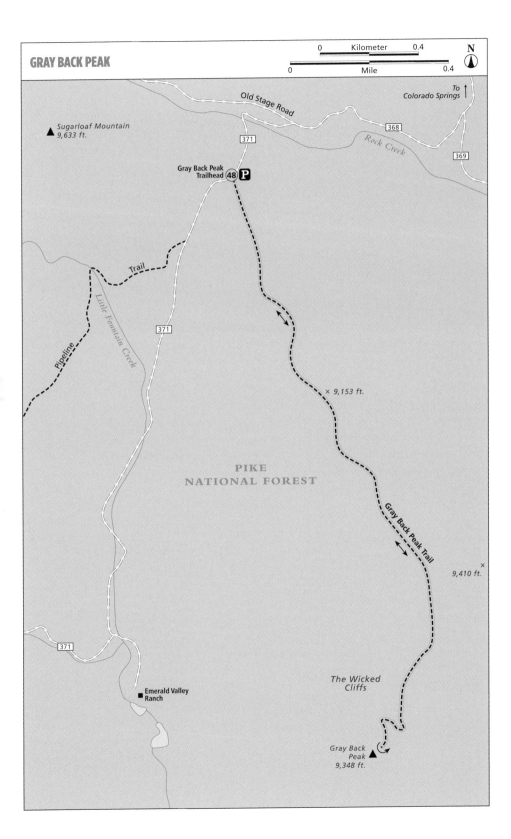

GRAY BACK PEAK

0   Kilometer   0.4

0   Mile   0.4

N

Old Stage Road

To
Colorado Springs

368

371

Rock Creek

369

▲ Sugarloaf Mountain
9,633 ft.

Gray Back Peak
Trailhead 48 P

Trail

Little Fountain Creek

Pipeline

371

× 9,153 ft.

PIKE
NATIONAL FOREST

Gray Back Peak Trail

×
9,410 ft.

371

The Wicked
Cliffs

Emerald Valley
Ranch

Gray Back
Peak ▲
9,348 ft.

Granite cliffs on Gray Back Peak frame pointed Mount Rosa and rocky Mount Vigil to the northwest.

THE HIKE

This fine hike climbs to the summit of Gray Back Peak, a mountain on the southeast edge of the Pikes Peak massif. The trail, beginning in a saddle, is easy to follow with moderate grades, though the trail's first part has been eroded and worn from the many strings of horseback riders from a nearby riding stable. Pay attention to the only trail junction, marked with a cairn, and be sure to go right and hike south toward Gray Back Peak. The mountain's summit offers spectacular views across the southern Front Range with deep canyons and rough peaks to the south and wooded Emerald Valley to the west.

MILES AND DIRECTIONS

0.0 Start at the unmarked trailhead in a saddle and hike east up the trail on a gravelly hillside.

0.7 Reach the crest of a wide ridge dotted with pines and clumps of kinnikinnik.

1.1 Reach an overlook with views of rugged Gray Back Peak to the south.

1.3 Descend to a saddle and a trail junction with a large cairn. Keep right here on the main trail and hike south across open, west-facing slopes with views west into the Emerald Valley.

1.6 Reach a wooded saddle between Gray Back Peak and an unnamed 9,410-foot mountain to the left. Begin climbing the steep east face of Gray Back Peak, making a couple of wide switchbacks through a mixed conifer forest.

1.9 Arrive at the small, rocky summit of 9,348-foot Gray Back Peak (GPS: 38.711628, -104.899865) and enjoy 360-degree views across the southern Front Range, including the bulky Wet Mountains and the distant twin Spanish Peaks. Retrace your steps, remembering to turn left at the trail junction.

3.8 Arrive back at the trailhead (GPS: 38.731404,-104.906671).

49 DRAGONS BACKBONE AND ROBBERS ROOST (CHEYENNE MOUNTAIN)

The challenging Dixon Trail climbs from a trailhead in Cheyenne Mountain State Park to the rocky tops of Dragons Backbone and Robbers Roost, two unranked subsummits of Cheyenne Mountain southwest of Colorado Springs.

Start: Limekiln Trailhead, Cheyenne Mountain State Park
Difficulty: Very strenuous
Trails: Talon Trail, North Talon Trail, Dixon Trail
Hiking time: 7–9 hours
Distance: 15.4 miles, lollipop
Elevations trailhead to summits: 6,043 to 9,170 feet at Dragons Backbone (+3,127 feet); to 9,210 feet at Robbers Roost (+3,167 feet)
Rank status: Unranked; Cheyenne Mountain is ranked
Restrictions: Fee area; open daily 5 a.m. to 10 p.m.; stay on designated trails; hikers only on Dixon Trail;

mountain bikes and horses allowed on lower trail segments; no dogs
Amenities: Restrooms, drinking water, picnic tables, and info signs at trailhead; visitor center; interpretive programs; park campground; picnic areas; services in Colorado Springs
County: El Paso
Maps: *DeLorme*: p. 62, C4; Trails Illustrated #137: Pikes Peak, Cañon City; USGS Cheyenne Mountain; Cheyenne Mountain State Park maps
Land status/contact: Cheyenne Mountain State Park (719) 576-2016 or (800) 678-2267

FINDING THE TRAILHEAD

From I-25 on the south side of Colorado Springs, take exit 135, the South Academy Boulevard exit, and drive west on South Academy past Pikes Peak Community College. Continue west to CO 115 and turn south on CO 115. Drive south on the divided highway for 1.9 miles to a stop light. The park entrance is on the right, opposite Fort Carson Gate 1. Turn right and drive west on JL Ranch Heights Road for 0.8 mile, passing the park visitor center, to the park entrance station. Continue another 0.1 mile and turn left into Limekiln Trailhead parking lot. The trailhead and Talon Trail are at the west end of the parking lot and right of the restrooms (GPS: 38.731287,-104.821429).

THE HIKE

This hike climbs more than 3,000 feet from Limekiln Trailhead to Dragons Backbone and Robbers Roost, the eastern subsummits of 9,565-foot Cheyenne Mountain. The strenuous 15.4-mile, round-trip trek, one of the hardest summit hikes in this book, is like climbing a 14er, or 14,000-foot peak, but without the altitude.

Only fit hikers should attempt the trail since the ascent and descent make for a long day with steep uphill sections, particularly the final 1.5 miles to the start of the Dragons Backbone Trail. The Limekiln Trailhead at the hike's start is the only place on the trail with restrooms and water. Sign in and out of a Dixon Trail register at the trailhead.

Cheyenne Mountain and its subsummit Dragons Backbone tower above meadows and scrub oaks at Cheyenne Mountain State Park.

Cell phone service is spotty on the trail, especially on the upper mountain. The Dixon Trail does not climb to the summit of Cheyenne Mountain, which rises a mile and a half southwest of the Antenna Field next to the trail's high point (not described in this chapter).

The Dixon Trail is open year-round, but it is best to hike between late April and late September when there is enough daylight to complete the hike. Carry plenty of water on hot days since no water is available on the trail.

The hike up Cheyenne Mountain from Limekiln Trailhead follows four segments:

The first segment follows the Talon Trail and North Talon Trail from the trailhead for 3.4 miles.

The second segment follows the difficult Dixon Trail for 3.8 miles.

The third segment follows the Dragons Backbone Trail for 0.9 mile.

The fourth segment follows the Mountain Loop Trail for 0.3 mile back to the junction with the Dixon Trail.

MILES AND DIRECTIONS

0.0 Begin at Limekiln Trailhead on the west side of the parking lot (GPS: 38.731282, -104.821442). Hike west on Talon Trail.

A granite prominence looms over the Dixon Trail on the south flank of Cheyenne Mountain.

DRAGONS BACKBONE AND ROBBERS ROOST (CHEYENNE MOUNTAIN)

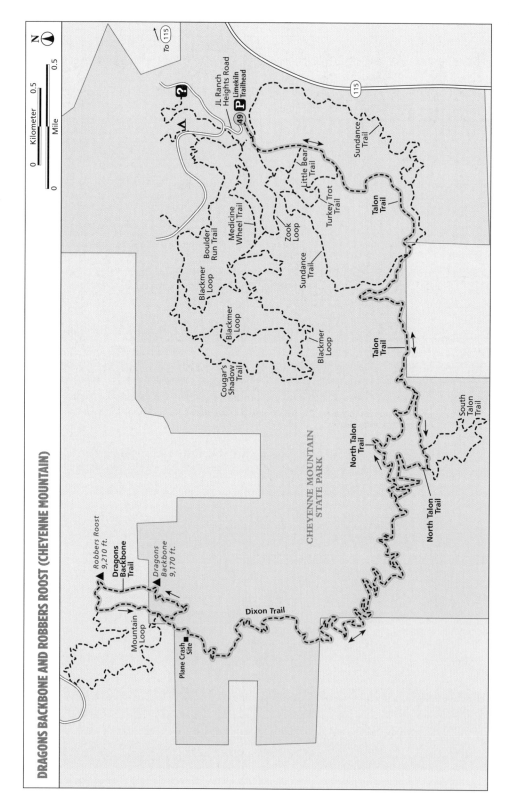

The Dixon Trail passes remains of a T-33 training plane that crashed below Dragons Backbone in 1957, killing the two pilots.

2.3 Reach a junction with North Talon Trail on the right. Continue straight on Talon Trail (GPS: 38.721003,-104.841383). (Note: If you go right on North Talon Trail, you can reach the Dixon Trail. This section shaves 0.2 mile off the hike, but the trail is steeper. This description continues along the Talon Trail and takes North Talon Trail on the return hike.)

2.6 Pass a junction with South Talon Trail on the left (GPS: 38.720586,-104.845670). Continue straight on Talon Trail.

2.7 Reach a second junction with South Talon Trail. Go right on North Talon Trail.

3.4 Reach a ridgetop and junction with the Dixon Trail (GPS: 38.722236,-104.849277). Go left on the Dixon and hike west.

5.9 Reach the mountain bike turn-around point on a high ridge. Here the trail narrows and steepens. This is the hike's most difficult section. Higher, the trail passes a 1957 plane crash site that killed two military pilots. If you stop at the plane wreckage, remember this is a historically relevant memorial. Out of respect for the dead and their families, do not touch or remove any artifacts. Cross an aspen-lined meadow (GPS: 38.728530,-104.858101).

7.2 Reach a signed trail junction in a meadow. Go right on signed Dragons Backbone Trail (GPS: 38.735973,-104.858198).

7.6 Arrive at the 9,170-foot rocky summit of Dragons Backbone (GPS: 38.736552, -104.856027). Continue north on Dragons Backbone Trail along a rough ridge.

7.9 Reach Robbers Roost, a rock outcrop on the trail's right side. Its 9,210-foot summit is reached by technical rock scrambling and not recommended without proper

Lower mountains and the tawny prairie spread eastward below Dragons Backbone.

Hazy mountains lie south of Dragons Backbone, a rough ridge at Cheyenne Mountain State Park.

gear and protection. Turn left on the trail and descend west on gentle slopes (GPS: 38.739870,-104.855712).

8.1 Reach the end of Dragons Backbone Trail at a junction with Mountain Loop Trail (GPS: 38.739801,-104.857700). Go left on it and hike south through meadows.

8.4 Reach the junction with Dragons Backbone Trail on the left. Continue south on Dixon Trail and steeply descend to the turn-around point and then down the mountain's east flank.

12.2 Reach the Dixon Trail's end and the junction with North Talon Trail. Go left on North Talon Trail. (This is not the same section of North Talon Trail you hiked up but for the return hike it is 0.2 mile shorter and joins the Talon Trail farther east.)

13.1 Reach a junction with Talon Trail. Go left on it.

15.4 Arrive back at the trailhead (GPS: 38.731287,-104.821429).

50 FREMONT PEAK

Fremont Peak, offering a scrubby desert hike to its rocky summit, towers above the Royal Gorge, a 1,250-foot-deep canyon west of Cañon City at the southern end of the Front Range.

Start: East Ridge Trailhead, Royal Gorge Park
Difficulty: Moderate
Trails: CR 389B (closed road), Summit Access Trail, Summit Trail, Far Out Trail, Cañon Vista Trail
Hiking time: About 3 hours
Distance: 4.35 miles, loop
Elevations trailhead to summit: 6,831 to 7,233 feet (+402 feet)
Rank status: Ranked
Restrictions: Day use only; CR 389B may not be passable to the trailhead in winter; leashed dogs only; no fires, alcohol, firearms, trapping, or hunting in park; no motor vehicles on trails
Amenities: Toilets in campground east of parking lot; East Ridge Campground at trailhead; services in Cañon City
County: Fremont
Maps: *DeLorme*: p. 72, A1; Trails Illustrated #137: Pikes Peak, Cañon City; USGS Royal Gorge
Land status/contact: Royal Gorge Park, City of Cañon City Parks Division, (719) 269-9028

FINDING THE TRAILHEAD

From Cañon City, drive west on US 50 for about 8 miles and turn left on paved Fremont CR 3A toward the Royal Gorge Bridge. Drive 3.3 miles to a road junction where the main road bends right. Turn left on gravel CR 389B. Drive 0.7 mile east to a fork. Keep right and continue for 0.1 mile to the East Ridge Trailhead, two parking lots, and a closed road that is the hike's trailhead (GPS: 38.464514,-105.293497).

Fremont Peak, one of the southernmost mountains in the Front Range, towers above the Royal Gorge west of Cañon City.

Pikes Peak rises beyond the twisting Summit Trail in the Gorge Hills.

THE HIKE

Fremont Peak, forming Cañon City's jagged western skyline, towers above the 10-mile-long Royal Gorge, a deep defile chiseled over the last three million years by the Arkansas River before it empties onto the Great Plains. The mountain, the high point of the Gorge Hills, and the Royal Gorge contain some of Colorado's oldest rocks. The 7,233-foot peak was named after explorer John C. Fremont, who searched for a transcontinental railroad route across Colorado in the 1840s and 1850s. The hike, lying in Cañon City–owned Royal Gorge Park, passes through a pygmy woodland of juniper, piñon pine, Gambel oak, yucca, and various cacti species. It is hot and dry in summer so bring water and sun protection.

The described route up Fremont Peak follows a closed road to a couple of communication towers, and then scrambles up a precipitous trail to the rock summit. This last short trail section is difficult, with loose rock and steep grades. Take your time and use trekking poles and MICROspikes, especially if the trail is icy. The reward is an unsurpassed summit view, including 14,115-foot Pikes Peak to the northeast, the Wet Mountains to the south, and the long ridge of the Sangre de Cristo Mountains rimming the western horizon.

MILES AND DIRECTIONS

0.0 Start at the East Ridge Trailhead located at the closed CR 389B road (signed "Do Not Enter") between the two parking lots. Hike southwest on the closed road. After 350 feet, reach the Cañon Vista Trailhead on the left (GPS: 38.463594,-105.293791). This is the end of the return trail loop. Continue straight on the dirt road.

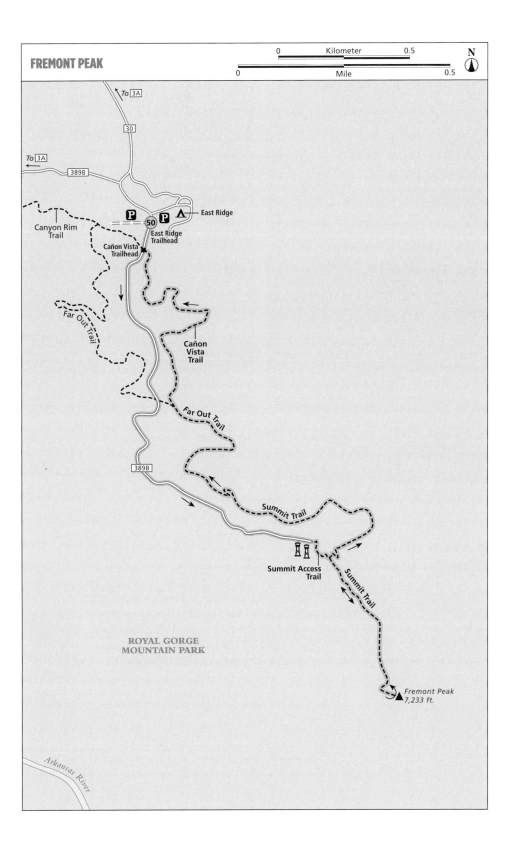

FREMONT PEAK

Kilometer
0   0.5

Mile
0   0.5

N

To 3A

30

To 3A

389B

Canyon Rim
Trail

East Ridge

East Ridge
Trailhead

Cañon Vista
Trailhead

Far Out Trail

Cañon
Vista
Trail

Far Out Trail

389B

Summit Trail

Summit Access
Trail

Summit Trail

ROYAL GORGE
MOUNTAIN PARK

Fremont Peak
7,233 ft.

Arkansas River

The trail up Fremont Peak gives spectacular views into the Royal Gorge, a deep canyon carved by the Arkansas River.

Steep slopes and cliffs scatter along the summit ridge of Fremont Peak.

0.1 Reach a locked metal gate across the road. Climb over or under it and continue up the road.

0.4 Reach a junction with Far Out Trail (GPS: 38.458455,-105.293143), which crosses the road here and goes east to Cañon Vista Trail. Continue straight on the road, steadily climbing south up a wide ridge. Look west for occasional views of the Royal Gorge and the Sangre de Cristo Mountains.

0.5 Pass another junction with Far Out Trail. Continue south on the old road.

0.6 After rounding a curve, stop at a scenic viewpoint on the right overlooking the inner gorge (GPS: 38.456449,-105.294126). Continue along the road, which bends southeast along the high eastern rim of the gorge.

0.9 Pass a communications tower on the right and continue southeast up the road.

1.1 Reach two towers, the dirt road's end, and a trail junction between the towers (GPS: 38.453864,-105.286526). Go straight on the singletrack Summit Access Trail down a slight slope on the wide ridge.

1.2 Reach a junction with signed Summit Trail (GPS: 38.453304,-105.285724) on the left and right. Continue straight on the trail's right fork and hike southeast along the ridge. The left trail is taken on the return leg.

1.5 Reach an obvious Y junction with Royal Cascade Trail on the left and Summit Trail on the right (GPS: 38.450349,-105.283555). Take the right trail. The final trail segment to the summit is steep and loose. Use extreme caution not to dislodge rocks and use MICROspikes and trekking poles in winter for traction.

Fremont Peak's summit offers dramatic views across its ragged east ridge to Cañon City and the Arkansas Valley.

1.55 Scramble up the steep side trail (which may be icy in winter) and reach the summit ridge. Go left and hike east along the ridge crest.

1.6 Arrive at the 7,233-foot summit of Fremont Peak (GPS: 38.448733,-105.282994), marked by a large stone cairn. Enjoy views of Pikes Peak to the northeast and the Wet Mountains, Sangre de Cristo Mountains, and Royal Gorge to the west and southwest. Return back down the steep Summit Trail. It is difficult to descend in icy conditions.

1.7 Reach the Y junction with Royal Cascade Trail. Keep left on the Summit Trail and hike northwest along the ridge.

2.0 Arrive back at the junction with the Summit Access Trail. Go right on the Summit Trail, which spirals around a knob and heads northwest across oak-covered slopes.

2.7 Reach a junction with Far Out Trail and the Summit Trail's end (GPS: 38.455678, -105.291053). Go right on Far Out Trail and hike around the head of a valley.

3.0 Reach a junction on the left with the west upper loop of Far Out Trail on a ridge. Keep straight on the main trail and hike northwest.

3.5 Reach a junction and the start of Cañon Vista Trail (GPS: 38.458435,-105.292540). The Far Out Trail goes left here and reaches the road after 100 feet (this is not your route). Go straight on Cañon Vista Trail.

4.3 Reach the closed road at the end of Cañon Vista Trail. Go right on the road toward the parking lot.

4.35 Arrive back at the trailhead (GPS: 38.464514,-105.293497).

APPENDIX: LAND STATUS CONTACT INFORMATION

CAMPGROUNDS

Colorado State Parks Camping
(800) 244-5613 (Phone reservations)
cpw.state.co.us/buyapply/Pages/
Reservations.aspx

Recreation.gov
(877) 444-6777 (Reservations)
recreation.gov

COLORADO PARKS AND WILDLIFE

Cheyenne Mountain State Park
410 JL Ranch Heights
Colorado Springs, CO 80926
(719) 576-2016 or (800) 678-2267
cpw.state.co.us/placestogo/parks/
CheyenneMountain

**Colorado Parks and Wildlife
Headquarters**
6060 Broadway
Denver, CO 80216
(303) 291-7227
cpw.state.co.us/

Golden Gate Canyon State Park
92 Crawford Gulch Rd.
Golden, CO 80403
(303) 582-3707
cpw.state.co.us/placestogo/parks/
GoldenGateCanyon

Lory State Park
708 Lodgepole Dr.
Bellvue, CO 80512
(970) 493-1623
cpw.state.co.us/placestogo/parks/Lory

Mueller State Park
21045 CO 67 South
Divide, CO 80814
(719) 687-2366
cpw.state.co.us/placestogo/parks/Mueller

Roxborough State Park
4751 East Roxborough Dr.
Roxborough, CO 80125
(303) 973-3959
cpw.state.co.us/placestogo/parks/
Roxborough

Staunton State Park
12102 S Elk Creek Rd.
Pine, CO 80470
(303) 816-0912
cpw.state.co.us/placestogo/parks/
Staunton/Pages/default.aspx

CITY PARKS AND OPEN SPACES

Boulder County Parks and Open Space
5201 St. Vrain Rd.
Longmont, CO 80503
(303) 678-6200
bouldercounty.org/departments/parks
-and-open-space/

Boulder Open Space & Mountain Parks
2520 55th St.
Boulder, CO 80301
(303) 441-3440
bouldercolorado.gov/government/
departments/open-space-mountain-parks

City of Black Hawk
City Hall
201 Selak St.
Black Hawk, CO 80422
(303) 582-2221
cityofblackhawk.org

City of Cañon City Parks Division
128 Main St.
Cañon City, CO 81212
(719) 269-9028 or (719) 269-9011
canoncity.org/348/Parks-Division

Colorado Springs Department of Parks, Recreation and Cultural Services
1401 Recreation Way
Colorado Springs, CO 80905
(719) 385-5940
springsgov.com

Denver Mountain Parks
201 West Colfax Ave., Dept. 601
Denver, CO 80202
(720) 865-0900
Park Rangers: (720) 913-1311
denvergov.org/Government/Agencies
-Departments-Offices/Parks-Recreation/
Parks/Mountain-Parks

Douglas County Open Space & Natural Resources
100 Third St.
Castle Rock, CO 80104
(303) 660-7495
douglas.co.us/open-space-natural
-resources

Fort Collins Natural Areas Program
1745 Hoffman Mill Rd.
Fort Collins, CO 80524
(970) 416-2815
fcgov.com/naturalareas

Jefferson County Open Space
700 Jefferson County Pkwy., Suite 100
Golden, CO 80401
(303) 271-5925
Jefferson County Dispatch (303) 980-7300
jeffco.us/open-space

Lakewood Parks and Recreation
Civic Center South
480 S Allison Pkwy.
Lakewood, CO 80226
(303) 987-7800
lakewood.org/Government/
Departments/Community-Resources/
Recreation

Loveland Parks and Recreation
500 E Third St.
Loveland, CO 80537
(970) 962-2727 or (970) 962-2000
lovgov.org/services/parks-recreation

Manitou Springs Parks and Recreation
606 Manitou Ave.
Manitou Springs, CO 80829
(719) 685-2610
manitouspringsgov.com/593/_Parks
-and-Recreation

Town of Palmer Lake
42 Valley Crescent St.
Palmer Lake, CO 80133
(719) 481-2953
townofpalmerlake.com

NATIONAL FORESTS

Arapaho and Roosevelt National Forests
2150 Centre Ave., Bldg. E
Fort Collins, CO 80526
(970) 295-6600
fs.usda.gov/arp

Pike National Forest
2840 Kachina Dr.
Pueblo, CO 81008
(719) 553-1400
fs.usda.gov/psicc

Roosevelt National Forest
2150 Centre Ave., Bldg. E
Fort Collins, CO 80526
(970) 295-6600
fs.usda.gov/arp

San Isabel National Forest
2840 Kachina Dr.
Pueblo, CO 81008
(719) 553-1400
fs.usda.gov/psicc

NATIONAL FOREST RANGER DISTRICTS

Boulder Ranger District
2140 Yarmouth Ave.
Boulder, CO 80301
(303) 541-2500

Canyon Lakes Ranger District
2150 Centre Ave., Bldg. E
Fort Collins, CO 80526
(970) 295-6700

Clear Creek Ranger District
2060 Miner St.
Idaho Springs, CO 80452
(303) 567-3000

Pikes Peak Ranger District
601 S Weber St.
Colorado Springs, CO 80903
(719) 636-1602

South Park Ranger District
320 US 285
Fairplay, CO 80440
(719) 836-2031

NATIONAL PARKS

Rocky Mountain National Park
1000 US 36
Estes Park, CO 80517-8397

Visitor information: (970) 586-1206
Campground reservations: (877) 444-6777
nps.gov/romo/

PASSES

CORSAR Card
dola.colorado.gov/sar/cardPurchase.jsf

National Parks Pass
nps.gov/planyourvisit/passes.htm
shop.usparkpass.com

State Parks and Wildlife Areas Pass
cpw.state.co.us/buyapply/Pages/
ParksPassInfo.aspx

HIKE INDEX

THE TEN ESSENTIALS OF HIKING

American Hiking Society

American Hiking Society recommends you pack the "Ten Essentials" every time you head out for a hike. Whether you plan to be gone for a couple of hours or several months, make sure to pack these items. Become familiar with these items and know how to use them. Learn more at **AmericanHiking.org/hiking-resources.**

 1. Appropriate Footwear

 6. Safety Items (light, fire, and a whistle)

 2. Navigation

 7. First Aid Kit

 3. Water (and a way to purify it)

 8. Knife or Multi-Tool

 4. Food

 9. Sun Protection

 5. Rain Gear & Dry-Fast Layers

 10. Shelter

PROTECT THE PLACES YOU LOVE TO HIKE

Become a member today and take $5 off an annual membership using the code **Falcon5**.

AmericanHiking.org/join

American Hiking Society is the only national nonprofit organization dedicated to empowering all to enjoy, share, and preserve the hiking experience.